Business Result

Advanced | Student's Book

Kate Baade, Christopher Holloway,
Jim Scrivener & Rebecca Turner

With additional material by
Gareth Davies, Andrew Shouler
& Shaun Wilden

D1493078

OXFORD

UNIVERSITY PRESS

Contents

Introduction

Welcome to *Business Result Advanced*. In this book you'll find:
| 12 units | Practice files | Language reference |
| Useful phrases | Information files | Audio scripts |
| Interactive Workbook on CD-ROM |

We hope you find this introduction useful, and that you enjoy using the course.

What's in a unit?

Starting point
- an introduction to the unit topic
- discussion questions

Working with words
- reading and listening based on themes from business and the world of work
- important new words and phrases that you can use immediately in your work
- practise the new vocabulary in a realistic final activity

Business communication skills
- presents key expressions for attending meetings, presenting information, communicating by telephone, and negotiating solutions to work-related issues
- helps you express yourself more clearly in real work situations
- lets you choose which phrases to use from the *Key expressions* list in every unit

Language at work
- reviews key grammar from *Business communication skills*
- helps you communicate more accurately in real work situations
- lets you check your knowledge of grammar and practise it in the classroom
- if you need more explanation, refer to the *Language reference* section

Practically speaking
- teaches really useful everyday phrases for small talk, telephoning, and short conversations
- helps you sound more natural when you speak English

Case study
- each unit ends with an authentic case study
- find out about situations related to the unit topic that affect real companies and organizations
- take part in a longer work-related activity with lots of opportunities to practise the language from the unit

Fast-track option

If time on your course is limited, *Business Result* has a unique fast-track option to use in class. For each unit, combine the *Business communication skills* section and the *Case study*. This creates a practical, highly communicative shorter course, enabling you to get the maximum benefit from your business English studies – fast.

What's in the Practice file?

The *Practice file* is like a mini-workbook in the back of the *Student's Book*. It allows you to think about and practise important words, phrases, and grammar. It has written exercises on the key language from each unit. When completing the *Language at work* exercises you can refer to the *Language reference* section for more detailed grammar explanations.
Use the *Practice file*
- in class to check your understanding
- after class for extra practice.
Follow the links to the *Practice file* in each unit.

>> For more exercises, go to **Practice file 1** on page 102.

What's the *Interactive Workbook* on CD-ROM?

Everyone's needs are different when it comes to using English at work. The *Interactive Workbook* gives you practical tools to use immediately in your work by helping you to practise the language and skills from the *Student's Book* and allows you to make them personal to you and your own work situation. It also helps you review and test your own progress.

Exercises and Tests
- review and practise key language with interactive exercises
- check your progress with unit tests

Glossary
- check the meaning of around 600 words and phrases
- personalize the vocabulary to your needs

Phrasebank
- listen to all the key expressions from the *Student's Book*
- learn new phrases for meetings, presenting, telephoning, negotiating, and socializing
- create your own personal phrasebook to match your needs at work

Email
- learn useful phrases for writing work-related emails
- copy model emails to your out-box, or create your own

Audio plus
- listen to dialogues and conversations in a variety of real-world business scenarios
- complete exercises to check your understanding

Listen again
- listen again to the *Student's Book* audio recordings, or download to your MP3 player

Wherever you see this link, it means you can access extra material on the *Interactive Workbook*.

ⓘ >> Interactive Workbook >>

Case studies with the Expert View from Cranfield School of Management

Each of the case studies in Business Result Advanced is accompanied by an Expert View from the Cranfield School of Management, one of Europe's leading management schools. It is part of Cranfield University, renowned for its high quality postgraduate teaching and research and its strong links to industry and business. The School of Management was established in 1967, and offers a range of MBA, Executive MBA, Executive Education, and Doctoral programmes.

For more information, visit: **www.som.cranfield.ac.uk/som**.

Your panel of experts are all from the faculty at Cranfield.

Cranfield
UNIVERSITY
School of Management

1 Jaime Bonache, Professor of International HRM (see page 13)

2 Peter Fennah, MSc MA Hons, Chartered Occupational Psychologist, Director, Career Development Service (see page 21)

3 Lester Coupland, Executive Development Consultant, Centre for Customised Executive Development (see page 29)

4 Ruth Bender, Senior Lecturer in Finance and Accounting (see page 37)

5 Joe Jaina, Senior Lecturer in Organizational Behaviour (see page 45)

6 Alan Cousens, MA MBA MSc PhD, Senior Research Fellow, Operations Management (see page 53)

7 Wendy Varney, Executive Development Consultant, Centre for Customised Executive Development (see page 61)

8 Professor Simon Knox, BSc PhD, Professor of Brand Marketing (see page 69)

9 Prof. David Grayson, CBE – Professor of Corporate Responsibility, Director of the Doughty Centre for Corporate Responsibility (see page 77 and 93)

10 Dr Donna Ladkin, Centre for Executive Learning and Leadership (see page 85)

11 Dr Stephanie Hussels, Lecturer in Entrepreneurship, Bettany Centre for Entrepreneurial Performance and Economics (see page 101)

1 | Connections

Learning objectives in this unit
- Describing cross-cultural experiences
- Reporting back on research
- Tenses review
- Introducing yourself to a group

Case study
- Planning for expansion

Starting point

1 Can you think of some examples where cultural awareness is important in your work?

2 To what extent do you think company culture is influenced by the country the company is based in?

Working with words | Describing cross-cultural experiences

1 Do you agree with the following statements about working across cultures?
1 Organizations generally have the same way of doing things.
2 Non-verbal messages carry more weight than verbal ones.
3 The concept of time is universal.
4 Individual differences can always be attributed to cultural differences.
5 Accepting and embracing ambiguity is essential when working internationally.
6 Consciously developing your cultural skills leads to better business relations.

2 Read this advice from intercultural consultant, Kate Berardo of culturosity.com, and compare your answers in 1. Which piece of advice do you find most useful?

Working across cultures
Kate Berardo

1 Do your homework
- Essential for building relationships when dealing with businesses across cultures.
- Each organization will have its own culture, personality, and way of doing things.

2 Keep your eyes open
- Your mind is processing a lot of information in new environments, so observation skills may be clouded or unfocused.
- Notice how people act, dress, and treat each other. Look for non-verbal messages. Being able to read a situation will greatly improve your ability to have a successful meeting.

3 Take your time
- Appreciate the need for more time. Communication may be slower and logistics may be different. You may be working in a culture with a different concept of time.
- Also, give yourself more time to process all the information before making decisions.

4 Take individuals into account
- Individuals may vary greatly from the stereotype of their native culture. Values and behaviour are also influenced by background, experience, and personality.
- Keep an open mind: be careful not to form an opinion too early or to attribute too much of what you see to a cultural difference.

5 Tolerate uncertainty
- This can be extremely difficult for people from some cultures where directness and precision are valued.
- Business is about managing unknowns. When working with a culture with a high tolerance for uncertainty, you may not get concrete answers. This, of course, can work both ways.

6 Build your intercultural skills
- When working with people from different cultures, you need a solid understanding of the norms of that culture.
- Greater cultural awareness will help you weigh up the pros and cons of your way of doing things and will give you a better insight into working across cultures.

3 Complete these phrases to form verb + noun collocations from the text in **2**.

1 _____ relationships

2 _____ your eyes open

3 _____ information

4 _____ a situation

5 _____ your time

6 _____ an open mind

7 _____ an opinion

8 _____ unknowns

9 _____ both ways

10 _____ your skills

11 _____ the pros and cons

12 _____ you an insight

4 Match the collocations from **3** to these definitions.

a avoid feeling rushed ____

b stay alert ____

c don't judge people / things too quickly ____

d succeed in creating rapport with others ____

e understand what is going on ____

f have a reciprocal effect ____

g consider the advantages and disadvantages ____

h make a judgement ____

i develop your ability in a certain area ____

j deal with and gain understanding of input you receive ____

k provide you with useful information to help you understand something ____

l deal successfully with unfamiliar situations ____

5 What advice would you give people from other cultures / companies who come to work in your culture / company? Try to use the collocations from **3**.

6 01▷ Listen to three people talking about their experience of working in other countries. Was each person's overall impression positive or negative?

7 01▷ Are the following adjectives used to describe people (*P*), places (*PL*), or experiences (*E*)? Listen again and compare your answers.

Extract 1

1 open-minded ____

2 out-of-the-way ____

3 time-consuming ____

4 tedious ____

Extract 2

5 up-and-coming ____

6 self-assured ____

7 outspoken ____

8 run-of-the-mill ____

Extract 3

9 down to earth ____

10 easy-going ____

11 low-key ____

12 unexpected ____

8 Work with a partner. Match definitions a–f to six adjectives from **7**, then write your own definitions for the other six adjectives.

a boring

b saying exactly what you think

c ordinary

d sensible / practical

e not intended to attract attention

f relaxed

9 Use adjectives from **7** to describe

• how you think you are viewed at work

• your workplace

• your experience of working at your present company.

>> For more exercises, go to **Practice file 1** on page 102.

10 Work with a partner. Think about a situation where you have

• been host to a business visitor

• worked in another country / city

• worked with a new colleague

• started a new job in a new company.

Now talk about your experiences with your partner and answer questions 1–4.

1 How did you feel to begin with?

2 Where did your first impressions come from?

3 Did your impressions change with time?

4 Were your first impressions right?

ⓘ >> Interactive Workbook >> **Glossary**

Peter works for Johanna, who runs one of the offices for an international operation finding locations for clients. One client, a chain of hotels, has asked them to find a new site for a hotel in Poland. Peter has just returned from a fact-finding mission to Poland. On his return he meets Johanna over coffee to report back on his trip.

Informal meetings | Reporting back

1 What type of information do you think Johanna will be expecting from Peter?

2 02▷ Listen to Extract 1 from the meeting between Johanna and Peter, and complete Johanna's notes. For each piece of information, note down whether it comes from
   1 personal observation
   2 a third party or another source.

---

premium
Premises

Poland – research
  Probable location = _____
  General details = up-and-coming place

Peter's feedback
  First site = city centre
  + points = • _____
              • the area is being pushed for development
  – points = • _____

Conclusions / action points
  • Several interesting sites worth considering outside Krakow.
  • Action = _____

---

3 02▷ Listen again.
   1 Note down the phrases used to indicate where each piece of information in Johanna's notes in 2 comes from.
   2 Why do you think Johanna and Peter present their information in this way?
   Example: Probable location: Krakow (information from third party – the client)
   'The client has told us that the site is likely to be around the Krakow area.'
   (Johanna may want to emphasize that this is not her decision.)

4 Work with a partner. Your company has come up with a potential new market, and you have been asked to conduct some initial research. Student A, read the newspaper extract below. Student B, turn to File 01 on page 136 and read the country briefing.

1 Report back to each other on your findings, using the phrases from **3**.
2 Discuss any differences in your information.

> Although lots of new investment is coming into the local market, the airport is insufficient for the volume of traffic expected. This will have a serious impact on the local economy. If a solution is not found, business will go elsewhere, possibly to new ascension countries, such as Bulgaria and Romania.

5 03, 04▷ Listen to Extracts 2 and 3 from the meeting between Johanna and Peter. Johanna makes some further notes while she is listening to Peter. Complete the details.

> 1 Mountain site – activities, location, local workforce
>
> 2 City outskirts site – infrastructure, facilities, possible site for purchase

6 03, 04▷ Listen again. In which extract is Peter

1 expressing doubts? ____
2 avoiding commitment? ____
3 being persuasive? ____
4 trying to avoid being negative? ____
5 dismissing any obstacles? ____
6 stating an advantage? ____

7 05▷ Listen to the pairs of sentences from the meeting between Johanna and Peter, and match them to 1–6 in **6**.

8 Work with a partner. Have the following conversations, using the prompts in brackets.

1 Student A wants to rearrange the open plan office you both work in.
 (Student A – state an advantage; Student B – express doubt)
2 You are discussing a proposal to buy out a small competitor.
 (Student A – express doubt; Student B – dismiss any obstacles)
3 Student A would like Student B to become involved in a long-term project.
 (Student A – be persuasive; Student B – avoid commitment)
4 Student B suggests working Saturday mornings, to meet a tight deadline.
 (Student B – be persuasive; Student A – try to avoid being negative)

>> For more exercises, go to **Practice file 1** on page 102.

9 Work with a partner. Think of a time when you had to report back to someone on one of the following.

- the result of a meeting
- what someone said
- how a project was going
- a success
- something that went badly
- a piece of research
- a trip abroad
- a course you'd been on

Practise reporting this to your partner. Alternatively, turn to File 02 on page 136 for some suggestions.

10 Discuss the impression you got from your partner in **9**. Did you give the impression you intended to give to your partner?

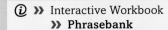 ⓘ >> Interactive Workbook >> Email

Key expressions

Reporting a personal observation
I get the impression that …
From what I could see, …

Reporting from another source
Apparently, it seems that …
According to …
I gathered from …
It was made clear that …

Expressing doubt
I'm just not 100% convinced.
I'm a bit wary of …
I'm a bit reluctant to …

Avoiding commitment
I wouldn't like to say.
I can't promise anything.
I wouldn't go so far as to say …

Being persuasive
I've got to say that …
I'm totally convinced.
I'm sure you'll agree …
I'm fully confident …
We can't go wrong.

Trying to avoid being negative
To be fair, it could have been worse.
It's more of a … than a …
I'm not saying … / It's not that …, it's just that …

Dismissing obstacles
That's not a reason to (delay).

Stating an advantage
The major advantage is …
The pros definitely outweigh the cons.

ⓘ >> Interactive Workbook
     >> Phrasebank

Language at work | Tenses review

1 Read extracts 1–7 from the meeting. Then match them to meanings a–g.

1 I *had planned* to spend an extra day in Krakow itself. ___
2 It was made clear that I *should go* exploring. ___
3 It's *going to be* a bit more complicated than we anticipated. ___
4 The client *has told us* that the site is likely to be around the Krakow area. ___
5 They*'re really pushing* the area for development. ___
6 I *had been looking* around Krakow for a couple of days. ___
7 I*'ll be writing* everything up later this week. ___

a something happening around the time of speaking
b a recent event affecting the present
c a recommendation
d a prediction made with some certainty
e something decided in the past, which did not happen
f an activity in progress at a particular time in the future
g an activity in progress up to a certain point in the past

2 Work with a partner. Turn to audio scripts 02–04 ▷ on page 150. Compare the **bold** section of sentences a–g with the scripts. Is the meaning in a–g different from the meaning in the scripts? If so, how?

a The client **has been telling us** that the site is likely to be around the Krakow area.
b They **have really been pushing** the area for development.
c I **was looking** around Krakow for a couple of days.
d I **planned** to spend an extra day in Krakow itself.
e It was made clear that I **should have gone** exploring.
f It **could be** a bit more complicated than we anticipated.
g I'll **have written** everything up later this week.

》 For more information, go to **Language reference Unit 1** on page 126.

3 Read this email and correct any tense mistakes. Then circle any verbs where you could use an alternative verb form. How would this change the tone of the email?

Dear Kaszia

In response to your enquiry about the feasibility of bringing forward the completion date, I had been skimming through the initial proposal and was gathering from talking to members of the team that unfortunately it won't be as straightforward as we had hoped.

I should have pointed out that the suppliers are being expected to deliver the raw materials required by the end of next week, but so far we had heard nothing from them. We try to get in touch with them and have been insisting that we'll need to know by the end of the week. However, if we haven't heard by then, we need to take legal action to resolve the matter. I'll have got back to you at the beginning of next week – by then I know what will be happening.

José Peres

》 For more exercises, go to **Practice file 1** on page 103.

4 Work with a partner. You share an office. Get to know each other. Talk about the following topics in relation to your work.

- an ongoing project
- a major change
- your responsibilities
- your regrets and hopes
- your predictions
- your career history

What did you learn about each other? What do you have in common?

Practically speaking | Introducing yourself to a group

1 Work with a partner. Discuss questions 1–3.
1. In what situations do you have to introduce yourself to a group in your own language / in English? How do you feel?
2. How much information about yourself do you provide?
3. What impression do you think you give?

2 06▷ A multinational company is holding a training session at its offices in Chicago. Listen to three participants introducing themselves. Would you have presented yourself in a similar way? What did they do well or badly?

3 The speakers include information about these topics. Put them in a logical order.
- aspirations
- reason for being there
- role
- achievements / activities
- who they are

4 06▷ Listen again and complete phrases 1–13. Then match the phrases to the topics in **3**.
1. Hi, _____ Holly Cheng. _____ the Singapore office …
2. _____ everything that goes on in Production Planning.
3. … _____ get on top of things and can see ways of …
4. _____ local production …
5. I guess _____ take on board anything I can about how to …
6. Hello. For _____ Elke Seifried from Graz in Austria.
7. _____ optimizing the quality assurance procedures …
8. _____ jettison any sub-standard products and _____ working out what went wrong.
9. _____ over the years, _____ procedures …
10. … _____ share some of my ideas with you here.
11. Hi, there. _____, I'm Harvey Benson from Atlanta.
12. … _____ coordinate what happens between departments …
13. … _____ talking, mailing, getting on people's cases, and so on …

▶▶ For extension and revision go to **Useful phrases** on page 134.

5 Take turns to introduce yourself to the class. Compare styles / use of language.

ⓘ ▶▶ Interactive Workbook ▶▶ **Exercises and Tests**

Key word | *point*

Match phrases 1–5 with *point* to definitions a–e.
1. To *get to the point*, we want to help out all the sites around the world.
2. *What's the point* of me being here today?
3. I'd like to *point out* that over the years, I have been continually improving procedures.
4. *There's no point* me rambling on if you can't understand what I'm saying.
5. *The point is*, we're finding it really tough to keep on top of demand.

a. make you aware of the fact that
b. stop digressing
c. what's important is
d. it isn't worth
e. what's the reason for

Culture question
- What criteria do you use to judge somebody when they introduce themselves?
- In your culture, when introducing yourself, is it appropriate to use humour, to be formal or informal, to list your achievements, to downplay the importance of your work?
- What else is important? Do you know what is appropriate in other cultures?

Company profile
Adventurous Appetites

Adventurous Appetites is an innovative start-up based in Spain which provides corporate event management services for visitors to Madrid. Since its creation in 2004, Adventurous Appetites has established partnerships with several web-based travel agencies in the US and European Union. Profits have been good and client feedback indicates how personalized and friendly the service is. The question is, where to go from here? James Fraser, the Managing Director, is considering expanding the company and has asked location scouts to investigate three possibilities.

Do Madrid the Spanish way from 8.00 p.m. till late

Want to get off the tourist track and experience the authentic 'Madrileño' ambience?

Join us on a 'gastronómico' tour and let us guide you round some of the delights that the real Madrid has to offer.

If you are the type of person who likes to get away from the main tourist areas and get a real feel for the cities you visit, come with us and let us show you why we love Madrid. We avoid the bustling main square, full of tourists, where the food and drink is expensive and frankly average. We like the local ambience with traditional food and drink and 'Madrileño' culture.

Adventurous Appetites offers a service for those people who, after visiting the tourist sites (or working!) during the day, want to soak up the atmosphere and culture of the real Madrid in the evening.

We do not offer one of those 'all-inclusive packages', but a personalized service. You choose what you want to eat and how much you want to pay – we are here to guide you and help you experience Madrid in an authentic and memorable way.

Hi David

It's great to hear you are available to visit Beijing for us next month. As you know, we have been talking for some time about the possibility of expanding Adventurous Appetites to a location outside Spain, and my preferences are for South East Asia, the UK, or Canada. As with Madrid, this needs to be a major city with an established culinary reputation. Beijing is one option, but we've also shortlisted Edinburgh and Vancouver, and I'm sending two other location scouts to each of these destinations.

Basically, I'd like you to submit a short report on your initial research in Beijing, but I'll call you over the next week or so to brief you in more detail on the kind of information I'm looking for.

Best wishes

James Fraser
Managing Director
Adventurous Appetites

Discussion

1 What are the strengths of Adventurous Appetites?

2 Would you / your company consider using the services of Adventurous Appetites? Why / Why not?

3 What issues do you think James needs to address when he expands?

4 What are your initial thoughts on the three locations proposed?

Task

1 07 ▷ You are the location scouts for Adventurous Appetites. You are about to visit one of the proposed locations. James has left you a voicemail message, giving instructions. Make a note of the key points to look out for.

2 Work in three groups. Group A, you are visiting Beijing – turn to File 28 on page 142. Group B, you are visiting Edinburgh – turn to File 04 on page 136. Group C, you are visiting Vancouver – turn to File 14 on page 139. In your working groups read the factfile about your city and discuss the strengths and weaknesses of the location.

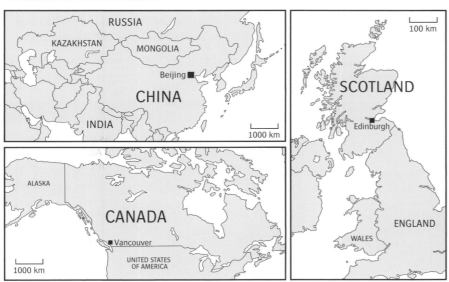

3 After your fact-finding trip, you meet the other scouts and James for the first time at an informal meeting. Introduce yourselves appropriately, then tell the others about your findings, making sure that you refer to
   • your impressions of the place
   • the pros / cons of the location
   • any other items James mentioned in his brief.

4 As a group, decide on
   • which location you believe should be the first location for expansion
   • action points – what you need to do next.

The Expert View

There's no doubt that the knowledge and experience acquired by a company in its initial location is a key asset for international expansion. However, internationalization can also provide learning opportunities for a company, through exposure to new cultures, ideas, etc. This experience can be used to create new expertise that complements and leverages the company's prior knowledge. Therefore the two basic dimensions defining multinational expansion should be both the effort to earn income from the diffusion and transfer of current knowledge, as well as the possibility of generating new knowledge to produce future income.

Jaime Bonache, Professor of International HRM

Cranfield School of Management

Unit 1 | Connections

Case study

2 | Careers

Starting point

1 **What is the best career decision you ever made? What happened?**

2 **Looking back at your career to date, is there anything you would change or do differently? Why? / Why not?**

Working with words | Comparing career paths and choices

1 On a global recruitment website, Professor Ben Fletcher of the University of Hertfordshire, UK, compares careers to the children's game of 'Snakes and Ladders'. Brainstorm what you think the snakes and the ladders might be.

2 Which of the lists below do you think are the typical 'snakes', and which are the typical 'ladders'? Why?

1	2
<ul><li>Being determined to succeed.</li><li>Keeping in with key people.</li><li>Being ruthless.</li><li>Taking more risks than others.</li><li>Appearing active and fast-moving.</li><li>Staying ahead of the game.</li><li>Managing 'others' in pursuit of your cause.</li><li>Holding on to successes and blaming failures on others.</li><li>Standing out from the crowd – getting noticed by the 'right' people.</li></ul>	<ul><li>Standing up for what you believe in.</li><li>Taking the initiative – coming up with your own list of priorities for job success.</li><li>Taking account of the ethical and moral dimension in business decisions.</li><li>Taking a minority position if you believe it is right.</li><li>Sticking up for your team blindly – taking the blame for mistakes they make.</li><li>Doing a good job quietly, without taking the credit.</li><li>Looking out for problems others have not seen in a decision, and highlighting them.</li><li>Getting on with your life outside work.</li><li>Looking out for your colleagues / team.</li></ul>

3 Read the rest of the text and see if you chose the correct list in 2. Do you find any of the real snakes and ladders surprising? Why / Why not?

Making the right move

To many aspiring corporate climbers, the first list appears to be the ladders to success, and the second list, the snakes of failure. Of course, this strategy doesn't stand up to scrutiny in a good company with good management, and in the end it is those companies that you will want to be in. If you really want to move on to the next rung of the corporate ladder you need to play by different rules. Yes, you guessed it; those things that look like the ladders are really the snakes. Of course, some people do get up the so-called snakes, but they are not what I call the True Super Achievers and they struggle to cling on to what they achieve.

4 Match the verbs in A to the preposition combinations in B, to form multiword verbs from the texts in **2** and **3**. Then read the texts again and check your answers.

A

stand _____	stick _____	stay _____	get _____
stand _____	cling _____	come _____	keep _____
hold _____	look _____	move _____	stand _____

B

on to (x3)	out for	up to	up for (x2)	ahead of
on with	up with	in with	out from	

5 Work with a partner. Think of definitions for the multiword verbs in **4**, using the context in the texts in **2** and **3** to help you.

6 Choose six of the multiword verbs in **4**, and write questions about careers or work. Join another pair. Take turns to ask each other your questions.

Example: *Is it important to stand out from the crowd in your company?*

7 08▷ Listen to the interview with career coach Susan Whittaker. Are the following statements true (T) or false (F)?

1 The interviewer becomes more convinced by Susan's views as the interview goes on. ____
2 Susan believes that career progress is the responsibility of the individual. ____
3 She thinks it is counterproductive for managers to allow staff to leave. ____

8 08▷ Match the verbs in A to the phrases in B to form fixed phrases from the interview. Then listen to the interview again and check your answers.

A	B
1 follow ____	a your horizons
2 move ____	b backwards
3 grow into ____	c a stage where …
4 reach ____	d in a better position
5 broaden ____	e your role
6 go beyond ____	f horizontally
7 take a step ____	g the scope of your job
8 put yourself ____	h less conventional paths

9 Work with a partner. Match the phrases you formed in **8** to the definitions a–h below. Can you use any of these phrases to talk about examples from your own career?

a do something original or unusual ____
b change jobs for a similar salary and responsibilities ____
c improve your situation ____
d increase your experience / knowledge ____
e get to a point where … ____
f develop to a point where you can do your job well ____
g develop further than current limitations allow ____
h cancel the effects of any progress you had made ____

» For more exercises, go to **Practice file 2** on page 104.

10 Work with a partner. Prepare to give a short talk for new employees about career development opportunities at your company. Consider some of the following aspects.

- training opportunities
- appraisals
- mentoring schemes
- job shadowing
- promotion prospects
- corporate culture
- sabbaticals
- teamwork

1 Discuss what you are going to talk about. Decide on six important points, and come up with an outline for the talk.
2 Take turns to practise the talk. Use as many of the new items of vocabulary from **4** and **8** as you can.

ⓘ » Interactive Workbook » **Glossary**

Context

The partners at Coben Walsh, a small, but expanding accountancy company, are considering making changes to their recruitment policy. In the past they have always recruited graduates, but they are finding it increasingly difficult to attract suitable candidates. Heidi Dawson, the HR Manager, and her new Deputy, Arun Chauhan, have been investigating the option of offering jobs to school-leavers. They have now called a meeting with the partners, Andy Coben and Rachel Walsh.

Meetings | Managing the discussion | Sharing ideas

1 Can you predict what kind of issues may be discussed during this meeting?

2 09 ▷ Listen to Extract 1 from the meeting while referring to the agenda. Heidi is chairing the meeting and the handwritten notes are prompts to herself. Note down
  1 the points on the agenda that are covered
  2 the points where any digressions or interruptions occur
  3 the phrases Heidi uses to express each of her handwritten prompts.

---

start meeting and establish meeting objectives

Agenda: Recruitment policy meeting

Attendees: Heidi Dawson (chair), Arun Chauhan, Andy Coben, Rachel Walsh

  1 Outline of current recruitment issues
  • recruitment difficulties *ask Arun to present his findings*
  • staff retention *get Arun to talk about this*
  2 Proposal to recruit school-leavers
  3 Discussion

---

3 10 ▷ Listen to Extract 2 from the meeting and answer questions 1–3.
  1 What are the proposed conditions for school-leaver positions?
  2 Why does Heidi think school-leavers would want to work for the company?
  3 Why does Rachel think it would be better to focus on improving graduate intake?

4 Match phrases a–d to categories 1–4.
  1 Putting forward ideas: _____
  2 Expressing reservations / disagreeing: _____
  3 Interrupting: _____
  4 Dealing with interruptions / digression: _____

  a You're absolutely right, but …
  b You probably won't like this idea, but …
  c Can I suggest we come back to this point a bit later on?
  d Could I just say something here?

5 09, 10 ▷ Listen to Extracts 1 and 2 again and make a note of other phrases you hear for the categories in 4.

6 Which phrases from **4** and **5** are used to put forward an idea which

1 you believe to be unpopular?
2 is under consideration?
3 you are confident about?

>> For more exercises, go to **Practice file 2** on page 104.

7 Work with a partner. In addition to the school-leavers programme, HR and the partners decide to look into ways of improving graduate intake / retention. Can you add any other ideas (and possible reservations) to their list?

Ideas for improving graduate intake / retention

• Greater presence at national graduate recruitment fairs.   Will this really help?

• Increase the starting salary.   Too costly for the company?

• Introduce penalties for graduates who don't stay beyond their training.
  Demotivating? May discourage some graduates from applying?

• Increase communication between graduates already working for the company and those considering applying, e.g. in blogs, podcasts on company website.
  No control over what is said about the company?

8 Have a meeting using the ideas from **7** and the flow chart below.

A Start the meeting and establish objectives.

B Ask for permission to speak.

A Give permission to speak.

B Put forward an idea that you are confident about.

A Express reservations.

B Put forward an idea which may be unpopular.

A Interrupt and disagree.

B Put forward an idea under consideration.

A Express reservations.

B Put forward a further idea.

A React to the idea.

9 Work in groups of three. Hold a meeting to discuss ways of improving staff efficiency. Use the agenda below or create one for your company.

Student A, you are chairing the meeting. Manage the discussion and make sure everybody keeps to the agenda.

Student B, turn to File 06 on page 137. Student C, turn to File 18 on page 140.

Agenda: Improving staff efficiency

1 Too much time wasted in the cafeteria
2 Messages are not being passed on
3 Complaints about attending training in off-site training centres
4 High absenteeism

(i) >> Interactive Workbook >> **Email**

Unit 2 | Careers

Key expressions

Managing the discussion
So let's get started.
The purpose of today's meeting is …
Can I suggest we come back to …?
Coming back to …
I'll get on to that in a moment.

Involving people
Perhaps you'd like to talk us through …
Did you want to talk about …?

Asking / giving permission to speak
Would this be the right moment to mention …?
Could I just say something?
If I could just come in there …
Go ahead.

Putting forward unpopular ideas
I know you're not keen on it, but …
You probably won't like this idea …
I'm not sure what your feelings are about this, but …

Putting forward ideas under consideration
We were wondering if …
Something else we've been thinking about is …

Putting forward ideas you are confident about
I'm sure you'll understand the need to …
The obvious solution to this problem must be to …

Disagreeing / expressing reservation
It's interesting you should say that, because actually …
You're absolutely right, but …

(i) >> Interactive Workbook
   >> Phrasebank

Culture question

• Do you openly criticize ideas that you don't like? Why? / Why not?
• Do you think that different cultures have different attitudes to open criticism?

Language at work | Expressing attitudes to the past

1 11 ▷ **Listen to two debriefing conversations where the participants from the meeting gave their impressions after the event. Complete sentences 1–12.**

Conversation 1

1 _____ a face-to-face meeting with the partners.

2 Yes, _____, Arun – as you're the one who's ...

3 If _____ one of the recruitment consultants ...

4 _____ a bit more progress today.

5 Yes, _____ how Rachel would react to the school-leavers proposal.

6 Well, _____ it really ...

Conversation 2

7 I _____ a bit too forthright, but I need to be sure ...

8 Well, it _____ we'd just gone round in circles.

9 But _____ the other side of the argument?

10 What _____ improving our graduate intake?

11 I _____ much to the discussion ...

12 Yes, but _____ to the meeting, though.

2 **Which sentences in 1 show that the speaker**

a is satisfied with something? _____

b is relieved about something? _____

c is dissatisfied with something? _____

d regrets something with hindsight? _____

Sometimes more than one answer is possible.

3 **Match the sentences in 1 to structures a–d below.**

a third conditional _____   c fixed phrase + past simple _____

b modal + perfect infinitive _____   d fixed phrase + past perfect _____

>> For more information, go to **Language reference Unit 2** on page 126.

4 **Work with a partner. Look at the 'nearly' CV below. The career choices made are in bold. Discuss the alternative career and the consequences.**

Example: *If only they'd known the employer abroad would go bankrupt!*

1 Graduate from university (business studies).

a Study for a postgraduate degree (e.g. MBA).

b Look for a first job to get some experience.

2 Offered first job abroad.

a Accept and move to that country.

b Refuse and eventually find a job at home.

3 Employer abroad goes bankrupt.

a Stay abroad and study for a postgraduate degree.

b Return to home country and change career path.

4 Back in home country, offered a new job which is really a sideways move.

a Accept the job.

b Reject and start your own business.

5 Shortly after you start your own business, a multinational offers to acquire it.

a Accept the offer from the multinational.

b Refuse the offer and keep going.

>> For more exercises, go to **Practice file 2** on page 105.

5 **Think of your own 'nearly' CV. Talk to your partner about some of the decisions you made. Consider**

• how you feel about these decisions with hindsight

• possible alternative decisions and their consequences.

   Example: *It's just as well I went to work overseas – or I would never have met my wife.*

Practically speaking | Getting your point across

1 What can you do to get your point across / make yourself understood?

2 12 ▷ Listen to five conversations and complete sentences 1–10.

1. Um, well … _____?
2. No, _____ the ones drawn up for internal purposes.
3. _____ the scale at the bottom of the page, _____ what I mean.
4. Yes, _____. Am I supposed to notify everybody …
5. _____ it's worth sending it to the people responsible for …
6. _____, there's no point in it sitting in your in-tray …
7. … but look, _____ that I need to see a dramatic improvement …
8. But _____ I'd like to see more evidence of how you deal with …
9. Yes, but _____, they'd have liked to be more involved with …
10. Look … _____, couldn't we consider letting them …

3 Match the phrases in **2** to these techniques for getting your point across.

a Reformulating: ___ c Illustrating or offering to illustrate a point: ___
b Clarifying what is meant: ___ d Summarizing: ___

4 Work with a partner. You are both in an update meeting and you are discussing the points on the agenda. Student A, turn to File 08 on page 137. Student B, turn to File 16 on page 139.

Have the meeting using the flow chart below. Student A, you have two minutes to get your point across. Student B, ask questions for further clarification. Then change roles, and continue with the next point on the agenda.

A Say what you think about the issue.

B Ask why / express surprise.

A Illustrate your point.

B Ask for further clarification.

A Clarify / reformulate / summarize.

▷▷ For extension and revision go to **Useful phrases** on page 134.

5 Work with a partner. Take turns to ask each other questions on the topics in the list. Ask for clarification where necessary. Respond using phrases from **2**.

- your performance this year
- how you deal with stressful situations
- your current work / project
- your team's strengths and weaknesses

Key word | *so*

Match sentences 1–4 to the uses of *so* in a–d. What other words could you use to replace *so* in each sentence?

1. *So*, what would you do if one of your key members of staff was off sick on the day of an important presentation?
2. Couldn't we consider letting them trial the products, *so that* they feel their views count?
3. I know Alex is looking for new contacts, and *so* is Thierry.
4. But it's been *so* difficult with all the changes.

a used to add a reason
b used for emphasis
c used to express *also* or *likewise*
d introduces a question

Agenda: Update meeting

1. Monthly reports
2. The competition
3. Sales figures
4. Travel budget

ⓘ ▷▷ Interactive Workbook ▷▷ **Exercises and Tests**

Axtrin: The case for establishing a career review process

- The organization was growing rapidly. It had plans to launch 22 new drugs on to the market in the next five years, and a further 15 in the following two years. Its share of the primary care sector – i.e. drugs prescribed by family doctors – had grown by 60% in one year.
- Axtrin found itself having to look outside the company to recruit new sales and marketing teams, rather than being able to find the necessary talent internally. For the longer term, it was essential that people in the organization were aware of the emerging career possibilities at Axtrin.
- As an innovation-focused company, Axtrin's success depends on the creativity, performance, and achievements of its staff at all levels. They have to anticipate and respond quickly to a fast-moving commercial environment.
- The company already had performance review procedures in place, helping individuals to develop in their role. A longer-term view, enabling staff to plan their careers and to be aware of the real possibilities in the company, was also needed.
- Without a formal career review process in place, there was a danger that talented people, painstakingly and expensively recruited, would leave. The costs to individuals and to the company were potentially enormous, and avoidable.
- Axtrin became a client of tpmg, the performance management consultancy, with expertise in HR-related services and software.

tpmg The Performance Management Group

At tpmg we fully understand the high-value areas of HR systems in terms of building and enhancing the capability of people, and we can help you to find ways of managing the performance and development of your people.

We provide leading companies with an innovative blend of HR-related services and software. We are the market leader in customer-focused web tools designed specifically to support top performance, and we focus on quality conversations between an individual and their colleagues, an individual and their line manager, or individuals collectively and their organization.

The software we have developed enables us to work with you on
- collecting 360-degree feedback via electronic questionnaires from managers, peers, and even external contacts and customers
- conducting employee surveys using an email-supported web tool for flexible, fast, powerful, and cost-effective results
- developing effective career review and performance management processes.

Our customers are in many sectors, such as financial and professional services, media, publishing, retailing, pharmaceuticals, transport, universities, and government. We are particularly proud of the fact that our relationships with these leading organizations are usually long-term.

13 ▷ **Listen to a manager from Training and Development at Axtrin explaining how they set up the career review process with tpmg's help.**

Discussion

1 How did the establishment of a career review process at Axtrin differ from the performance review process that was already in place?

2 In what ways do you think the establishment of a career review process helped Axtrin / its staff?

3 How do you think the input from tpmg helped with setting up the process?

Task

1
> Zylapharm is a young, medium-sized pharmaceutical company which is undergoing rapid expansion. It has taken on a lot of new staff recently and the HR department is in the process of setting up a formal career structure. Having heard of the successful Axtrin case, they have now decided to work with tpmg to find ways of encouraging new talent to stay in the company.

Work in two groups. Each group should read the information and discuss initial ideas.

Group A, you are HR managers. Turn to File 21 on page 141 for details about the current career structure in your company and decide what you would like tpmg to do for you.

Group B, you are consultants for tpmg, and you are about to start working with Group A. Turn to File 35 on page 144 for some possibilities for the client.

2 Hold an initial meeting to put forward ideas for what could be done when you work together. Follow the agenda below. One person from Group B will chair the meeting. Make sure some decisions are reached.

Meeting agenda

- Current situation in the company
- Where we want to be in five years' time
- tpmg propositions
- Conclusion of discussion

The Expert View

The essence of good career management is firstly to clarify your career goals. It is also important to clarify why these goals have meaning to you as well as the organization, since this will ensure motivation from both you and your company. You then need to take time to consider how you can achieve these goals and who can help you access the information that will enable you to do so. It is also essential that you have regular conversations to receive feedback and discuss your progress in achieving these goals.

Peter Fennah, MSc MA Hons,
Chartered Occupational Psychologist,
Director, Career Development Service
Cranfield School of Management

Unit 2 | Careers

Case study

21

3 | Change

Starting point

1 What do you like or dislike about your place of work? Think about space, layout, lighting, equipment, noise, location, etc.

2 What does 'flexible working' mean to you?

3 Will the way you work in the future be different? If so, how and why?

Working with words | Discussing working practices

1 Read this text. Which description is closest to your organization?

Quite a few organizations invest in new offices and information systems in order to improve efficiency, but they do comparatively little to **transform** a corporate culture that is often rooted in a previous era. Others seek to **implement** innovations in their working practices and **procedures** – such as flexible hours, teleworking, policies for work-life balance – without **putting in place** the necessary infrastructure of facilities and technology. Some companies manage to combine a poor infrastructure with an aversion to any kind of cultural change. But of course there are a few that get it right, combining both innovative working practices and the **means** to make them work.

2 How good is your organization at changing with the times? Decide to what extent you agree with the statements below in relation to your company.

1	The company buildings create a **dynamic** working atmosphere.	1 2 3 4 5
2	Staff are judged by the hours they work, not what they achieve.	1 2 3 4 5
3	Staff need to have excellent IT skills.	1 2 3 4 5
4	In order to be able to work here you need to **access** paper files.	1 2 3 4 5
5	Staff can work wherever and whenever is most **effective** for the job in hand.	1 2 3 4 5
6	Meetings have a sense of **purpose**, and result in decisions.	1 2 3 4 5
7	The demands of working at the company put pressure on people's home lives.	1 2 3 4 5
8	Seamless technology across all our sites enables us to perform competitively.	1 2 3 4 5
9	Most staff aren't given the **option** to work flexible hours.	1 2 3 4 5
10	Staff are consulted before any new procedures are put in place.	1 2 3 4 5

Strongly agree 1 2 3 4 5 Strongly disagree

3 Look at the texts in **1** and **2** again. Find words in **bold** that are similar in meaning to the words in *italics* in sentences 1–10.

1 We need to come up with ways of being more *efficient* in our work.

2 We're *entering* quite a difficult period, and there are plenty of challenges ahead.

3 At the interview you have to prove you have the *ability* to do the job well.

4 We like to give all staff the *opportunity* to come back to us with any comments.

5 We have *changed* the job description quite significantly.

6 It's important to *carry out* thorough research before redesigning jobs.

7 It's quite a lengthy *process* from agreeing the changes to implementing them.

8 I don't really understand the *meaning* of the last paragraph.

9 He's in his sixties, but he's still an *energetic* man with lots of new ideas.

10 Call IT and ask them to *install* all the software you need.

4 Can you use the words in **bold** from the texts in the sentences in **3**? If so, does the meaning change?

5 14▷ Listen to an interview with Iñaki Lozano, a consultant specializing in space management and new ways of working, and answer questions 1–3.

   1 What three organizational aspects of companies do BICG focus on?

   2 Why is their work necessary, and what are the advantages?

   3 Who is most likely to resist change / embrace change?

6 14▷ Listen to the interview again. What nouns collocate with verbs 1–8?

   1 accommodate _____   5 generate _____

   2 achieve _____   6 exchange _____

   3 anticipate _____   7 assess _____

   4 facilitate _____   8 measure _____

7 What other nouns do the verbs 1–8 in **6** collocate with? Match them to a–h below.

   a targets / objectives   **e** progress / productivity

   b special requirements / requests   **f** development / growth

   c ideas / interest   **g** performance / a situation

   d knowledge / points of view   **h** potential difficulties / objections

8 Work with a partner. Ask and answer questions about working conditions in your companies using the collocations from **6** and **7**.

   ▶▶ For more exercises, go to **Practice file 3** on page 106.

9 Work with a partner. You work for a manufacturing company and meet to discuss a problem with morale in the factory. Read about the possible causes in the email, then follow steps 1–3.

   1 Briefly outline the main points.

   2 Discuss possible approaches to improve morale.

   3 Decide on an action plan for change.

Dear all

Following a series of low productivity figures, I've been looking into the situation in the factory. I have talked to a number of staff and the general impression is that they are not motivated and they are doing the bare minimum to achieve their daily targets. From my point of view, this seems to be a self-perpetuating cycle of low morale – the figures are down so the supervisors are applying more pressure, which means people feel less valued, etc. Anyway, I thought I ought to let you know my findings so far (see below).

Possible causes of low morale:
- the impact of recent technical changes in production
- work-life balance issues
- working by output / result, not by time spent
- cost-saving initiatives
- instability of jobs in the sector

Let me know if you'd like to discuss this further.

Best regards

Brian

ⓘ ▶▶ Interactive Workbook ▶▶ **Glossary**

Context

A large insurance company is creating a strategy for facing the future and one of its managers has been asked to attend a seminar on the future of working practices. The manager is expected to report their findings to the management team including the CEO. As the management team is cross-functional, specialist terminology and jargon may not be understood by everyone.

Presenting | Giving a formal presentation

1 Work with a partner. Discuss the following questions.
- How often do you give presentations and what kind of audiences do you present to?
- How do you feel about giving presentations?
- How often do you listen to presentations and who gives these presentations?
- What difficulties do you have when listening to a presentation in English?

2 15–18 ▷ Listen to four extracts from a formal presentation. Fill in the notes on the slides below.

1 Facing the future

Introduction:
Flexible working – by 2050 most people will have been working flexibly for more than a decade.

Presentation outline (x3 sections):
1 current research
2 effects on the workforce
3 effects on employers

Notes

3 Effects on the workforce

- 'Binge-time careerism', employees working non-stop for a period, and then taking time off.
- 'Shadow careers' encouraging personal development.
- 24 / 7 access to work email and phones / BlackBerries leading to longer hours.

Notes

2 Current research

- Rise in 'demuting' – 12 million people in UK will be working from home by 2020.
- New generation of 'career nomads', employees moving around changing jobs / careers.

Notes

4 Effects on the employer

- Competing for talent.
- Faced with dilemma as employees gain the power to make choices.

Notes

3 15–18▷ Listen to the four extracts from the presentation again and refer back to the slides in **2**. Note down the phrases which are used for the following functions.

Extract 1

1 Put the presentation in context: _____

2 Refer to a point that will be raised later: _____

3 Outline the structure: _____

Extract 2

4 Introduce the second slide: _____

5 Explain the terms 'demuting' and 'career nomads': _____

Extract 3

6 Introduce the third slide: _____

7 Explain the terms 'binge-time careerism' and 'shadow careers': _____

8 Introduce the information on 24/7 working: _____

9 Refer to a point that was made earlier: _____

10 Talk about a point not included in the presentation outline: _____

Extract 4

11 Introduce the last point: _____

12 Finish the presentation: _____

4 Turn to audio scripts 15–18▷ on page 153. Check your answers to **3**.

» For more exercises, go to **Practice file 3** on page 106.

5 Work with a partner. You are going to report back to your colleagues and CEO on your findings from the presentation. Using your notes in **2**, prepare an outline for your own presentation summarizing your findings.

1 Decide who will present which parts of your presentation, and what phrases from **3** you will use to structure and signal the different parts of the presentation.

2 Practise giving your part of the presentation to each other. When listening to your partner, check against your notes in **2** that they include all the relevant information, and that they use appropriate language from **3**.

6 Think of a change you would like to make at your company. Prepare to present your proposal for change to the board of directors. As the presentation will be formal, you need to prepare well. Sketch out the structure of your presentation on a series of slides. Include

- background information
- an outline of the structure
- explanation of specialist terms
- a reference to something you will say later
- a reference to something you said earlier
- a digression
- links from one section to another
- a conclusion.

7 Work in groups. Listen to each other's presentations, and make notes of the key points. When you have finished, check your understanding and ask questions.

ⓘ » Interactive Workbook » **Email**

Key expressions

Outlining a structure
I've divided my talk up into …
First of all, I'll … After that, I'll …
I'll conclude with …

Beginning the presentation
I'd like to start by saying …

Referring forwards / backwards / sideways
I'll return to … later.
As I said earlier, …
I'll say more about … in a moment.
Just to digress for a second, …

Signalling the next section
OK, moving on …
Turning to …
This brings me to …

Ensuring understanding of a specialist subject
Just to fill you in on some of the background, …
By … I mean …
Now I don't know if you're familiar with …
Well, … refers to …
This is where …
And perhaps here I should explain what I mean by …
That's when …
So, for example, …

Ending the presentation
And this is my key point.
To sum up, …
I'll be happy to take any questions now.

ⓘ » Interactive Workbook
» **Phrasebank**

Culture question

- Is it appropriate in your culture to use humour in presentations?
- How else can you vary the pace?
- What difficulties can be caused when humour is used?

Language at work | Speculating about future changes

1 Look at extracts 1–10 from the presentation. For each one, answer questions a–d.

a What structure is used?

b How certain is the speaker in each sentence?

c Could the structure used be replaced by any other future structure?

d How would an alternative structure change the meaning of the sentence?

1 The flexible working revolution means that management **will become** more about resourcing and measuring results.

2 It's estimated that by 2050 most people **will have been working** flexibly for more than a decade.

3 It's anticipated that as many as twelve million people in the UK **will be working** from home by 2020.

4 The 21st century **is going to be** about a new generation of 'career nomads'.

5 The trend towards home working **could have** other positive social side-effects.

6 We anticipate that this trend **will** only **increase**.

7 Home-based businesses **are likely to** revive local communities.

8 By the mid-21st century a major cultural change **will have taken place**.

9 People **are expected to be working** more flexibly in the future.

10 Solving this dilemma **must surely become** a key priority.

>> For more information, go to **Language reference Unit 3** on page 127.

2 19▷ **Members of the Federation of European Employers were asked: 'Do you think there will be a major change in the way we work in the future?' Listen and note down phrases they use to make predictions.**

3 Put the phrases you noted in **2** into these categories.

1 certain _____

2 probable _____

3 possible _____

4 unlikely _____

4 19▷ **Listen again. Make a note of four phrases the speakers use to refer to a point or period in future time.**

>> For more exercises, go to **Practice file 3** on page 107.

5 Work with a partner. Give your predictions for possible changes in your company / department. Think about the aspects below.

- the business
- budgets
- the competition
- technologies

- your working day
- relationships with colleagues / boss
- your role / prospects
- your colleagues' roles / prospects

Practically speaking | Showing understanding

1 20▷ **Listen to four conversations. What are the problems? How do the listeners respond?**

2 20▷ **Listen again and complete phrases 1–10.**

1 I know _____.
2 It's quite _____.
3 No, it _____?
4 It _____ sending an email …
5 I hear _____. I mean …
6 I _____ for a lot of you …
7 I can _____.
8 I _____ at my last company …
9 I _____ the request again, though.
10 Well, _____ word it so that …

3 **Match the phrases in 2 to categories a–c. Can you add any other phrases?**

a Showing that you understand the problem: _____
b Explaining why you are able to understand the problem: _____
c Offering practical solutions: _____

4 **Work with a partner. Look at sentences 1–4. Discuss how you would respond in order to show understanding.**

1 'My workload has increased dramatically since we merged with the Cork office.'
2 'I don't think my presentation was very convincing.'
3 'This report just doesn't make sense.'
4 'I need to change offices – mine is getting too noisy.'

>> For extension and revision go to **Useful phrases** on page 134.

5 **Think about a problem you currently have at work. Alternatively, use one of the problems below. Take turns to explain the problem, and to respond appropriately.**

Problem 1: Time differences
You work for a company with offices all round the world. You need to coordinate a project, but it is very difficult to call a meeting at a suitable time for everyone.

Problem 2: Holiday planning
You have to plan staffing over the Christmas period. Everyone wants time off, and you feel priority should go to those with small children. However, there are childless staff who feel unfairly treated because they always have to work at Christmas.

6 **Discuss your partner's reaction to your problem with the class. How sympathetic / understanding / practical was it?**

ⓘ >> Interactive Workbook >> **Exercises and Tests**

Key word | *quite*

Replace *quite* in phrases 1–5 with synonyms a–e.

1 It's *quite* hectic over here too.
2 Not *quite*.
3 There were *quite a few* technical problems.
4 I'm finding it *quite a task* to manage my work.
5 **A** I don't want it to look like I'm badgering them.
   B *Quite*. Well you might want to word it so it's not too aggressive, in that case.

a exactly
b several
c very
d absolutely
e very difficult

Parelect is a multinational group operating in the energy, manufacturing, and healthcare sectors, which specializes in electronics and electrical engineering. The company has around 400,000 employees working to develop and manufacture products around the globe. There are a number of companies in the Parelect group. For example, RM-Circuit, an international supplier of automotive electronics, and Isustain, which focuses on sustainable energy.

Planning office space
Background

Phil Marsden, Facility Management Director at Isustain, has written to Carlos Medici at Parelect HQ about plans for changes to the working environment at Isustain. He has also sent Carlos plans of the current building layout for reference. Carlos has now sent a reply.

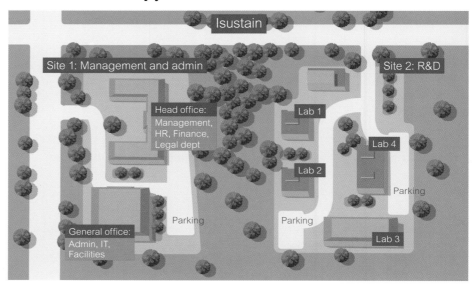

Hi Phil

Thank you for your email. As you know, we have been looking at redefining work space standards across our industry, and it is good that you are now thinking about how this could be achieved at Isustain.

Please find attached for reference a summary of a report from RM-Circuit, where they initiated the first project of its kind. This is now the benchmark in the Parelect group for redefining office space.

Some key points worth noting about this new workspace concept are:
- Improved communication between staff and management.
- Flexible design, e.g. identical desks used in the computer-aided design department (CAD), laboratories, and office areas makes it possible to change the composition of teams and working processes without great expense. Change within a team's working space doesn't have to affect neighbouring work spaces.
- Ergonomics and healthy workspaces, e.g. desk height can be adjusted electronically.

Kind regards

Carlos Medici
Facility Management Director
Parelect HQ

Office space planning project at RM-Circuit

Project

Aim: to promote communication through effective office space planning. Four main sites were set up at Head Office with 20 buildings for production, development, and administration. All activities were concentrated in one building. This building was designed to increase productivity and to act as a benchmark within the industry.

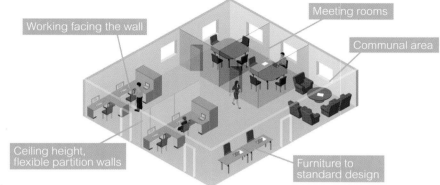

Process

1 Analysis of present-day and future working methods in over 80 discussions.
2 A flexible office concept was defined in workshops, so that the composition of teams and working processes could be changed without great expense, and working areas could be provided when greater concentration was required, as well as spaces for meetings. The management could sit with their teams in the open-plan structure, as well as being able to withdraw for confidential conversations.
3 A pilot project was carried out a year before the company moved into the development centre. Space configuration was mapped out with its variations of furniture. Some twenty staff also worked in these areas for almost twelve months, and changes were made in consultation with these pilot users.

Result

The project has been successful, with the positive reaction of users. An essential contributory factor to the success of such large-scale change has been the involvement of staff at an early stage in the project.

The Expert View

Managing any kind of change is a complex process and in order for it to be successful, the guiding team needs to generate trust, commitment, and teamwork. Firstly they need to encourage staff to feel dissatisfaction with the current situation, so that it's recognized change is required. Secondly, the vision must be right and should be communicated in clear, simple, and sincere ways. The first steps in implementing the change must then be taken in order to keep up the momentum. Tackling these three drivers (dissatisfaction, vision, first steps) and addressing organizational inertia and resistance help increase positive energy for change.

Lester Coupland, Executive Development Consultant, Centre for Customised Executive Development

Cranfield School of Management

Discussion

1 What problems can you see with the layout of Isustain?

2 Why do you think the office space planning concept at RM-Circuit is used as a benchmark in the industry?

3 What key issues do you think need to be addressed when relocating employees and designing office space?

Task

1 Work in groups. You are office space consultants for Isustain. Discuss what solutions you would propose for the company's office space planning issues.

2 In your groups, prepare a presentation that could be given to the staff at the company.

3 Give your presentations to the rest of the class.

4 As a class, decide which proposal would work best for Isustain.

Case study

4 | Risk

Starting point

'Living at risk is jumping off the cliff and building your wings on the way down.'
Ray Bradbury 1920–, novelist

'You can't cross a chasm in two small steps.'
David Lloyd George 1863–1945, British Prime Minister

'Expert prediction is rarely better than rolling the dice.'
Tom Peters 1942– , management writer

1 Discuss the quotes. Do you agree or disagree? Why?

2 Do you consider yourself a risk-taker? Why / Why not?

Working with words | Talking about different kinds of risk

1 What kinds of risks do businesses face?

2 Read this review of a new risk management software package called 'Watchman'. What does the writer say about the following points. Do you agree?
- risks in our everyday lives
- risks in the telecommunications sector
- the link between survival and change
- technology versus human skills

A bold new solution for Risk Management

The world is often a dangerous place to do business in. For an organization to survive it must become adept at **identifying** and managing possible risks. In our personal lives we do this every day, often without thinking about it. Before we cross the road, we look around to make sure there isn't a vehicle heading towards us. And every parent **weighs up** all potential dangers before allowing their child to **run the risk of** riding a bike outside. Businesses have to make **predicting**, **recognizing**, and **minimizing** risk as natural and habitual as this.

Some risks affect all businesses, such as the unpredictability of economics (e.g. inflation), politics (e.g. new legislation), and business realities (e.g. late payments). However, there are also risks specific to each sector. In the volatile telecommunications sector, a mobile phone company has to **anticipate** shifting customer taste in a market that is moving so fast it's hard to look one year into the future, let alone ten.

It's been said that the species most likely to survive is the one most responsive to change. The problem in risk assessment is that progression and change in today's world is no longer linear and predictable. The only successful business will be one that **accepts** uncertainty and is flexible enough to respond to change as it comes. That's where Watchman can help. This impressive software accepts a variety of inputs and then produces a stunning three-dimensional graphic display that allows you to view various risk factors at a glance, all against an interactive timeline. Intuitive controls allow you to filter the output to compare probabilities, **determine** the relative importance of each risk factor, and **evaluate** potential impact. And, of course, you can alter the variables to **gauge** how different conditions make an impact – in the hope that this knowledge will help you to avoid **exposing** your organization to unnecessary risks.

So it's great as far as it goes, but there is a problem. If the input you provide is incomplete this will affect the quality of the risk analysis. Watchman can't do the thinking for you and it can't determine whether a threat is directly relevant to your company. It's a sound program, but it's no replacement for the skilled, intuitive work done by an experienced risk manager.

3 Match the verbs and verb phrases in **bold** in the text in **2** to definitions 1–9.

1 make an informed guess that something will happen (2 verbs)
2 think carefully about something and decide its value or importance (2 verbs)
3 see something and know what it is (2 verbs)
4 consider good and bad aspects of something before making a decision (1 verb)
5 reducing something to the smallest possible level (1 verb)
6 put something in a situation where it is not protected from something (1 verb)
7 encounter the danger of something bad happening (1 verb)
8 carefully calculate and decide something (1 verb)
9 able to regard and understand a situation or future situation as true (1 verb)

4 Work with a partner. Using the verbs and verb phrases in **3**, discuss what advice you would give to someone considering the following decisions.

- accepting a job with another company
- becoming self-employed
- investing savings in the stock market
- relocating to another city / country

5 21 ▷ Listen to three different people discussing risk. In each case, decide

1 what their job might be
2 what risks they have to deal with.

6 21 ▷ Listen again and note which speaker uses these adjectives.

*sensible   cautious   rash   risk-averse   prudent   foolhardy
reckless   bold   imprudent   over-cautious*

7 Which of the adjectives in **6** have a positive connotation (+) and which have a negative connotation (−)?

8 Read these four extracts from employee appraisal reports. Which of the adjectives in **6** could you use to describe their attitudes towards risk?

1 'Luis takes no or few risks.'
2 'Anastasia has a balanced, realistic view of risks.'
3 'Victoria doesn't take a sufficiently careful view of risks.'
4 'Lothar completely ignores obvious dangers and is largely unworried by risks.'

9 Work with a partner. Think about someone you know, e.g. a friend, a current or previous colleague / boss, a famous person, a relative. Describe their attitude towards risk. How similar is their attitude to your own?

≫ For more exercises, go to **Practice file 4** on page 108.

10 Work with a partner. Read this information about a PEST analysis.

PEST analysis is a way of analysing four key external factors that may affect an organization, a business, or a project.
Political (e.g. change of government; change of legislation; impact of corruption)
Economic (e.g. change of labour supply and costs; impact of competitors' behaviour)
Social & Cultural (e.g. change of public opinion, taste, or attitudes; population changes)
Technological (e.g. new technologies; changing costs of communications)

Think about your company. For each category in the PEST analysis
1 brainstorm possible changes in your sector, your country, or the world
2 think about the associated risks for your company / project and any possible action points in response to these risks.
Example: *(Economic) One of our competitors is getting stronger. They might launch a rival product at a lower price. We would then run the risk of losing market share. We should try to be bold with new product ideas to keep ahead of the competition.*

11 Report back to your colleagues on your PEST analysis.

ⓘ ≫ Interactive Workbook ≫ **Glossary**

Context

Frangipani Travel organizes luxury specialist tours and safaris in Kenya, Brazil, India, and Egypt. Their main target clientele is well-off European couples. However, more potential Frangipani customers are organizing holidays for themselves via the Internet and there is less demand for ready-made packages.

The company is considering a bold reorientation to focus exclusively on ecologically-sound 'green holidays'. Jean-Luc, a senior manager based in France, has organized a teleconference with the regional managers to discuss the risks. The participants in the teleconference are – Joana in Brazil, Khalid in Egypt, Thomas in Kenya, and Greta in India.

Telephoning | Taking part in a teleconference

1 Work with a partner. What advice would you give to someone participating in a teleconference in English for the first time? Compare your ideas with the guidelines in File 10 on page 138.

2 22▷ Look at the agenda, then listen to four extracts from the teleconference and note which guidelines from 1 are (or aren't) followed by the participants.

Agenda

Conference call 23 November 10:00 GMT
Moderator: Jean-Luc Boyer

1 Introductions.
2 Proposal 1: redirect Frangipani entirely towards 'Green-Stay' tours (Joana).
3 Proposal 2: introduce 'Green-Stay' tours alongside traditional holiday offers (Greta).
4 Decide on conclusions to take to the board. Agree action points.
5 AOB
6 Set date for follow-up meeting.

3 Put phrases 1–15 from the teleconference into these categories.
   a Inviting / nominating someone to say something: _____
   b Checking if you have understood something correctly: _____
   c Stating that you are not persuaded or have doubts about something: _____
   d Managing the discussion and the behaviour of the participants: _____
   e Summarizing / ending the discussion: _____

   1 I'd be interested in hearing what you think about this.
   2 I'm not fully convinced as yet.
   3 Can I just ask everyone to sum up their views?
   4 Maybe we're digressing a little.
   5 Am I right in saying that the general opinion is we can go ahead on this?
   6 Could you let Greta finish, please?
   7 Maybe we can let Joana answer that.
   8 You're saying that it's not worth reconsidering?
   9 I'd like to draw things to a close.
   10 Can I just check – we are now talking about the alternative smaller-scale proposal?
   11 I still have serious reservations.
   12 Joana, could you talk us through this?
   13 I'm having some second thoughts about it.
   14 We seem to have some sort of consensus.
   15 If I could just bring the conversation back to the agenda.

4 Look at the phrases from the teleconference in A and the alternative phrases in B. What are the differences between them?

A

1 Could you talk us through this?
2 Am I right in saying that the general opinion is we can go ahead on this?
3 I'd be interested in hearing what you think about this.
4 Can I just check …?
5 We seem to have some sort of consensus.

B

Tell us about it.
Do you all agree to go ahead on this?
Tell us what you think.
Can I check …?
We all agree.

5 23 ▷ Listen to these extracts from the teleconference. Decide what the speaker really means in each case. Follow the example.

1 That's interesting, Thomas.
  That's not relevant. I don't want to continue talking about this topic.
2 Maybe we can let Joana answer that.
3 With respect, Joana …
4 Sorry, Khalid …
5 I'm not sure this is getting us anywhere.

6 Work with a partner. Your company is investigating the possibility of introducing performance-related pay in all offices around the world. Some key staff took part in a short teleconference to compare initial reactions to the idea.

One of the participants is describing the call to his colleague. For each underlined section, discuss what each speaker might have said.

By five minutes past two we were all online. The moderator ¹nominated the HR Manager to talk about the proposal and our options, because he's championing the suggestion. I wasn't sure if I had properly understood what he said, so I ²asked for clarification to check if I had understood correctly. He gave a much clearer response. After that we all started discussing the main proposal quite usefully. Then the moderator ³invited the representative from Finance to give her opinion, but she started making a long and irrelevant speech about executive bonuses, so the moderator ⁴interrupted her and ⁵tried to get the discussion back on topic. We talked for about 25 minutes and then the moderator ⁶ended the meeting by asking us to ⁷summarize the main points that had been made.

» For more exercises, go to **Practice file 4** on page 108.

7 Work in small groups with people in the same company or in a similar field of work. Think of a current issue or problem in your work and follow points 1–3.

1 Make notes about the issue under the headings below.

Issue: _____

What needs to be decided: _____

Important factors to consider when making a decision:

_____

2 Write a short agenda for a teleconference about this issue.
3 Now take part in the teleconference to discuss the issue and reach some conclusions.

Alternatively, turn to File 11 on page 138. Work in small groups, choose a moderator, and have the teleconference.

(i) » Interactive Workbook » **Email**

Key expressions

Checking understanding
Am I right in saying that the general opinion is …?
You're saying that …?
Can I just check – we are now talking about …?

Nominating or inviting someone to say something
X, could you talk us through this?
I'd be interested in hearing what you think about this.
Maybe we can let X answer that.

Expressing doubts / disagreement
I still have serious reservations.
I'm not fully convinced as yet.
I'm having second thoughts …
With respect …

Managing the discussion / the participants
Sorry, X. Could you let Y finish, please?
Maybe we're digressing a little.
That's interesting X, but I think …
I'm not sure this is getting us anywhere.
If I could just bring the conversation back to the agenda.

Ending the meeting
We seem to have some sort of consensus.
I'd like to draw things to a close.
Can I just ask everyone to sum up their views?

(i) » Interactive Workbook
    » **Phrasebank**

Culture question

• Are you often interrupted in meetings? If so, how does this make you feel?
• What factors would you consider before making an interruption?
• Do you think people from different cultures might react differently to interruptions?

Language at work | Referencing

1 Turn to page 154 and read audio script **22** ▷. Then look at these extracts. For each one, say exactly what the underlined pronouns *it*, *this* and *that* refer to.

> *Example:* *How about now, Greta? Is <u>that</u> any better?*
> *The word 'that' refers to the sound quality of the call, probably after some technical difficulties.*

1 <u>That</u>'s interesting Thomas … but I think <u>it</u>'s probably best left for another meeting.
2 Well, if you remember, we did explore <u>this</u> last year – <u>that</u> was just before you joined us Khalid – and we decided … <u>it</u> wasn't the route to go down.
3 Greta – I'd be interested in hearing what you think about <u>this</u>.
4 What do you think of <u>this</u>? We offer customers the option of paying …
5 I think <u>that</u>'s where we've got to. Is <u>that</u> right? Joana?
6 To me, <u>it</u> sounds a lot more manageable.
7 <u>It</u>'s been quite hard – but I think we've made the right decision. <u>It</u> would have been too risky to …

2 Look at sentences 2 and 4 in **1** and choose the correct answer from the words in *italics*.
1 If you want to refer to something that is clearly distant or in the past, use *that / it*.
2 If you want to refer to something new, important, more current or relevant, use *this / that*.

➤➤ For more information, go to **Language reference Unit 4** on page 128.

3 <u>Underline</u> the correct answer from the words in *italics*.
1 **A** We used to use QuarkXpress for all our desktop publishing.
  B *That / This* was a really good design application.
2 **A** We hope to double Central European sales within two years.
  B *It / That* is excellent news.
3 **A** Do you think we've made the right choice?
  B Yes. *That / It* would have been a mistake to raise our prices now.
4 **A** He left the company five years ago.
  B Yes – *this / that* caused big problems for our department.
5 **A** Agnetha – do you have any other suggestions?
  B Well, what do you think about *this / that*: we open a new outlet in Medina?
6 **A** Have you seen the new photocopier in the resources room?
  B Yes. *This / It* is very impressive, isn't it?

➤➤ For more exercises, go to **Practice file 4** on page 109.

4 Work with a partner. Choose a topic from the list or think of your own. Discuss your opinions on the topic using referencing language where possible.

> *Example:* **A** *Have you seen that email about bonuses? What do you think it's going to mean for us?*
> **B** *I think it's going to be pretty negative for us. It's going to mean we get less money. This is going to make a lot of people angry.*

- a recent presentation
- a notice on the staff noticeboard
- a recent email giving news about your company
- a news article
- a conference
- a meeting

Practically speaking | Establishing rapport and showing interest

1 Which of the methods a–j for establishing rapport would you use

  1 when meeting someone for the first time?
  2 when meeting a colleague or friend again after a long time?
  3 when meeting a business contact who could help improve your career prospects?

  a recalling past events in common
  b paying a compliment
  c asking a follow-up question
  d asking about someone's journey
  e showing that you already know something about a person you have just met
  f giving a brief summary of your recent history
  g echoing the other person to encourage them to say more
  h joking about yourself
  i being modest about achievements
  j picking up on a key word in order to extend the conversation

2 24▷ Listen to five extracts from conversations. For each conversation decide on the possible relationship between the speakers, the methods from **1** they use to establish rapport, and the phrases that enable them to do so. Complete the table.

Extract	Relationship	Methods	Phrases
1			
2			
3			
4			
5			

>> For extension and revision go to **Useful phrases** on page 134.

3 It is five years in the future – after the course you are doing now has long finished. You have been invited to a social event to meet up with the people who were in your class (and the teacher). You haven't seen any of them for a long time.

  1 Take a minute to think where you might be and what you might be doing in five years' time. Make notes below about your future life.
  The date today is: ⎯⎯⎯⎯⎯⎯⎯⎯⎯⎯
  My work mainly involves: ⎯⎯⎯⎯⎯⎯⎯⎯⎯⎯
  Now I'm living in: ⎯⎯⎯⎯⎯⎯⎯⎯⎯⎯
  The biggest difference compared with my life five years ago is: ⎯⎯⎯⎯⎯⎯⎯⎯⎯⎯
  I work at / in: ⎯⎯⎯⎯⎯⎯⎯⎯⎯⎯

  2 Talk to each person. Use as many methods for establishing rapport from **1** as you can.

ⓘ >> Interactive Workbook >> **Exercises and Tests**

Key word | *matter*

Match phrases 1–7 with *matter / matters* to synonyms a–g.

  1 What's the *matter*?
  2 It's *no laughing matter*.
  3 We'll do it, *no matter what*.
  4 That will make *matters* worse.
  5 *As a matter of fact*, I do smoke.
  6 This *matters*.
  7 It's *a matter of urgency*.

  a a serious topic
  b problem
  c is important
  d the situation
  e despite any difficulties that occur
  f something that must be dealt with immediately
  g actually, you're wrong

Company profile
McCain Foods Ltd

McCain is one of the world's most important makers of frozen food, drinks, snacks, and ready meals. It specializes in potato products including potato chips (French fries) as well as waffles, hash browns, croquettes, wedges, and roast potatoes. McCain is believed to supply around a third of the worldwide market for chips.

Out of the frying pan

Recently, there has been growing concern in Europe about the prevalence of obesity, especially among children. Newspapers, magazines, and TV have all taken up the call for a healthier diet. In order to remain successful McCain needs to be aware of such trends and the potential risks they pose to the company. It has always seen itself as careful to listen to and respond to public demand – and has a successful track record in introducing new products to meet the changing environment. Back in 1979 the company was the first to introduce a chip that could be cooked in the oven rather than the deep fryer and this is now widely seen as a healthier and easier-to-prepare alternative to the fried chip. The more recently launched McCain Home Fries™ oven chip is a huge seller. The challenge for McCain now is to ensure that they are able to market their products in increasingly hostile conditions.

PEST analysis for McCain

Political
The growing pressure to make foods healthier has led to widespread discussion of the possibility of higher taxes on unhealthy food, restrictions on advertising (e.g. during children's TV), regulations limiting what may be sold in schools, requirements to label fat, sugar, and salt content more clearly and even the suggestion of health warnings on packets.

Economic
Because all adults work in more and more households, the market for quality prepared food seems likely to continue growing. People generally have more money but less time, and seek products that allow them to prepare good food quickly. People have been prepared to spend more on sophisticated, higher-quality prepared products, but a downturn in the economy could see a choice of more basic items.

Social & Cultural
Recent health advice given to the public has led to a change in consumer demand. There have been many warnings about eating too much salt and saturated fat. The media regularly include chips within the category of unhealthy or junk food.

Technological
New technology has led to new kinds of 'functional food' items (e.g. margarine that helps reduce your cholesterol levels, yoghurts that help your digestion, etc.) to appear on the shelves, claiming to offer positive health benefits. Potatoes are naturally high in vitamin C and natural carbohydrates – but the technological challenge is retaining nutritional value and flavour while making the product easier to use, or usable in new ways.

Discussion

1 McCain Foods Ltd needs to assess the potential risk factors for the company. Look at the PEST analysis of McCain and decide which factors have the most potential to cause problems.

2 Choose three of the factors and think of ways that McCain might respond to the risk involved.

3 25▷ Listen to a journalist explaining what McCain actually did. Make a note of the actions they have taken. Did they use any of your ideas in 2?

Task

1 Read the information about Asian Spice Traders.

> ### FACTFILE
>
> Asian Spice Traders (AST) is a large food company, exporting hot-spiced Thai, Indonesian, Malaysian, and Indian microwaveable ready meals to Europe. Although it is based in Thailand, the company has found that its Indian food range has been the most successful, outselling the other lines by a factor of three.
>
> After many years of growth, the company recently decided to enter the US market. However, the timing has been problematic as there have been a number of health scares about food quality that have affected confidence in imported food. Despite some expensive advertising, none of the five launch products (all hot Indian and Thai curries) has sold very well. Some of the managers are now wondering whether there really is a market for spicy Asian foods in the US.

2 Work with a partner and discuss questions 1–2.
   1 Based on what you know about current attitudes to food, health, and the present economic situation, what do you think are the biggest risks and opportunities for the company over the next five years?
   2 Which of McCain's strategies would be useful to AST?

3 Asian Spice Traders have employed your team as consultants to advise them about their future strategies. Work with your partner from 2 and join another pair. Decide which pair is A and which pair is B.

   Pair A: Read the extracts from three recent articles about food and health issues in File 12, page 138 and follow steps 1–4.
   1 Decide which information from the articles might be important for AST to consider.
   2 Prepare concrete suggestions for AST based on your own ideas and the information you have read.
   3 Make notes about the reasons for your suggestions.
   4 Outline any potential risks for AST and strategies to deal with them.

   Pair B: Read notes from a brainstorming session about possible strategies for AST in File 56, page 149 and follow steps 1–4.
   1 Discuss your reactions to the notes.
   2 Prepare concrete suggestions for AST based on your ideas and the information you have read.
   3 Make notes about the reasons for your suggestions.
   4 Outline any potential risks for AST and strategies to deal with them.

4 Now work in a group of four with pair A and pair B. Hold a meeting to exchange ideas and reach a consensus about what advice you should give to the company.

The Expert View

Risk assessment should be done regularly, both 'top down', from management, and 'bottom up' by operating units, because each bring a different perspective. It is helpful to have a structured process for the evaluation. Checklists can be useful in ensuring that key areas are considered. However, they may focus managers' attention on the known risks instead of making them think about new risks arising from a changing commercial environment. Too much focus on checklists and risk registers can lead to complacency: noting down that a risk exists is not the same as managing that risk. So the best approach incorporates structured procedures, alongside more intuitive risk assessment methods.

Ruth Bender, Senior Lecturer in Finance and Accounting

Cranfield School of Management

Unit 4 | Risk

Case study

5 | Teamwork

Starting point

1 What problems can occur when working with other people?

2 What different types of personality are needed for a successful team?

Working with words | Exploring team relationships

1 Dr Meredith Belbin of the Henley Management College developed nine team roles to show how different individuals behave in teams. Read the text and compare these team roles with your ideas in *Starting point*.

What kind of team player are you?

Meredith Belbin

1 Plant
Valued in a team for their ability to come up with strange and innovative solutions. Like the absent-minded professor-inventor, they often spend time quietly working alone, which results in solutions to problems, but they may have trouble communicating their ideas effectively.

2 Resource investigator
This person contributes to the team with boundless enthusiasm at the start of the project. They are excellent networkers who express themselves clearly and they vigorously pursue opportunities outside the team. They tend to lose momentum towards the end of a project.

3 Coordinator
The natural chairperson, able to detach themselves from the detail, to see the bigger picture. They are mature, good at delegating and at helping the rest of the team to reach decisions. Their management and delegating powers may mean they don't **pay** enough **attention to** their own duties at work.

4 Shaper
They spur their team into action. You have to tread carefully with this person; they thrive on pressure and challenge, and often get results by pushing others hard to do the same. In their drive to get things done, they may upset other team members by seeming to treat them unfairly.

5 Team worker
Working closely with everyone, they like to **steer clear of** confrontation. They are good listeners and can help to calm situations by talking through problems with colleagues. However, as they don't like taking sides, they may find it difficult to make decisions.

6 Completer – Finisher
The team's perfectionist. They take themselves very seriously – **keeping to** schedules and maintaining quality are equally important to them, and they pay painstaking attention to detail. Colleagues may have trouble relating to them as they are poor delegators and they tend to worry excessively about minor details.

7 Monitor – Evaluator
They are good at judging the situation due to a great ability to analyse logically. They assess periodically and look at all the available options objectively. However, their work can **fall short of** expectations as they can lack drive and find it difficult to relate passionately to their work.

8 Implementer
This person is disciplined and can be relied on to perform to a high level and to **cope with** things practically. They tend not to deviate from a set path and can find it difficult to take new ideas on board.

9 Specialist
They are highly skilled and are usually viewed positively for providing specialized knowledge. They tend not to see the bigger picture, **focusing on** technicalities.

2 Read the text again and discuss questions 1–2 with a partner.

1 What is the main positive and negative characteristic of each role?

2 Which team role best describes you?

3 Underline the adverb in *italics* which collocates with each verb in 1–8. Then check your answers in the text in **1**.

1 communicate their ideas *thoroughly / effectively*

2 express themselves *understandably / clearly*

3 tread *carefully / well* with this person

4 push others *hard / roughly*

5 treat employees *unfairly / carelessly*

6 work *tightly / closely* with a colleague

7 look at (available options) *objectively / deliberately*

8 be viewed *satisfactorily / positively*

4 Work with a partner. Use as many of the verb + adverb combinations in **3** as you can and give each other advice for successful working relationships at your work / in your job.

5 26▷ Three people are talking about the roles they play in their teams at work. Listen to the extracts and identify the strengths and weaknesses of each person.

6 Which of the two Belbin roles best fits each of the people you listened to in **5**?

1 Shaper / Team worker   3 Resource investigator / Implementer

2 Coordinator / Completer – Finisher

7 Work with a partner. Discuss which of the three people you would choose to work with you / in your team, and why.

8 Work with a partner. Replace the <u>underlined</u> words in sentences 1–6 with multi-word verbs in **bold** in the text in **1** with a similar meaning. Change the form of the verb where necessary.

1 I didn't <u>spend enough time on</u> the sales figures – I think they're actually incorrect. _____

2 I'm capable of <u>handling</u> most complications by myself. _____

3 There are some particularly tight deadlines to <u>meet</u>. _____

4 I prefer to <u>avoid</u> any last-minute changes. _____

5 Otherwise we would <u>not achieve</u> our sales targets, would we? _____

6 I think we should <u>concentrate on</u> solving the problem, rather than discussing who was to blame. _____

>> For more exercises, go to **Practice file 5** on page 110.

9 Work with a partner. Take turns to describe a colleague / team leader you work with, using vocabulary from **3** and **8**. How similar / different are their working styles?

10 Work with a partner. Ask and answer questions about recent projects you have worked on to find out which Belbin role you think you each play in a team. Consider the following aspects.

1 task / project   4 issues / problems

2 colleagues / fellow team members   5 confrontation / fairness

3 schedules / pressure

Alternatively, turn to File 15 on page 139, for some project outlines. Discuss the projects, and work together to establish the best mix of Belbin roles for each.

ⓘ >> Interactive Workbook >> **Glossary**

Context

Duverger is a well-established European kitchenware company and it is about to launch an exciting new range of branded kitchenware. The company intends to create a 'big splash' with an extensive promotional campaign across Europe, starting with a product launch at a convention in Vienna next week. The Sales, Marketing, and Production departments in Duverger are working together on the promotional campaign. The first box of brochures for the company's stand in Vienna has just been delivered, but they don't look quite right.

Negotiating | Dealing with conflict

1 What can go wrong when brochures are printed? Why do these things happen?

2 27▷ A meeting takes place between three managers – Jenny, Riccardo, and Paul – to discuss the situation. Listen to Extract 1 from the meeting. Compare your answers to **1** with what actually went wrong.

3 27▷ The three managers handle the discussion and deal with conflict in different ways. Listen again and decide who – Jenny (*J*), Riccardo (*R*), or Paul (*P*) –
1 attempts to clarify the situation _____
2 encourages the others to keep to the facts _____
3 expresses their concerns diplomatically _____
4 expresses their concerns more directly. _____

4 Match phrases a–i from Extract 1 to these categories. Can you add any more phrases?
1 Keeping to the facts / being objective: _____
2 Talking about concerns directly: _____
3 Talking about concerns more diplomatically: _____
4 Clarifying / checking understanding: _____

a Do you understand what I'm trying to say?
b Would I be right in thinking …?
c I don't know if you are aware, but …?
d Let's try not to get personal here.
e Can we try and stay focused on the facts?
f I'm really not happy with …
g Can I just make sure I've understood this correctly?
h I'm a bit worried about …
i The real issue here is …

5 Work with a partner. Discuss what you would say in these 'conflict' situations. Then have the conversations.

Situation 1
- **Student A** Tell B about your boss's plans to get rid of the coffee area.
- **Student B** You are surprised. Try to clarify what A has said.
- **Student A** Confirm.
- **Student B** You are very concerned and want to know what staff can do about this decision. Express your concerns directly.
- **Student A** Tell B to focus on the facts – there has been no final decision yet. You are concerned that staff don't have enough informal meeting space. Be diplomatic.

Situation 2
- **Student A** Tell B (the senior manager) you are not happy that a colleague who has been at the company for less time than you has been promoted above you and is now your line manager. Express your concerns directly.
- **Student B** Tell A to focus on the facts – the new line manager is very capable and is qualified for the job. Be diplomatic.

6 28▷ Listen to Extract 2. What are the options for Duverger? What course of action do they successfully negotiate?

7 During the negotiation in Extract 2, who
a plays the role of chairperson?
b expresses points of disagreement?
c offers a compromise?

8 28▷ Listen to Extract 2 again. Replace the words in *italics* with phrases from the audio with a similar meaning.

1 Well, Riccardo, *what do you think we should do about this*?
_____

2 To be frank, *don't expect me to* sit around and wait for you to sort this out.
_____

3 And *how can you possibly* be contemplating a reprint?
_____

4 OK, Paul, *that's fair enough, but* surely we need to get this right now?
_____

5 Oh, come on, that's just not practical. *I'm cancelling* the launch in Vienna if …
_____

6 Look, Paul, Riccardo, *I don't want* any serious setbacks …
_____

7 Thinking about this sensibly, the problems with the artwork *I can live with*, if …
_____

8 I mean, *why don't I give* the printer another call?
_____

9 Paul, *do we have* your approval on this?
_____

10 In which case, Riccardo, *would you be happy to* liaise with the printer …?
_____

9 Match the phrases you noted in **8** to a–c in **7**.

》》 For more exercises, go to **Practice file 5** on page 110.

10 Work in groups of three. Student A, turn to File 17 on page 140, Student B, turn to File 36 on page 144, and Student C, turn to File 49 on page 147. Negotiate the situations, following the steps below.
1 Establish the point of conflict.
2 Discuss any disagreements.
3 Try to reach a solution / compromise.

ⓘ 》》 Interactive Workbook 》》 **Email**

Key expressions

Clarifying the situation
Can I just make sure I've understood this correctly?
Would I be right in thinking …?
Do you understand what I'm trying to say?

Staying focused on the facts
Let's try not to get personal here.
Can we try and stay focused on the facts?

Expressing concerns diplomatically
I'm a bit worried about …
I don't know if you are aware, but …?

Expressing concerns directly
I'm really not happy with …
The real issue here is …

Chairing the negotiation
How do you propose we deal with this issue?
Look, can we try and avoid any …?
I need to know …
Can I leave you to …?

Expressing points of disagreement
I can't just …
I just don't understand how …
I see what you mean, but …
I just won't be able to …, if …

Offering a compromise
I'm prepared to … if …
Look, would it help if …?
I'd be more than happy to …

ⓘ 》》 Interactive Workbook
　　　　》》 **Phrasebank**

Culture question
- How do you deal with conflict in your culture?
- Do you know how it is dealt with in other cultures?
- How can differences in the approach to conflict affect working relationships?

Language at work | Adding emphasis

1 29▷ Listen to extracts 1–9. How do the speakers add emphasis to each sentence (e.g. word order, intonation, adding words or phrases)?

1 The reason why I say this is because if we get it right this time, any future campaigns should run more smoothly.
2 Which is why this whole thing is just so frustrating.
3 How we resolve this is the issue now.
4 It's the Vienna convention which really worries me.
5 In which case, Riccardo, can I leave you to liaise with the printer …?
6 What really concerns me is the way this has been handled so badly by the printers.
7 The problems with the artwork I'm prepared to overlook.
8 The thing that bothers me is that we just don't have time.
9 Not only do we have a major error on our hands, but we're also not sure how this happened.

2 Which techniques for adding emphasis from a–d are used in the sentences in 1? More than one technique may be used in each sentence.

a cleft sentences: *it's … which / that; what … is …* _____
b fixed phrases used to add emphasis _____
c fronting (putting a topic at the start of a sentence for emphasis) _____
d adverbs of degree _____

>> For more information, go to **Language reference Unit 5** on page 128.

3 Look at conversations 1–6 below. In each case, add emphasis to B's reply using one of the phrases from the list.

What we must be clear about is …   *What I'd really like to know is …*
It's … which …   *Not only … but also …*
Which is why …   *In which case …*

1 **A** I really don't know how to fill in this document.
  B Wouldn't it be a good idea to sit down and sort this out properly?
2 **A** Apparently there are hardly any tickets left for the conference.
  B I told you to book early.
3 **A** How should I reply to their email?
  B It's absolutely essential that the contract is signed by the 5th.
4 **A** I can't believe there's no budget left to complete the project!
  B What'll happen to the team if the project is abandoned?
5 **A** So they didn't attend?
  B They didn't attend the meeting. They forgot to let us know.
6 **A** The job is challenging enough, without all these extra changes they're asking for.
  B The changes make the job interesting.

4 Add emphasis to the following sentences, using the fronting technique.

1 We need to think about how we go about this.
2 It's absolutely crucial that we get this right.

>> For more exercises, go to **Practice file 5** on page 111.

5 Work in groups of three. You are members of a team set up to produce the company news section on the intranet. The deadline for a first draft is the end of next week. However, poor communication in the team has slowed the project down. You decide to hold a meeting to discuss the problems. Student A, turn to File 20 on page 140, Student B, turn to File 40 on page 145, and Student C turn to File 27 on page 142.

1 Discuss each problem on the agenda. Use techniques for emphasizing the points you make to each other.
2 End the meeting by deciding how you are going to resolve these issues.

Agenda

Communication problems in the intranet team

1 Unfocused meetings
2 Team members with different working styles
3 Lack of communication outside team meetings

Practically speaking | Responding to feedback

1 Work with a partner. Discuss the following questions.

1 Is feedback necessarily the same as criticism?
2 How can negative feedback be made constructive?
3 How do you normally react to negative / positive feedback?

2 30▷ Listen to three conversations. In which conversation does somebody

1 respond to positive feedback?
2 accept negative feedback?
3 challenge negative feedback?

3 30▷ Match phrases a–k to 1–3 in **2**. Then listen again to check your answers.

a I see what you're saying ..., but ... ____
b Thanks for your support – it's good to know I'm on the right track. ____
c I'm sorry, I didn't realize – thanks for pointing that out. ____
d Oh, I see, well it seems a pity to ..., but maybe you're right. ____
e Oh, really? Why do you think that? ____
f ... to be honest, I just don't have time to ... ____
g No, I'm sorry, I don't see what you're getting at. ____
h Thanks. Though I have to admit, I got the idea from ... ____
i Actually, I'm very happy to have some honest feedback. I'll just keep working on it. ____
j So how do you think I could improve it? ____
k Look, you're entitled to your opinion, but ... ____

>> For extension and revision go to **Useful phrases** on page 134.

4 Work with a partner. Discuss how you would respond to the feedback in 1–6 below. Use phrases in **3** to help you.

1 'I basically liked the way you presented your arguments, but I did feel you need to sound more sure of yourself.'
2 'Some of the ideas you came up with in that meeting were really creative. I'm sure Gian Luca is going to want to explore some of those further.'
3 'Did you read the report through before submitting it? It's just that there were several inconsistencies. It just doesn't seem like your normal standard, that's all.'
4 'We've just had some feedback from the client – I know it's a bit late, but basically they're not very happy with the colours we've selected.'
5 'I know the team's been under a lot of pressure recently, but I can't help feeling it's compromising the quality of the work.'
6 'We've got deadlines to meet, and we all have to do our bit. The delay from your group has meant that the production team are sitting around waiting for us to deliver.'

5 Work with a partner. Student A, turn to File 22 on page 141, Student B, turn to File 39 on page 145. Take turns to respond to each other's feedback.

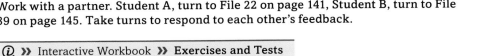

ⓘ >> Interactive Workbook >> **Exercises and Tests**

Key word | only

Match phrases 1–5 with *only* in *italics* to synonyms a–e.

1 I'm sorry, *only* I didn't realize.
2 I'm *only too* happy to have some honest feedback.
3 I'm *only* trying to help.
4 I think my *only* real doubt is the line you've taken on absenteeism.
5 Apparently the same issue came up *only* last week.

a very
b as recently as
c single
d just
e but

Southwest Airlines

Southwest Airlines is the largest airline in the world based on numbers of passengers. It's also the sixth largest US airline based on revenue. The company was founded in 1971 by Herb Kelleher in Dallas, Texas. It now operates more that 5,000 Boeing 737 aircraft between 64 cities with more than 3,300 flights a day. The company boasts that the 2006 year-end results marked their 34th consecutive year of profitability.

The power of teamwork

How does a major airline turn a plane around and get it ready for take-off within 20 minutes of landing? Whereas some airlines say this is impossible, Southwest Airlines pride themselves on their ability to get a plane ready for departure in record time, and they put it all down to teamwork. Everyone helps out; the cabin staff double as cleaners, the captain helps people on to the plane or helps with the cleaning, while outside the plane is being serviced by ground staff who work with the precision of a grand prix pit lane crew.

The efficiency of the turnaround shocks first-time Southwest flyers, who moments before can often be heard grumbling that they will be late taking off. This turnaround time means Southwest can fly up to 35 fewer planes than their competitors, which leads to lower prices and higher profits. The teamwork ethos all started back in 1971 when Southwest was facing financial meltdown. They had just sold a plane to a competitor to raise capital to pay staff, but needed to continue to meet demand with one less aircraft. It was then that they realized the importance of tight turnaround times. This led to a policy of everyone pitching in. Since then Southwest has become a model for successful teamwork and employee relations.

It's an inspiring company to work for and is well-regarded by its employees – they know that success will be rewarded. 'Everyone works hard', says one blogger on the company website, 'but it doesn't feel like hard work when you're having so much fun'.

Come and work for Southwest Airlines!
Here are just some of the benefits we offer!

- **Continuing education** – We offer personal and professional development in our state-of-the-art educational facilities. Why not try our 'Days in the Field' programme to see life in another department?
- **Stay connected** – Feel part of the Southwest family by keeping up to date with all company developments through weblogs, emails, toll-free phone lines, and even our own TV channel.
- **Work hard and play hard** – Have fun, because happy employees equal happy customers. Why not join our haunted headquarter weekends, chilli cooking competitions, and spirit parties?

What we require at Southwest

We ask one thing of our employees – the willingness to fit into the team. So we expect you to be ethical, honest, and trustworthy. We ask for a warrior's spirit, a servant's heart, and a fun-loving attitude.

Discussion

1 Based on the approach at Southwest Airlines, what are the main principles for fostering good teamwork in a company?

2 What are the pros / cons of the Southwest Airlines approach?

3 How does your company's attitude to teamwork compare to Southwest Airlines?

Task

1 Alligator Sandwiches has outlets throughout Britain. It has a well-publicized 'all-for-one' principle, meaning that everyone in the company should have equal status – if a server has a business idea they are free to share it, and likewise managers are expected to take their turn behind the tills. The company has become very successful. However, this success has led to some serious problems at many of its outlets. Read this email to the CEO from a former employee at the Manchester outlet and make a note of the key problems.

RE: Reasons for leaving Alligator Sandwiches
From: Alison Whittaker
To: Russell Summers

Dear Mr Summers

I've recently handed in my resignation to my outlet manager and I feel that I have to inform you about the issues that led me to do this.

I've worked at Alligator Sandwiches in Manchester right from the beginning and at first it was a great place to work. I really felt part of the team and the management weren't separate from the rest of us – they were really involved. They listened to our ideas and made us feel that we were just as important to the company as they were.

But now it feels like it's a 'them and us' situation. They don't help out in the stores any more and they certainly don't seem to care about any feedback or suggestions from their staff or customers. I realize they're under pressure because of the expansion and increased competition, but the 'all-for-one' principle has gone out of the window. Most of the staff are unhappy and a lot of us are leaving. We've also had a lot of customer complaints recently. I hope you can do something to re-establish the teamwork ethic and to stop the company from destroying itself.

Kind regards

Alison Whittaker

2 Head Office has organized a meeting to discuss the problems and negotiate ways to improve teamwork. Work in groups of four.

Student A, you're Head of Finance. Turn to File 24 on page 141.

Student B, you're an outlet manager. Turn to File 44 on page 146.

Student C, you're a server. Turn to File 26 on page 142.

Student D, you're a representative from Head Office. Turn to File 51 on page 148.

Read the information and prepare for the meeting. Student D should start the meeting when all participants are ready.

3 Report back to the rest of the class on what was agreed during your negotiation.

The Expert View

Teams are usually constructed because there is a belief that that the whole (team) could be greater than the sum of its parts (individuals) – i.e. the group can achieve more. In general, teams outperform individuals when tasks require multiple skills, judgement, and experience. However, often the biggest issue for managers is to decide if they need a specifically selected team or just a work group that already exists within the structure of the company. In a working group the skills of the group members are varied and random and there is individual accountability, whereas in a team the skills of the group members are complementary, there is individual and collective accountability, and everyone contributes to the overall outcome.

Joe Jaina, Senior Lecturer in Organizational Behaviour

Cranfield School of Management

Case study

6 | Progress

Learning objectives in this unit
- Discussing factors for success
- Problem-solving and brainstorming ideas
- Using adverbs to qualify attitudes
- Using vague language

Case study
- Handling rapid growth and progression

Starting point

1 What do you think a company needs to do to stay ahead of the competition?

2 How can companies ensure continued progress?

Working with words | Discussing factors for success

1 The Creativity Lab is part of ITRI, a Taiwanese publicly-funded organization helping local companies develop their products and manufacturing techniques. Read the text and answer the questions.
1 What does the Creativity Lab do?
2 What is Hsueh Wen-Jean's attitude towards creativity and success?

Thinking outside the box

With Taiwan's successful track record in manufacturing, local electronics companies concentrated on **figuring out** ways to reduce cost and improve existing products, rather than on developing new products. Taiwan's niche was as an outsourcer for large American IT firms, but that market is now so mature that Taiwan's manufacturing sector has lost ground to lower-cost countries. Taiwan's IT elite realize change is needed in order to get back on track, and product innovation could hold the key to new business opportunities.

Hsueh Wen-Jean is the driving force behind the recently launched Creativity Lab. She is responsible for helping to green-light new projects, and is well aware that she and her colleagues need to think outside the box, **looking beyond** their technical training to find creative answers and innovative solutions.

The Lab conducts workshops to help their customers, a diverse group of companies known as the Next Consortium, to develop their creative thinking. Ideas are **bounced around**, after which two or more companies are able to collaborate on projects based on these ideas.

The principle is that because so many ideas fall by the wayside, it is best to come up with as many as possible. This should help increase the chances of **hitting on** a few good ideas that can generate real income, and help these companies stay ahead of the game. Although most ideas never come to fruition, the Consortium's members can work together to **try out** different possibilities while avoiding the problems a company can **run into** by pursuing a bad idea on its own. 'A culture of success can tolerate mistakes, and all great entrepreneurs learn from their mistakes,' Hsueh says.

So far, the Lab has not laid down hard and fast criteria for judging whether, or how far, to explore a concept. At this stage Hsueh is reluctant to impose revenue targets, as there are numerous projects that do not get off the ground or prove to be impractical. That is all part of the process at The Creativity Lab.

2 Work with a partner. Match phrases 1–6 from the text in 1 to definitions a–f.

1	get back on track	a	be realized
2	think outside the box	b	be started
3	fall by the wayside	c	find the path to success again
4	stay ahead of the game	d	come up with creative / unusual ideas
5	come to fruition	e	keep in front of the competition
6	get off the ground	f	fail to make it

3 Replace the <u>underlined</u> words in these sentences with a verb phrase in **bold** in the text in **1**. You might need to change the form of the verb phrase.

1 I know that you're not impressed with what John suggested, but why don't you <u>test</u> his ideas and see how they work in practice?

2 We might suddenly <u>face</u> some big problems if we don't plan this carefully.

3 I'm trying to <u>work out</u> how we can reorganize the team once David has left.

4 You have to <u>stop concentrating only on</u> what's been done before, and focus on the future.

5 He suddenly <u>came up with</u> an excellent idea.

6 You should <u>see what other people think about</u> the ideas – someone might know how to develop them further.

4 Look at the text in **1**. Find the nouns that collocate with the verb phrases in **bold**.

5 Read the quotation from George Buckley, CEO of 3M. What dilemma do you think the company might have faced?

6 31 ▷ Listen to Jost Van der Saar, a business analyst, talking about the situation at 3M, and answer the questions.

1 What is the dilemma that is discussed in the interview?

2 What has been 3M's traditional approach to creativity?

3 How did McNerney change things?

4 What is the company's current approach?

7 Match verbs 1–12 to the most suitable noun, a or b, to form collocations.

		a		b	
1	cut into	a	the success	b	the bottom line
2	undergo	a	change	b	progress
3	pursue	a	the competition	b	ideas
4	boost	a	earnings	b	money
5	tolerate	a	mistakes	b	progress
6	cause	a	a stir	b	a discussion
7	shift	a	the emphasis	b	the competition
8	explore	a	a concept	b	difficulties
9	control	a	profits	b	costs
10	impose	a	targets	b	problems
11	demand	a	process	b	precision
12	outperform	a	earnings	b	the competition

8 31 ▷ Look at the text in **1** and listen to the interview again and check your answers.

9 Work with a partner and put the collocations from **7** in the table below. Then compare your answers with another pair and discuss any differences.

Profitability	Change	Creativity	Quality

➤➤ For more exercises, go to **Practice file 6** on page 112.

10 Work in groups. Think of a recent project you have been involved in. Think of

- how you came up with the idea
- how you ensured quality
- changes / problems with the project
- the success of the idea.

Hold a post-project review meeting to discuss what happened and what you could have done differently.

ⓘ ➤ Interactive Workbook ➤ **Glossary**

Context

Skion PCs is a small computer hardware store set up by two IT graduates, James Logan and Gareth Newman. Currently it has one shop on the high street, and a website for online sales. It prides itself on the expertise and specialized knowledge of its employees. However, competition from the large, well-known national / international PC chains is threatening business. Skion PCs needs to find an innovative niche market to maintain its position. James and Gareth decide to hold a brainstorming meeting with two key members of staff – Sue Edwards and Jessica Williams.

Meetings | Problem-solving | Brainstorming ideas

1 32–34 ▷ Listen to three extracts from the problem-solving meeting at Skion PCs.
1 Complete the table below with the four ideas.
2 Note down the pros and cons that are mentioned for each idea.

Ideas	Pros	Cons
1		
2		
3		
4		

2 32 ▷ Listen to the first extract again and complete these sentences.
1 I mean, _____ ways to develop our image …?
2 Also, _____ 'caring'.
3 _____, what about moving into the area of recycling?
4 _____ collect a customer's old computer …
5 _____ something charitable … and send X% off to developing countries, _____?
6 _____ set up a programme where staff can choose to …
7 To tell you the truth, _____.
8 _____ that would work in practice …
9 … and _____ it would really be cost-effective.
10 Well, no, but _____ that it's profitable, _____.

3 Work with a partner. Put phrases 1–10 in **2** into categories a–e.
a Putting forward an idea: _____.
b Asking for clarification: _____.
c Clarifying the idea: _____.
d Building on the idea: _____.
e Evaluating the idea: _____.

4 Work with a partner. Brainstorm alternative ways of saying sentences 1–9. The meaning should be the same or similar.

Example: *That's not such a bad idea.* → *I actually quite like this idea.*

1 I can't help wondering whether it would be really cost-effective.
2 I'm not sure how this would work in practice, but how about a wider policy on environmental issues?
3 What did you have in mind?
4 I was thinking along the lines of solar-powered laptops.
5 Supposing we were to sell recovered parts … back to the manufacturers?
6 And there's nothing stopping us from setting up as brokers ourselves, is there?
7 It's certainly worth thinking about.
8 We should at least consider it.
9 In terms of marketing, I think it has potential.

>> For more exercises, go to **Practice file 6** on page 112.

5 Work in groups of four. You work for a company that has grown rapidly over the last few years. Growth is now slowing due to high staff turnover. Read the following information from HR about this issue.

- One of the reasons for high staff turnover is the lack of company perks – apparently competitors are offering better conditions.
- Money is available to fund one or two perks within reason. Perks without costs would be preferable.

Prepare to hold a brainstorming meeting about the issue. Students A and B turn to File 23 on page 141. Students C and D turn to File 54 on page 149.

During the meeting
- put forward all your ideas and note them down
- clarify and then evaluate the ideas
- decide on the best options.

6 Think of a work-related problem you've each had which needed a creative solution. Hold a problem-solving meeting to brainstorm possible solutions.

Solution 1:	Solution 3:

The problem:

Solution 2:	Solution 4:

Alternatively, look at one of the problems below.

1 You have just found out that key features of the new product or service you are working on are very similar to one that your competitors launched last week.
2 You work in a sector where it is extremely difficult to recruit suitable employees. You are seriously understaffed and demand for the company's services is huge.

ⓘ >> Interactive Workbook >> **Email**

Key expressions

Putting forward an idea
Couldn't we consider …?
I would have thought it would be possible to …
I'm not sure how this would work in practice, but how about …?
Supposing we were to …?

Asking for clarification
It's not clear to me what you mean by …
Oh I see, so you're thinking … am I right?
What did you have in mind?

Clarifying the idea
Well, for example, …
I was thinking along the lines of …

Building on the idea
Thinking about it, we could even …
And there's nothing stopping us from … is there?

Evaluating the idea
I'm concerned about how …
I can't help wondering …
I would certainly need to know … before -ing …
It's certainly worth thinking about.
We should at least consider it …
In terms of … I think it has potential.
That's not such a bad idea.

ⓘ >> Interactive Workbook
>> **Phrasebank**

Culture question

Think about the 'company culture' in your organization.
- Are ideas developed hierarchically or can they come from any level?
- How is support generated for these ideas?
- Do you know how this compares to other company cultures?

Language at work | Using adverbs to qualify attitudes

1 **35▷ Listen to sentences 1–10 and match the adverbs in *italics* to their uses a–d below. There may be more than one possible answer.**

1 Could I *just* explain in a bit more detail? ＿＿

2 You've *obviously* given this some thought. ＿＿

3 I'm not *totally* convinced. ＿＿

4 It's been a *surprisingly* difficult year. ＿＿

5 It's *easily* the best idea I've heard so far. ＿＿

6 I'm *just* not convinced. ＿＿

7 It was *actually* one of the most rewarding things I've ever done. ＿＿

8 Look, I *only* say that because there's big money in energy saving. ＿＿

9 I'm not *so* keen on the idea. ＿＿

10 I don't *really* think we could get away with that – do you? ＿＿

a emphasizing a comment
b expressing an attitude contrary to expectation
c persuading others to listen to you
d softening a negative reaction

2 **36▷ Listen to these pairs of sentences, where the meaning changes according to the position of the adverb. What is the difference in meaning?**

1 a Could I explain in just a bit more detail?
   b Could I just explain in a bit more detail?

2 a Surprisingly, it's been a difficult year.
   b It's been a surprisingly difficult year.

3 a It was actually one of the most rewarding things I've ever done.
   b Actually, it was one of the most rewarding things I've ever done.

4 a I really don't think we could get away with that – do you?
   b I don't really think we could get away with that – do you?

>> For more information, go to **Language reference Unit 6** on page 129.

3 **Work with a partner. Discuss what B might have said in conversations 1–6.**

1 A I don't have much time – what is it you wanted to talk about?
   B (Needs to run through some ideas. Persuades A to listen.)

2 A Do you have any thoughts on my idea for a new staff car park?
   B (Thinks the money could be better spent elsewhere. Softens this negative reaction.)

3 A The conference wasn't as well attended as last year, was it?
   B (Thinks there were a lot more people than expected. Responds contrary to expectation.)

4 A I hear you're not happy with the way the new project's going.
   B (Doesn't understand why it's delayed. Emphasizes this negative reaction.)

5 A Are you pleased with the outcome from this morning's meeting?
   B (Thinks the best proposal got accepted. Emphasizes this positive reaction.)

6 A Are you happy with our choice of candidate?
   B (She wouldn't have been the first choice. Responds contrary to expectation.)

4 **Choose your most favourite and least favourite technological innovation from the list (or think of your own). Work with a partner and take turns to explain your choices using adverbs from 1.**

- BlackBerry
- online teleconferencing software
- memory sticks
- digital television
- air conditioning
- automatic doors
- self check-outs in supermarkets
- central locking in cars
- electric windows in cars
- MP3 players

>> For more exercises, go to **Practice file 6** on page 113.

Practically speaking | Using vague language

1 37▷ **Listen to three conversations where people are being asked for information. For each conversation, answer questions 1–2.**

1 How does the person being asked for information sound (e.g. knowledgeable, tentative, vague, encouraging, lazy)?

2 Why isn't the information more precise?

2 37▷ **Look at the phrases used to show that the information is imprecise in the table below. Then listen again and add any other similar phrases.**

Conversation 1	Conversation 2	Conversation 3
Something about … I think!	I'd say you're on the right track.	No, not really.
… you've put me on the spot there.	… it's the kind of thing …	It's difficult to explain, really.

>> For extension and revision, go to **Useful phrases** on page 135.

3 **Work with a partner. Student A, read the information below. Student B, turn to File 30 on page 143. Have the conversations.**

Situation 1

You have been asked to give a tour and presentation of your company to a group of graduates. You are busy planning the event, and you know Student B organized the same day last year. Speak to Student B and find out what she / he did to prepare for the event.

Situation 2

In order for the MD to authorize a new project, you need to present a written proposal with Student B. Student B has written the first draft. However, it looks long, and you haven't had time to read it in detail. Student B asks you for feedback.

- Student B needs to add the long-term benefits for the company.
- The basic structure looks OK.
- The text looks very wordy – you'd prefer to see more bullet points.

4 **Work with a partner. Ask each other about a topic from the list. Answer your partner's questions, using vague language where necessary.**

- a training session you've been to
- a hotel you've stayed in
- a business trip you've been on
- a city you've visited
- a product from a competitor
- a presentation you've been to

ⓘ >> Interactive Workbook >> **Exercises and Tests**

Key word | *still*

Look at sentences 1–5. In which sentence is the word *still* used to

a emphasize a comparison?

b say what remains to be done?

c say you continue to wait for something which is overdue?

d offer a contrasting viewpoint?

e refer to a possibility in the future?

1 That should *still* give you time to revise your draft.

2 I *still* need to bring it all together.

3 *Still*, there was one place that was quite interesting.

4 He *still* hasn't got back to me.

5 More worrying *still* is that it's only a month away.

Company profile
Mobile Interactive Group

Mobile Interactive Group is the UK market leader in providing interactive services via mobile phones. The company was founded in 2004 by three ex-O2 employees – Barry Houlihan, Anthony Nelson, and Nick Aldridge – and since then has grown rapidly to become a multi-million pound business and a key player in mobile software innovation. In four years the annual revenue grew from £252,000 to around £40 million and the number of employees went from three to more than 40. It specializes in mass participation events such as voting on reality shows, and provides billing solutions for premium SMS services, as well as interactive marketing services. Their clients include ITV (UK), TV3 (Ireland), Freemantle Media, and O2.

Background

How to manage rapid growth effectively

It's every entrepreneur's dream to start a new company and to see it grow rapidly to become one of the leading players in the industry. However, companies that grow too quickly can face unexpected difficulties, such as inadequate cash flow, loss of control, and problems associated with diversifying too quickly. Often these are due to a simple lack of management experience, but they can cause a company to lose sight of their core purpose and, ultimately, to fail.

Here are five tips for managing rapid growth effectively and avoiding some of the major pitfalls.

1 **Make sure you have the money to expand.** It's essential that adequate financial resources are in place to support the cash-flow problems that often accompany rapid growth.

2 **Employ qualified people to run the company.** Promoting from within can be tempting, but just because people have been with the company since the start, it doesn't mean they have the management skills to deal with the challenges the company faces.

3 **Don't try to run before you can walk.** Rapid success brings with it the temptation to diversify away from your core business. This can lead to a 'watering down' of the company's overall strengths.

4 **Always remember who your core customers are.** Customer service is a vital part of any business – if your customers feel you are neglecting them in order to chase new business opportunities, they will look elsewhere.

5 **Stay true to your original vision.** Companies that grow too fast can sometimes lose sight of the core values that made them a success in the first place. Never forget who you are and why you're doing this.

Mobile Interactive Group (MIG) is recognized as one of the fastest-growing businesses in the UK, operating in a sector where technological developments happen constantly. A key factor in the company's success has been its apparent ability to avoid many of the usual pitfalls associated with new businesses experiencing accelerated growth over a relatively short period of time. So how have they achieved this?

Firstly, adequate financing was in place from the start in the form of a loan from the British government. Then in their second year, when things were really beginning to take off, the company secured a further £250,000 from a Canadian investor. Since then, with their track record established, there has been no shortage of potential investors.

Secondly, MIG has recruited carefully. CEO Barry Houlihan has appointed experienced people to key positions within the company to ensure that growth is managed appropriately and expansion plans are met. On top of this MIG has also appointed an advisory committee to bring wider expertise to the decision-making process.

MIG has also chosen its customers carefully. Instead of pursuing every potential contract, the company has taken a long-term view, carefully selecting who it wants to work with, and has built and maintained close relationships with these clients.

Discussion

1 Which tips for managing rapid growth in the article do you think are the most important? Why?

2 Do you think the fact that MIG managed its growth so effectively was due to luck, judgement, or both? Why?

Task

1 Work with a partner. Read about Adamo Automotive's company history and discuss what the company's key strengths are.

Adamo Automotive

Adamo is an independent specialist car manufacturer. The company was established in the 1990s by Adam Crees and Morgan Terry who had previously designed and built vehicles for international racing teams. At the time, the company filled a niche in providing high-performance, 'no frills' two-seater sports cars at an affordable price.

Company situation in the 1990s

Typical customer profile: young, well-paid professionals aged 25 to 45

Models: the AV1 and the more powerful Capra

Financial performance: Within five years Adamo had a turnover of over £30 million and was producing more than 1,000 cars annually. Strong European and American economies and relatively low fuel prices supported growth.

Staff: The workforce were highly skilled and motivated – all employees received stock options. Starting out with a team of only eight, within five years Adamo employed 45 people.

Strengths: The cars gained a reputation for innovative construction and distinctive styling.

Weaknesses: Despite being a high-status brand, Adamos offered little in the way of luxury features – the cars were about performance and the driving experience.

2 Turn to File 31 on page 143 to find out what has happened to Adamo in recent years. Discuss the information with your partner and make a list of the main problems they are now facing.

3 Adamo's directors have asked a team of consultants to advise the company on how to reverse its decline. You and your partner are two of the consultants. Prepare for a brainstorming meeting by discussing the following questions and making notes on your answers.

  1 Based on what you know about the current economic climate, what do you think are some of the ways the company can address the problems?

  2 Which (if any) of the advice offered in the article could be followed by Adamo?

4 Work with another pair. Follow the agenda and hold the brainstorming meeting.

Agenda – Adamo Automotive

1 Each idea to be put forward, then clarified and recorded
2 Ideas to be evaluated and built on if possible
3 Best ideas and recommended strategy for Adamo to be decided on
4 Decision to be made on who will report suggestions to the board

The Expert View

Some entrepreneurs have been able to take their vision from its initial conception to market success, creating and sustaining a growing organization. Creativity is part of the process of bringing new products and services to the market, but truly innovative organizations are able to select the new ideas that they are best placed to exploit and then implement them successfully. They must be expert at 'making things happen'. To nurture creativity and to ensure that rapid growth can occur, organizations must be comfortable with experimentation, novelty, and uncertainty – they must not fear failure. They must also have excellent processes – they must manage risk and control resources.

Alan Cousens, MA MBA MSc PhD, Senior Research Fellow, Operations Management
Cranfield University School of Management

Case study

7 | Learning

Starting point

1 'Some people stop learning the moment they leave school. Others go on learning all their lives.' Do you agree?

2 What is different about the process of learning in each of these situations?
- learning about historical events in school
- learning how to cook
- learning how to negotiate successfully
- learning how to balance your work and private life

3 Think about any training courses you have done at work. What was good or bad about them? What did you learn?

Working with words | Talking about training and learning

1 Have you ever heard of the terms 'learning organization' and 'systems thinking?' Read the first part of the text and find out what they mean.

Becoming a 'learning organization'

Peter Senge, an American business strategist, came up with the concept of 'learning organizations' in his best-selling business management book, *The Fifth Discipline*. He defined them as companies '… where people continually expand their capacity to create the results they truly desire, where new and expansive patterns of thinking are nurtured, where **collective aspiration** is set free, and where people are continually learning to see the whole together.' At the heart of this vision is what he called 'systems thinking' – an ability to see and think about the organization as a whole, not just as a lot of disconnected parts. It emphasizes the need for the whole team to focus, learn, and build a **shared vision**.

2 Work with a partner. Read the text in 1 again and discuss questions 1–2.
1 What potential benefits might there be for a learning organization?
2 Do you work in a learning organization?

3 How realistic is it for a company to become a learning organization? Read the next part of the text and note the arguments for and against.

It sounds great, but does it actually work in practice? Those who maintain that it does, suggest that although it tends to cause upheaval and a real **paradigm shift** within a company, it usually leads to improved results. This is because 'systems thinking' means all levels of staff are actively encouraged to be creative and to take a holistic view of the business. **Performance management** and **personal development plans** play a key role in ensuring this happens, and the result is that all staff become far more engaged in the success of the company.

Conversely, there are some who question whether creating a learning organization is possible in the real world. They argue that in most cases a radical **structural change** to a company's culture is needed for it to stop thinking about training individuals and to start focusing on learning at the wider organizational level. There is also a suspicion that while the ideal is to have total **employee participation** and engagement in the learning process, in reality management will continue to impose values on a reluctant but deferential workforce. The argument against the 'learning organization' concept is that in the long run, what employees really need is to be able to do what they do better, not to spend time worrying about the bigger picture, and that companies should simply direct training towards addressing any **skills deficit** and encouraging professional development across the board in response to individual training needs.

4 Match the phrases in **bold** in the texts in **1** and **3** to definitions 1–8.

1 a written record of how an employee would like to progress in their career _____
2 a lack of ability and knowledge amongst a group of people _____
3 a view of the future that everyone is committed to _____
4 facilitation of staff achievement and progression by a company _____
5 personal involvement of a staff member in an activity _____
6 a radical change from one way of thinking to another _____
7 when a company reorganizes itself and introduces new systems _____
8 ambition and a desire for success that is shared by the group _____

5 Complete these sentences with the <u>underlined</u> phrases in the text in **3**.

1 'I just don't believe in this idea that anyone can become a millionaire if they try hard enough. How often does this actually happen _____?'
2 'Yes, of course this project is going to be a nightmare to organize – but stop worrying about all the minor details – you need to focus on _____.'
3 'We've increased profitability in every single division of the company. It's been an incredibly successful year _____.'
4 'I know that we're spending a lot on training at the moment, but give it a few years – we're going to see huge benefits from this _____.'

6 Work with a partner. What advice would you give in situations 1–5? Use vocabulary from **4** and **5** and phrases below to help you.

They need …   There's a lack of …   There isn't any …   There needs to be …

1 'A lot of the staff feel that no one is looking out for them and their career progression.'
2 'Everyone's just concentrating on their own tasks, so there's no team spirit.'
3 'There's a very rigid hierarchical management structure here, and staff feel that they're never going to get promoted because higher positions rarely become available.'
4 'We're having real problems recruiting people with the right kind of expertise.'
5 'We set up lots of training courses, but hardly anyone has signed up.'

7 38▷ Jane Willis is a training manager at a large publishing company. Listen to the interview and answer questions 1–3.

1 Does her company's training approach encourage 'systems thinking'?
2 How does Jane categorize the two types of training offered at her company?
3 What are the advantages and disadvantages of her company's approach?

8 38▷ What adjectives were used in the interview to describe the nouns *training* and *approach*? Listen again and check your answers.

9 Match the adjectives you noted in **8** to these definitions.

1 answering a wide range of needs (two adjectives): _____
2 coming from key departments / management (two adjectives): _____
3 coming from all areas and levels of a company (two adjectives): _____
4 answering particular work-related needs (one adjective): _____
5 coming from the individual member of staff (one adjective): _____

>> For more exercises, go to **Practice file 7** on page 114.

10 Work with a partner. Turn to File 32 on page 143. Read the information about training approaches at the two companies and discuss questions 1–2.

1 How would you describe each approach?
2 What are the advantages and disadvantages of each approach?

11 Work in small groups. Think about your own company.

1 How would you describe your company's approach to training and learning?
2 What are the advantages and disadvantages of that approach?
3 What changes would you suggest? What would be the results of these changes?

ⓘ >> Interactive Workbook >> **Glossary**

Kirsten Marr is the training manager at Thurn Biotechnology. This morning she had a phone call with her line manager, Tamara Soledo, head of HR, to plan next year's training programme.

Telephoning | Communication strategies

1 39▷, 40▷ Listen to Tamara calling Kirsten back and a follow-up call received by Kirsten. What is the main problem and what is the eventual solution?

2 39▷, 40▷ Listen again and complete phrases 1–13.
1 Did _____ Friday?
2 I'm not quite _____.
3 Could you _____ again?
4 And, what _____ is, you don't think we have …
5 No, it's _____ we don't have the trainers. We don't have the expertise.
6 Could you _____ what the problems were?
7 What was _____ again?
8 Consuelo _____ say?
9 Could I ask you _____ some details – how many participants …
10 What _____, it's annoying for us because …
11 … do you _____ you can't do this training for us?
12 Sorry, I'm not _____ I understand.
13 That's not what I mean. _____ is that …

3 Match the phrases in **2** to categories a–f.
a Checking a fact: _____
b Saying that you haven't heard or fully understood what was said: _____
c Asking for repetition of a whole idea: _____
d Checking understanding: _____
e Requesting more information about something: _____
f Clarifying following a misunderstanding: _____

4 41▷ Look at these extracts and correct the mistakes. Then listen and check your answers.
1 Just a thought. It may not be entirely relative, but …
2 Actually, no, it doesn't matter – I guess it's a bit outside the topic right now.
3 Oh, that recalls me. Have you heard that Leon's leaving to go and work for another training provider?
4 Anyway, … sorry. That's a bit of a digress.
5 Let's get back at the main issue.
6 By this way, talking about costs …

5 Which corrected phrases in **4**

a move away from the main topic to talk about something else? _____

b move the conversation back to the main topic? _____

» For more exercises, go to **Practice file 7** on page 115.

6 Look at these topics and choose one that you find interesting. Make notes of some true things you can say about it.

1 a new product proposal you are considering making

2 problems with a current project

3 something that was decided at a recent meeting which you disagree with

4 a suggestion you have for improving efficiency in your company

5 something that annoys you at work

7 Work with a partner. Make a call to a friend who works in another company. Discuss your topic from **6** and get help and advice from your friend. Use the flow chart to help you structure the conversation. When you have finished, change roles and repeat the task.

Student A	Student B
1 Greet.	
	2 Respond.
3 Start talking about your topic.	
	4 Ask for repetition and clarification.
5 Repeat. Then add more information.	
	6 Show interest. Then request more information about something.
7 Respond to the request.	
	8 Check you've understood. Then make a suggestion.
9 React. Then move off topic.	
	10 Bring the conversation back to the main topic. Check a fact.
11 Respond. End the call by asking about plans for the weekend.	

ⓘ » Interactive Workbook » **Email**

Key expressions

Checking facts
Did you say …?
… did you say?
What was … again?

Checking understanding
What you're saying is that …
Do you mean that …?

Asking for clarification
I'm not quite clear about your last suggestion.
I'm not quite sure I understand. Could you run it by me again?
Could you clarify exactly what the problems were?
Could I ask you to spell out some details?

Dealing with a misunderstanding
It's not that we don't …. We don't …
What I'm saying is …
That's not what I mean. What I mean is …

Digressing
Just a thought. It may not be entirely relevant, but …
That reminds me. Have you heard …?
By the way, talking about …

Resuming
Actually, it doesn't matter – it's a bit off-topic right now.
Anyway … sorry. That's a bit of a digression.
Let's get back to the main issue.

ⓘ » Interactive Workbook
» **Phrasebank**

Culture question

One reason that communicating by telephone can be difficult is because you are unable to use gestures or body language.

• How important are gestures, eye contact, and body language in your culture?

• Are there any gestures or body language that are not acceptable?

• Are there any gestures / body language typical of your own culture that may be misinterpreted in international business meetings?

Language at work | Participle clauses | 'The future in the past'

1 **42▷ Complete extracts 1–5 with these phrases. Then listen and check your answers.**

Working   Given the   Having discussed   Knowing how   Faced

1 _____ with the need to be fully compliant with the new legislation by early next year … I think we have at least 70 staff who need to …

2 _____ on the principle that they can all pass the content on to their own staff, we should have everyone trained up by January.

3 _____ limited number of companies offering this training, we don't actually have much choice.

4 A Have you heard that Leon's leaving to go and work for another training provider?

   B _____ demotivated he's been about his job recently, I'm not too surprised!

5 _____ it with the relevant people, we now think we need to ask an external training provider to do this.

2 **The phrases *working*, *faced*, *knowing*, *given*, and *having discussed* in the sentences in 1 all help to form what are called 'participle clauses'. Match these phrases to descriptions a–d.**

a this is a present participle (two answers) _____

b this could be replaced by *because there is a* _____

c this is *having* + past participle _____

d this could be replaced by a passive, e.g. *as we are confronted* _____

3 **Look at sentences 1–2. Why would you use 1 rather than 2? How could you make 1 negative?**

1 Knowing how demotivated he's been about his job recently, I'm not too surprised!

2 Because I know how demotivated he's been about his job recently, I'm not too surprised!

4 **Look at this extract from audio 41▷ and answer questions 1–4.**

Tamara   … I haven't seen that report on the e-learning project yet.

Kirsten   Ah, yes, I remembered that yesterday. I **was going to** write it this morning, but …

1 Is Kirsten trying to explain her schedule or make an excuse?

2 Has Kirsten written the report or not?

3 When did she decide that she would write the report 'this morning'?

4 Why do you think the structure in **bold** is known as 'the future in the past'?

5 **Look at other examples of 'the future in the past' in a–d. Which one expresses**

1 a prediction? ____   3 an obligation? ____

2 an arrangement? ____   4 an intention? ____

a I **was meeting** Jim at 9.00 a.m. tomorrow, but he's just cancelled.

b We gave her the Sales Manager job and we thought that she **would** increase profits.

c I **was going to** contact her this week, but apparently she's on holiday.

d They **were supposed to** call me before 1.00 p.m., but I haven't heard anything.

>> For more information, go to **Language reference Unit 7** on page 129.

6 **Work with a partner. Turn to File 47 on page 147.**

>> For more exercises, go to **Practice file 7** on page 115.

7 **Work with a partner. For each of the following situations, think of examples from your own life or work. Take turns to tell your partner about it using 'the future in the past' and a participle clause. Your partner can ask questions.**

Example: I was supposed to go to a conference in Tokyo, but it was cancelled. Given my current workload, this was probably a good thing.

1 A time when you had to change your plans at the last minute.

2 Something you believed someone else was planning to do, but they didn't do it.

3 A task you were responsible for. Explain what other people expected you would do.

Practically speaking | Expressing dissatisfaction

1 43▷ **Listen to three conversations. In each case decide**
1 where the people are
2 what they don't like
3 if they both have the same views.

2 43▷ **Complete extracts 1–11. Then listen again and check your answers.**
1 Though I have to admit, I'm not getting _____ it.
2 And the pace is so slow! It's _____!
3 I know what you mean. It's really _____, too.
4 In fact, I think I've _____.
5 Well, I agree it hasn't _____ so far …
6 I have to say that I _____ professional.
7 Well, the cover for example – _____.
8 And to be frank, I'm _____ the wording either.
9 I _____ staying.
10 To be honest, I'm _____ that I have to be here at all.
11 … I just _____ my time.

3 Match sentences 1–11 in **2** to these categories.
a The speaker says that something does not reach the right level of quality. _____
b The speaker says that something is not as good as they hoped beforehand. _____
c The speaker says that something isn't useful for them. _____
d The speaker says that something is making them impatient or bored. _____
e The speaker says that they cannot stand any more of something. _____

4 Sometimes it's important to soften what you say to make it sound less direct. Look at sentences 1–4 and <u>underline</u> words the speaker uses to soften what they say.
1 To be honest, I think this seminar is a bit of a waste of time.
2 I can't really see the point of everyone being here if they're not contributing.
3 I have to admit, I'm not really enjoying my new job.
4 I'm afraid that this report still needs some work.

5 Work with a partner. Decide how you would soften sentences 1–5.
1 Your performance this year has been substandard.
2 I hate the project I'm working on at the moment.
3 You need to completely rewrite your presentation.
4 This meeting is a waste of time.
5 Why are we here if there's nothing for us to do?

▶▶ For extension and revision, go to **Useful phrases** on page 135.

6 Read situations 1–4 and think of phrases from **2** that could be used in each one. Then work with a partner and practise the conversations.
1 You meet your colleague at the coffee machine. Discuss how bad the coffee at work is and how poor the canteen food is.
2 You are both attending a long presentation given by a regional manager about last quarter's turnover, but it's very boring. Find out if your partner is also finding it boring.
3 You have both just seen an announcement about the annual staff bonus. It is surprisingly low. Discuss this with your partner.
4 You are both very busy, but have been asked by your boss to attend an informal presentation given by another department about their work. It is not relevant to you or your current tasks. Discuss this with your partner.

ⓘ ▶▶ Interactive Workbook ▶▶ **Exercises and Tests**

Key word | *say*

Match phrases with *say* in *italics* in 1–5 to alternatives a–e.
1 Let him *have his say.*
2 *Let's say* … the 24th? Do you think you'll be able to do it by then?
3 *Say that we go ahead with this* – what will happen?
4 *I say let's forget it.*
5 If you had, *say*, a bad cold, you might not come to work.
6 *You can say that again.*

a for example …
b assuming …
c my opinion is …
d You've made a really good point and I agree with it.
e give his opinion
f how about …

Leyland Trucks

Leyland Trucks, originally founded in 1896, is based in North West England. It manufactures over 14,000 trucks each year and employs over 1,200 people. Since 1998 it has been a subsidiary of PACCAR Inc, a global manufacturer of commercial vehicles. Leyland is now the PACCAR group's established centre for light and medium truck design, development, and manufacture.

Tackling the skills shortage
Background

Lack of skilled workers affects future of UK economy

A recent report commissioned by the government has found that the UK could face a significant decline in economic growth if nothing is done to address the current skills deficit.

Despite recent improvements in education standards, the report found that over 20% of school leavers have difficulties with numbers and are unable to read or write properly. Even university graduates are part of the problem, as employers often report them to be unable to communicate effectively and thus lacking in the soft skills that are essential in the majority of graduate positions. There is also a distinct lack of highly-trained individuals in IT and engineering, causing serious recruitment problems for companies in these sectors.

The report concludes that, in the face of increasing competition from emerging economies such as China and India, action needs to be taken now if the UK is to remain competitive in the global environment. And the recommended changes are not just limited to schools and universities – employers will also be part of the process and will be encouraged to train more employees at work.

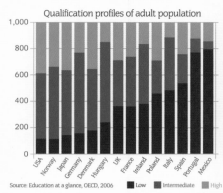

Qualification profiles of adult population

Source: Education at a glance, OECD, 2006   ■ Low ■ Intermediate ■ High

Tackling the skills shortage

Leyland Trucks is a company that has already been affected by the UK skills deficit. Over the last few years the company has become aware that there is a growing shortage of trained professional engineers. There are two main causes for this. Many of the firm's most highly-qualified and longest-serving employees have recently retired. At the same time, fewer young people are choosing to study engineering and enter the profession. The combination of these two factors means that Leyland faces the risk of a serious shortage of professional engineers in years to come if nothing is done to tackle the problem.

Discussion

1 **What action can be taken to deal with a countrywide skills shortage?**

2 **What could the HR department at Leyland Trucks do to solve their skills-related problem?**

3 44▷ **Listen to an interview with a consultant who worked with the company. Compare Leyland Trucks' strategy with your suggestions in 2.**

4 **What advantages does their strategy have? Are there any possible disadvantages?**

Task

1 Read this information about XM22.

> XM22 is a small web marketing agency based in the UK. It has developed several highly successful websites for various clients and is aiming to expand over the next few years. In order to expand, the company needs more staff, but is finding it difficult to recruit employees with the right skills. The roles that are particularly difficult to fill are the creative positions and IT development positions. The HR department has to find solutions to this problem.

2 Work with a partner. You work together in the HR department of XM22, but you have different ideas about how to solve the problem. One of you regularly works from home, so you need to discuss your ideas by telephone. Student A, look at the information below. Student B, turn to File 33 on page 143.

3 Read your suggested action points and prepare to explain them to your partner in a telephone call.

Student A

Suggested action

1 Recruit internationally – research suggests it should be quick and easy to recruit skilled people in India for the development roles and possibly in Europe for the creative roles.
   Why?
   • Although it can be complicated recruiting abroad, it will be easier to find people who already have the necessary skills and this will solve the problem very quickly.
   • It's cheaper than recruiting in the UK and then paying for extensive training courses.
   • It will give the company more of an international feel and perspective.

2 Introduce low-cost training / learning solutions including mentoring / shadowing programmes, and self-managed learning.
   Why?
   • Mentoring / shadowing programmes will enable less experienced employees to seek advice and support from a more experienced colleague, and learn new skills – this is a great way of sharing knowledge and skills. It also builds relationships between staff members and is low-cost (although it could be time-consuming).
   • Self-managed learning (allowing staff access to books, DVDs, and e-learning packages) – encourages employees to take responsibility for their own learning and is also low-cost.

4 Have the telephone call. During the call
 • explain your suggestions and deal with any misunderstandings
 • check you have understood your colleague's suggestions
 • if you wish, digress from the main topic / resume discussion of the main topic
 • decide which suggestions the company should follow.

5 Work with your partner and present your suggestions from **4** to the class.

The Expert View

In today's competitive environment more employers are looking for an approach to learning and development that requires less time away from the place of work. The use of e-learning, coaching, job shadowing, and self-directed learning all provide employers with a potential solution. For work-based learning to be successful a joint commitment is needed from both the trainee and their manager to ensure that short-term productivity is not continually prioritized over longer-term development needs. By working in partnership with an external provider, an employer can increase the organizational commitment to workplace learning. The provider will help the employer define time commitments, communicate expectations, and monitor progress.

Wendy Varney, Executive Development Consultant, Centre for Customised Executive Development

Cranfield School of Management

Case study

8 | Performance

Learning objectives in this unit
- Discussing employer / employee expectations
- Giving an impromptu presentation
- Using questions
- Dealing with difficult questions

Case study
- Increasing staff and customer satisfaction

Starting point

1 What benefits can employees bring to their companies?

2 What do organizations do to recognize and reward employees?

Working with words | Discussing employer / employee expectations

1 Make a list of what makes you happy to work for a company.

2 Read this text about what employees are looking for at work and compare your ideas in 1.

Happiness at work

Employees **make a difference to** companies, and they are **gaining recognition for** their contribution. More and more employers are realizing that there is a real correlation between happy staff and a strong bottom line. But what makes us happy at work?

According to the HR Consultants Chiumento's 'Happiness at work' index, employees have interests that rank higher than a big pay cheque, which comes in at a lowly tenth place. Instead, it's people first – **feeling part of** a friendly, supportive atmosphere, where you **have a say in** what happens, and where people take care of each other. At Google, for example, they **take pride in** the fact that employees enjoy a 'fun workspace'.

Second in line on the 'Happiness at work' index comes enjoyable work, where employees derive satisfaction from their achievements. It also helps if you can relate to the values of the company where you work. According to a recent newspaper survey, Innocent, a young, fast-growing fruit drinks company, attracts employees who **see a future for** themselves in a company with clear values. Innocent 'innocently' claims they want to 'leave things a little better than we find them'. At Google, where they receive 100,000 job applications a month, their philosophy is to make money 'without doing evil'. Employees are clearly keen to make the most of their opportunities, especially if they feel they are making a worthwhile contribution to their company while helping to improve the world they live in.

3 The combinations below follow the pattern: verb + noun + preposition. Complete each one with a noun from the list.

Example: make a contribution to

pride   recognition   a difference   a say   a future   part

1 make _____ to   3 feel _____ of   5 take _____ in
2 gain _____ for   4 have _____ in   6 see _____ for

4 Match the combinations in 3 to definitions a–f.

a get public praise or reward for work / actions _____
b be able to influence a decision by giving your opinion _____
c get satisfaction from doing something well _____
d have an effect on something _____
e know that you are included and involved _____
f think that something / someone will do well _____

5 Work with a partner. Discuss how satisfied you are at work at the moment / in a previous job you had using the combinations from **3**.

> *Example:* *I gain recognition for the extra hours I do. My boss gives me time off in lieu at the end of each month.*

6 45–47▷ Listen to three employers being interviewed at a graduate careers fair about working in their companies.

1 What are the companies and what do they each look for in their employees?

2 Do you think you would like to work for these companies? Why / Why not?

7 45–47▷ Combinations 1–8 follow the pattern: verb + preposition + noun, and combinations 9–11 follow the pattern: verb + noun + preposition. Complete each one with the correct preposition(s), then listen and check your answers.

1 seek _____ opportunities

2 believe _____ the need to …

3 benefit _____ diversity

4 build _____ rapport

5 live _____ expectations

6 strive _____ a healthy work-life balance

7 think _____ your feet

8 put someone _____ the test

9 demonstrate the ability _____

10 show a willingness _____

11 show a desire _____

8 Work with a partner. Replace the <u>underlined</u> sections of sentences 1–5 with a combination from **7**.

1 We had to fire Joanna. She didn't <u>achieve the results that we thought she would</u>.

2 <u>I'm convinced that we need</u> to improve communication between teams.

3 He isn't improving. He needs to <u>convince us that he is prepared to</u> change.

4 I didn't expect to have so many difficult questions after the presentation. I had to <u>react very quickly</u>.

5 You need to <u>show us that you can</u> accept criticism and move forwards.

>> For more exercises, go to **Practice file 8** on page 116.

9 Choose four of the combinations from **7** and give examples from your own experience at work.

> *Example:* *I had to think on my feet when my boss was taken ill, and I had to give a presentation in his place.*

10 Work in two groups and prepare for a careers fair.

Group A, you are the employer. Work together to decide on your ideal employee. What would you offer in order to attract / keep this ideal employee? What would you expect in return? Base your ideas on the company you all work for, or turn to File 34 on page 144 for some alternative company profiles.

Group B, you are the employees. Ideally, what do you each hope to gain from working for Group A?

11 Work with a partner from the other group. You meet at a careers fair. Have an informal discussion about

- what Student A's company looks for in an employee
- Student B's expectations of an employer
- what Student B has to offer as a potential employee.

Then decide how well-suited you are to each other.

(*i*) >> Interactive Workbook >> **Glossary**

Context

Ovanta is an international financial services company which has been created from the recent merger of three smaller companies. The company holds regular briefing meetings to update the senior management team on key initiatives following the merger.

The Operations Director, Ian Dungannon, has invited two project team leaders to the latest briefing. Anya is in charge of a project looking at training needs across the organization; Pavla is leading an initiative to improve relations between management and the union. Both women are knowledgeable about their subjects, but neither has been specifically asked to make a presentation at this meeting.

Presenting | Giving an impromptu presentation

1 **Work with a partner. Discuss the following questions.**

1 How is an impromptu presentation different from a formal presentation?
2 How do you feel about giving impromptu presentations? Do you find them easier or more difficult than formal presentations? Why?

2 **48, 49 ▷ Listen to extracts 1 and 2 from the management briefing at Ovanta. Choose the best answer for questions 1–5.**

1 How does Anya begin her impromptu talk?
  a She explains in detail what she is going to say.
  b She gives an informal overview of the current situation.
2 How would you describe Anya's way of signalling what she wants to talk about?
  a informal and conversational
  b formal and structured
3 How does Anya deal with Ian's questions?
  a She's negative and defensive.
  b She's positive and constructive.
4 In her update, Pavla chooses to
  a emphasize the key points of the discussion.
  b give a detailed account of the discussion.
5 How do both Anya and Pavla respond to unexpected requests for details?
  a They just say they don't know / aren't sure.
  b They say they don't know / aren't sure and promise future action.

3 **48 ▷ Listen again to the first part of extract 1 and complete these sentences.**

1 Well, to be honest, we haven't got as far as I'd hoped. _____
  … er, we've just completed the initial consultation stage.
2 However, _____ the initiative will be complete and in place before the annual review.
3 _____ give you a more precise date, _____ do that at the moment.
4 _____ run the details by Jean-Paul and the team leaders first …

4 48▷ Listen again to the second part of extract 1 and complete these sentences.

1   So, now, _____ went through some of the other training programmes we are running.

2   So if it's OK, _____ the core elements of the plans …

3   I don't know if you've heard of a 'balanced scorecard'? _____ this approach and how it works in practice …

4   … And that's more or less it … _____.

5 Match the phrases you noted in **3** and **4** to the following categories.

a   Signalling what you intend to talk about next: _____

b   Setting a context for the whole talk: _____

6 Work with a partner. Turn to File 07 on page 137. Read the information and decide what you would you say in an impromptu presentation to

a   set the context

b   signal the key points you intend to cover.

7 Work with a partner. Brainstorm phrases you could use to highlight your main points in an impromptu presentation (e.g. *So, the first thing is …*). Then turn to audio script 49▷ on page 160 and compare your ideas with the phrases that Pavla uses.

8 48, 49▷ Listen to both extracts again. Note down what Anya and Pavla say in response to the following questions from Ian.

1   Anya, you haven't said anything about management training.

2   And you've still got time to do that, have you?

3   If it was just one or two individuals, then just how useful are the results?

4   … it might also be worth touching on the numbers of complaints per business unit.

>> For more exercises, go to **Practice file 8** on page 116.

9 Work with a partner. Look back at the situation in **6** and decide how you would respond to the following questions from your audience. Then take turns to ask and answer the questions.

1   'The process is taking quite a long time, isn't it?'

2   'How confident are you that you have time to process all the data?'

3   'Could you say something about the kind of questions you asked?'

4   'How many people were interviewed in each area?'

5   'Isn't there a danger that the data will be out of date before we can process it?'

6   'I assume you have further research planned – can you give us details?'

10 Work in groups. You are going to take part in a team meeting. Think about your current projects at work. Write an agenda with your names and a list of these projects. Then follow points 1–2.

1   Take turns to give an impromptu presentation of the project you are working on to your group.

2   When listening to the other presentations, ask questions to get more information or check details.

ⓘ >> Interactive Workbook >> **Email**

Key expressions

Setting the context
Where we are at the moment is …
What I can tell you is that …
I'd like to be able to … but unfortunately I can't …
You'll appreciate that I still need to …

Signalling intention
Perhaps it would be a good idea if I just …
I'd just like to sketch out …
Let me just touch on …
I think that's covered everything.

Responding to questions and challenges
I was coming to that.
I have to admit that …
You're quite right, we need to address this.
That's a good point.

Highlighting key points
So, the first thing is …
And I think you should be aware that …
So that's one key point right there.
… and I think this is a really important point …
So, the main thing to remember is …

Responding to requests for detail
Let me check … and I'll get back to you.
I can't remember exactly, but off the top of my head …
I can double check if you like?
I don't have the exact figures, but what if I …?

ⓘ >> Interactive Workbook
    >> **Phrasebank**

Language at work | Using questions

1 Look at questions 1–10 from two impromptu presentations. The letters in brackets tell you who is asking the question, the presenter (P) or the audience (A). Match the questions to categories a–d below (more than one match may be possible).

1 Now, how can I put this? (P) _____

2 If it was just one or two individuals, then just how useful are the results? (A) _____

3 Anya, can you give us an overview of where we are with this? (A) _____

4 I assume everyone participated in the brainstorming, did they? (A) _____

5 I don't know if you've heard of a 'balanced scorecard'? (P) _____

6 It's probably best if I just highlight some of the ideas we came up with, don't you think? (P) _____

7 And you've still got time to do that, have you? (A) _____

8 Would you like to run through the union complaints briefly? (A) _____

9 OK. How long do I have? (P) _____

10 Anya, you haven't said anything about management training? (A) _____

a buying time to think

b challenging the presenter or checking the facts

c prompting or leading the presenter

d previewing the topic

2 Which of the questions in **1**

1 are *wh-* / *how* questions? _____   3 are statements used as questions? _____

2 use a question tag? _____   4 include a modal auxiliary verb? _____

3 Which of the questions 1–10 in **1**

1 don't expect an answer (rhetorical questions)? _____

2 expect a *yes* / *no* answer? _____

3 expect more than a *yes* / *no* answer? _____

>> For more information, go to **Language reference Unit 8** on page 130.

4 Work with a partner. Ask questions using prompts 1–8 and the information in brackets.

1 Is it a good idea? **(challenge speaker)**

2 Latest figures? **(prompt speaker)**

3 Send a draft to the listener first? **(check facts)**

4 Best way to present the information? **(give yourself time to think)**

5 Familiar with this new software? **(preview topic)**

6 Present findings to the client without showing them to senior management first? **(challenge speaker)**

7 The research phase has been completed? **(check facts)**

8 Initial impressions from research trip? **(prompt speaker)**

>> For more exercises, go to **Practice file 8** on page 117.

5 Work in groups of three. Student A and Student B are in an update meeting.

Student A Student B asks you for an update on your work over the last two weeks. As you start to speak, give yourself time to think. Ask questions to ensure that Student B is interested and is following what you are saying.

Student B Ask Student A for an update on her / his work over the past two weeks. Interrupt as often as you can with a variety of questions. If necessary, prompt Student A to move on and talk about a new point.

Student C Listen and make a note of the questions asked and their function.

Now change roles.

Practically speaking | Dealing with difficult questions

1 **What can you do if someone asks you**
  a a question you don't know the answer to?
  b a question you don't want to answer?

2 **50▷ Listen to six questions and the responses. In each conversation (1–6), tick (✓) the strategies used by the person responding to the question.**

Strategies	1	2	3	4	5	6
admit ignorance						
directly refuse to answer						
avoid the question						
distance yourself from the situation						

3 **50▷ Listen again and note down the phrases the speakers use for the strategies in 2.**

>> For extension and revision, go to **Useful phrases** on page 135.

4 **Work with a partner. Student A, read the information below. Student B, turn to File 37 on page 144. Take turns to ask / respond to two difficult questions, using the information / prompts given.**
Student A
1 You've just heard that the budget on your project will be cut significantly, and the launch date for your product will be pushed back by a year. Find out from Student B
   • if this is true
   • what the implications are for you.
2 You've been involved in a series of secret meetings where the decision has been taken to restructure Student B's department. Student B has just found out. Respond to Student B's difficult questions by
   • admitting ignorance
   • directly refusing to answer.

5 **Think of two difficult questions for your partner about his / her job. Then take turns to ask / respond to each other's questions.**

(i) >> Interactive Workbook >> **Exercises and Tests**

Key word | *just*

Match phrases 1–5 with *just* to synonyms a–e.
1 It's *just* that everyone is dying to know who …
2 We've only *just* started looking at the figures.
3 Could I *just* ask how you got to hear about the problems in the factory?
4 You know I *just* might do that.
5 *Just* the man I'm looking for!

a very recently
b precisely, exactly
c only
d take this opportunity to
e actually, really

Unit 8 | Performance

Culture question
• In your culture when (if at all) is it acceptable to ask questions about a) someone's salary b) someone's latest appraisal c) someone's family situation?
• How would you respond if someone from another culture asked you a question that you found unacceptable or inappropriate?

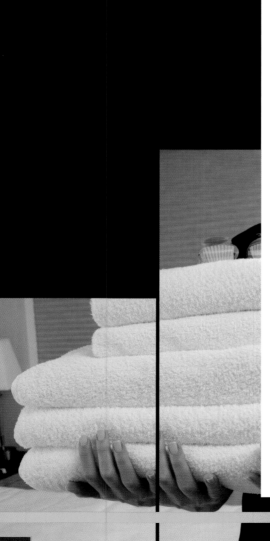

Company profile
The Ritz-Carlton

The Ritz-Carlton Hotel Company, L.L.C. has grown to over 70 hotels worldwide with plans for further expansion in Europe, Africa, Asia, the Middle East, and the Americas. It has won numerous awards, and its business practices provide a benchmark not only in the hotel industry, but also in other sectors. Its corporate philosophy is based on an unwavering commitment to service.

The Portman Ritz-Carlton, Shanghai

In 1998 The Ritz-Carlton Hotel Company, L.L.C. took over management of The Portman Shangri-La, which was to become The Portman Ritz-Carlton, Shanghai.

Prior to 1998, The Portman Shangri-La in Shanghai was a five-star property much like any other in the city. Employee and guest satisfaction ranged between 70% and 80%, and finances were unspectacular. But fortunes changed under Ritz-Carlton management – employee satisfaction soared, guests were much happier, and finances improved. For five consecutive years, its annual employee satisfaction rate has been the highest among all the Ritz-Carlton hotels worldwide.

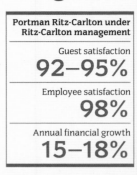

Portman Ritz-Carlton under Ritz-Carlton management

Guest satisfaction
92–95%

Employee satisfaction
98%

Annual financial growth
15–18%

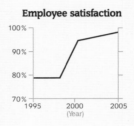

Employee satisfaction

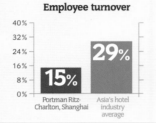

Employee turnover
15% Portman Ritz-Carlton, Shanghai
29% Asia's hotel industry average

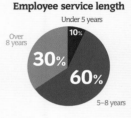

Employee service length
Under 5 years **10%**
Over 8 years **30%**
60% 5–8 years

Leadership and management practices at The Portman Ritz-Carlton, Shanghai

1 Leadership consistency: The executive team works with employees when issues arise, no matter how small. They lead by example: 'People believe what they see, not what is said.'

2 Selecting the right employees: The General Manager (GM) is involved in the interview process of all employees to show how important that individual is to the company. The GM will try to determine whether candidates are seeking a long-term relationship with the hotel.

3 Training and daily briefing: After an initial two-day orientation and 30 days of training, every employee receives at least 130 hours of training a year in company culture, their department, language, and computer skills. There is also a daily briefing.

4 Listening and communication: This is ensured through breakfast meetings between the GM and employees, regular meetings between the executive team and department managers, talks by the executive team to the entire staff, and sessions with HR and randomly selected employees to discuss concerns. Every employee can speak in private with the GM or HR Director and there are also employee satisfaction surveys.

5 Empowerment and continuous improvement: Employees are empowered to spend up to $2,000 to resolve customer complaints. Employees are also encouraged to be innovative and creative in improving their jobs, without a lengthy and bureaucratic approval process.

6 Information support: Employees record a guest's check-in, room service, and housekeeping preferences. These are then entered in the Ritz-Carlton's worldwide database, so whenever guests make a reservation at a Ritz-Carlton hotel, their needs are known and taken care of.

7 Reward and recognition: Employees are recognized for outstanding customer service at staff meetings, on the HR bulletin board, and also by colleagues, who send first-class compliment cards for service excellence. The Five-Star Employee Award rewards the winner with a five-night stay for two at a Ritz-Carlton anywhere in the world.

Discussion

1 How has The Portman Ritz-Carlton, Shanghai achieved such radical improvements?

2 To what extent do you agree with Ritz-Carlton leadership and management practices? Which of the practices do you find most innovative?

3 What other factors could contribute to
- your satisfaction as a hotel guest?
- staff satisfaction at a hotel?

Task

1 Work in groups of three. You are HR managers at GS International Hotel Group. You have just taken over the four-star Katisha Hotel in Buenos Aires and have been asked to devise a proposal for improving the hotel's staff and customer satisfaction levels. Look at the graph below and briefly discuss the areas for improvement.

The Katisha Hotel, Buenos Aires

2 51▷ Shortly after the takeover, the newly-appointed General Manager of the Katisha has an update meeting with the Business Development Director of GS International. Listen to the extract from their meeting and make further notes about the current problems at the Katisha on the graph above.

3 Work in your groups of three. Spend ten minutes devising your plan for improvements at the Katisha Hotel. You have heard about how Ritz-Carlton management turned the Portman Shangri-La around, and you may wish to use some of these ideas, together with your own.

4 Present your ideas to the class.

The Expert View

A leadership focus on improving both employee commitment and, consequently, customer satisfaction can lead to gains in shareholder value. These causal linkages have now been widely embraced across many industry sectors and the reasons for this are clear. As the business model in most developed economies shifts from 'make and sell' to 'listen, serve, and customize', the provision of service has become a key means of differentiation between competing firms. As a consequence, senior management have engaged in developing the means to empower, incentivize, train, and retain personnel directly involved in delivering customer services to improve both customer satisfaction and the commitment of these front-line personnel.

Prof. Simon Knox, BSc PhD,
Professor of Brand Marketing

Cranfield School of Management

Case study

9 | Resources

Learning objectives in this unit
- Talking about resources
- Discussing options and reaching decisions
- Using conditionals
- Dealing with misunderstandings

Case study
- Starting a CSR project

Starting point

1 Think of examples of
   - natural resources
   - company resources.

2 In which of the four basic resource areas (financial, human, physical, or intangible) would you find these resource types?
   - production facilities
   - existing staff
   - ability to raise funds
   - existing funds
   - changes to staff
   - goodwill / reputation / brands
   - IT

Working with words | Talking about resources

1 Marks and Spencer plc is an international company. What do you know about it? In what ways could it show that it uses both natural resources and company resources in a responsible way? Read the text and compare your ideas.

M&S pledges to manage resources responsibly

1 _____

Ask anyone in the UK what Marks and Spencer plc stands for and you'll get a range of answers. This is because the company has had to refocus several times in an attempt to retain its **competitive advantage**. In today's business world companies have to accept that **corporate accountability** is now fundamental to company strategy. Businesses now need to ensure that they deploy all resources in a responsible way. M&S has embraced this challenge.

2 _____

M&S knows that with its staff it commands a huge **knowledge base** that it needs to protect and enhance, therefore it has recognized its responsibility to nurture current employees and to offer employment opportunities to the wider community. As a result, resources have been allocated to various HR projects, including staff secondment to charities, and providing up to 2,600 work experience placements in stores.

3 _____

Marks and Spencer also listened to its customers, something it has an excellent **track record** for, and ensured its resources were being maximized by creating a new, all-embracing Corporate Social Responsibility (CSR) programme. It realized that one **critical success factor** for CSR was transparency, so it set out to consult customers about the issue of social responsibility. It became clear that public awareness of the **sustainability of resources** was on the increase. Mike Barry, head of CSR explains, 'Four years ago 50% of customers said it mattered

to them that Marks and Spencer was a responsible business. By last year that proportion had grown to 97%,' proving its customers supported a company with green credentials that would also optimize its use of resources.

4 _____

Marks and Spencer plc responded by pledging to introduce a range of changes. It began by analysing the utilization of existing resources with the intention of running a greener business. Some small-scale changes include recycling coat hangers, discouraging the use of plastic bags, and allowing its own-brand chickens more room to roam.

5 _____

Cynics might say that such well-publicized HR and CSR projects are simply a way to enhance the company's image. There's no doubt these projects allow Marks and Spencer to publicly demonstrate how both company and natural resources are being put to good use, rather than being squandered or mismanaged. However, it's also clear that many areas of society can benefit.

2 Match these headings with paragraphs 1–5.

- Respecting customer opinion
- Just a PR tool?
- Becoming a more responsible company
- Responsibility and business
- Being a responsible employer

3 Match the noun phrases in **bold** in the text to definitions 1–6.

1 a company's obligation to justify its actions to its stakeholders, customers, and society
2 the skills and expertise of a company's employees
3 the efficient use of materials and energy in a way that minimizes harm to the environment
4 the benchmark which measures how well a project / strategy has been implemented and is running
5 how well a company / person has achieved something over a number of years
6 something that helps a company be more successful than other companies in the same market

4 Find eight verbs in the text in **1** that collocate with *resources*.

5 Put the verbs you noted in **4** into categories 1–3 based on their meaning.

1 get the best out of resources   2 waste resources   3 do something with resources

6 52▷ Listen to three people talking about CSR and answer questions 1–3.

1 What's the first person's argument against CSR projects?
2 What's the second person's argument for CSR?
3 What's required of a CSR partner with the third person's company, and why?

7 Work with a partner. Complete sentences 1–9 with these words and phrases.

*short-term profit   drain on resources   return on investment   bottom line
assets   market value   quantifiable data   cost-benefit analysis   long-term viability*

1 To find out if the project's worth doing we need a …
2 This project is costing us far too much; it's a real …
3 We'll have to do some forward projections to check the project's …
4 Before I commit a lot of money to the project I need to be sure of a good …
5 We need to be sure that our projected figures are based on …
6 Our highly-skilled workforce is one of our key …
7 Rather than future stability, the company's strategy is all about …
8 Our reputation as a responsible employer has enhanced the company's …
9 The shareholders were disappointed because the drop in sales had an impact on our …

≫ For more exercises, go to **Practice file 9** on page 118.

8 Work with a partner. Using vocabulary from **3** and **7**, discuss the pros and cons of investing in projects 1–4 for

- the current employees
- the customers
- the shareholders.

Projects

1 Invest in extensive IT and skills-based training programmes for all members of staff, and include residential team-building weekends for managers.
2 Offer work to asylum seekers in the local area: train them and provide them with free language lessons to enable them to work effectively.
3 Invest in a project to protect the environment – encourage staff to leave their cars at home and install solar panels on the roof of office buildings.
4 Relocate the customer services department to a developing country. Pay the staff in that country a higher salary in comparison with other companies.

---

9 Would your company invest in any of the projects in **8**? What projects does your company currently have? What new projects would you suggest, and why?

i ≫ Interactive Workbook ≫ **Glossary**

Context

Floralope is located in Hungary and manufactures seed packets for companies in neighbouring countries. Floralope is part-owned by a Dutch company, so any major decisions have to be discussed with them. Recently, Floralope has found it hard to keep up with its competitors, due to outdated systems and a more demanding customer base. Investing in a new IT system would help keep existing customers and could enable expansion. The question is whether this is a wise investment and if long-term expansion is the right strategy. Zoltan and Judit from the Hungarian company, and Margit from the Dutch parent company, meet to discuss the situation.

Meetings | Discussing options and reaching decisions

1 How might the company's current resources affect the decision to expand and invest in a new IT system?

2 53–56▷ Listen to four extracts from the meeting. Check your ideas in 1 and answer questions 1–2.
   1 What type of company resources were discussed?
   2 Which resources are problematic?

3 53–56▷ Listen to the four extracts again and answer questions 1–2.
   1 Who takes a positive lead in the meeting? How do you know?
   2 Who seems quite negative throughout? How do you know?

4 Put the phrases in **bold** in sentences a–l into these categories.
   1 Summarizing / bringing the meeting to an end: _____
   2 Talking about the future of the company as a whole: _____
   3 Discussing options: _____

   a So, **looking at the situation from a long-term perspective**, if the IT system is updated, you'll be more efficient in terms of your customer admin …
   b **We need to develop a clear strategy to move the business forward.**
   c **Well, we have a number of options.**
   d OK, that's all very positive, but **I think we need to look at the bigger picture.**
   e **I think our options are quite clear here.**
   f **How would it work if** you took on some younger people?
   g And we're in a great location, so I think **we're in a really strong position to** find new staff.
   h **Basically we don't have much choice** for a long-term plan like this – **we can either** provide training for everyone, which will be a substantial investment, **or we** accept that it's totally unfeasible.
   i **We have to bear in mind the long-term viability** of a commitment like this.
   j **So the general consensus is** that long-term we have the human resources for the strategy.
   k **Are there any other points to consider?**
   l **Right, so we're decided.**

5 Look at phrases 1–6 from the meeting and answer questions a–d.

1 Yes, but we do have some employees who've worked on SAP-type systems in previous jobs.

2 I mean, there's no point in investing in a system upgrade if we don't have the space, the personnel, or the finances to carry it through.

3 Provided we check out the feasibility of these options thoroughly, I'm convinced we can find a system upgrade that will work for us.

4 I'm not sure that would work.

5 Realistically, would we be able to finance this strategy?

6 Assuming we decided to commit to the full amount, we could also look at ways to save money in other areas.

a Why is *do* used in phrase 1?

b Are phrases 2–6 used for *deciding not to follow an option* or for *evaluating an option*?

c Which phrases from 2–6 focus on positive results?

d Which phrases from 2–6 focus on negative results?

» For more exercises, go to **Practice file 9** on page 118.

6 Margit discussed the strategy proposed by Floralope with a senior manager at the Dutch parent company. Some ideas were rejected and alternative suggestions were made. Work in groups of four. Students A and B, turn to File 38 on page 145. Students C and D turn to File 19 on page 140.

Agenda

Impact of new IT system

1 Human resources – training and staff issues?

2 Financial resources – how will the IT system and training be funded?

3 Timescale – when will the new system be introduced?

Follow the agenda and hold a meeting to discuss the alternative suggestions. Try to reach a decision.

7 Work with a partner. Discuss projects 1–6 in relation to your company and answer questions a–c.

1 new computer system

2 new building / relocating

3 new product / service

4 refurbished offices

5 increase in staff numbers

6 merger / restructuring

a Which projects would be appropriate for your company?

b What resources would be necessary?

c How would the resources be managed?

8 Present your ideas to the rest of the class.

ⓘ **»** Interactive Workbook **»** **Email**

Key expressions

Setting the context / discussing strategy

Looking at the situation from a long-term perspective …

We need to develop a clear strategy to …

I think we need to look at the bigger picture.

We have to bear in mind the long-term viability …

Stating / discussing options

We have a number of options.

I think our options are quite clear here.

How would it work if you / we …?

Basically, we don't have much choice …. We can either … or we (accept that) …

We're in a really strong position to …

Discussing feasibility / evaluating options

There's no point in … -ing, if we don't / can't …

Provided we …, I'm convinced we can …

I'm not sure that would work.

Realistically, would we be able to finance this strategy?

Assuming we decided to …, we could also …

Reaching agreement

So, the general consensus is that …

Are there any other points to consider?

Right. So we're decided.

ⓘ **»** Interactive Workbook
» **Phrasebank**

Language at work | Using conditionals

1 Look at these extracts from the strategy meeting and <u>underline</u> all the verbs.

1 … if the IT system is updated, you'll be more efficient in terms of your customer admin …

2 Provided we check out the feasibility of these options thoroughly, I'm convinced we can find a system upgrade that will work for us.

3 … there's no point in investing in a system upgrade if we don't have the space, the personnel, or the finances …

4 … if we'd invested in our production facilities five years ago, … we would have knocked down the old building and had one purpose-built.

5 If we made them our key users, we could gradually train up the rest.

6 … if you'd recruited more young employees at the start, they would have had some IT knowledge from school.

7 If we only had a couple of people initially who could use the system, how could they cope with the extra work?

8 … if we hadn't invested in the system, we'd be way behind the competition.

9 If we work more efficiently with the customers, our reputation can only improve too.

2 Work with a partner. Look at the conditional sentences in **1**. Identify the conditional type (zero, 1st, 2nd, 3rd, mixed) for each sentence.

3 Match the sentences in **1** to these categories. Do you notice any connection with your answers in **2**?

1 Predicting the results of a decision in the future: _____

2 Making a suggestion: _____

3 Stating a fact: _____

4 Questioning the results of a future situation: _____

5 Expressing regret for past inaction: _____

6 Talking about the present results of a past action / inaction: _____

>> For more information, go to **Language reference Unit 9** on page 131.

4 Work with a partner. Take turns to discuss these situations. Use conditionals to talk about past, present, or future consequences. See the example.

Example: Last year your company outsourced catering. Now the standard of food in the canteen is lower and the number of employees eating there has fallen by 40%.
→ *If we hadn't outsourced catering, we would still have a good canteen.*

1 Your company is making a loss – it needs to cut costs because it is close to bankruptcy.

2 The government is considering raising interest rates, but they are concerned about the effects on consumer spending.

3 Your department hired a bad manager, Ian. Since his arrival, three people have left.

4 You chose the wrong career path. You are now bored and disillusioned with your job.

5 Some staff will be relocated to Berlin (it might be you). You have lots of friends there.

6 Your annual pay review is coming up. You want to go on holiday to the Caribbean, but you can't afford it at the moment.

>> For more exercises, go to **Practice file 9** on page 119.

5 YP fitness studio is having its yearly review meeting. Work with a partner and turn to File 13 on page 139. Talk about what happened and the future plans.

6 Think about the past year in your company, department, or team. Make notes about what happened and add some suggestions for next year using headings 1–3. Then discuss your notes with a partner.

1 Past action / inaction and past results

2 Past action / inaction and present results

3 Suggestions / predictions for next year plus results

Practically speaking | Dealing with misunderstandings

1 57▷ **Listen to five conversations. In which conversation(s) does the person react to the misunderstanding**

  1 in a polite way?

  2 in a less polite way?

Key word | *look*

Match sentences 1–6 to the uses / definitions of *look* a–f.

1 *Look*, you've got this wrong.

2 It *looks* as if Nadine's left the office.

3 You *look* great in that new outfit!

4 I have to *look* for my car keys every morning.

5 Could you take a *look* at this email before I send it?

a it seems / it is apparent

b to focus on something, think about it, and give a reaction

c to describe appearance

d to indicate you're highlighting something

e to search

2 57▷ **Listen again. In which conversation (1–5) do you hear these phrases?**

  a I didn't mean that! ___

  b I don't know what you're talking about. ___

  c Sorry if I didn't make that clear. ___

  d I was thinking more along the lines of … ___

  e Look, you've got it wrong. ___

  f What do you mean? ___

  g That's not really what I meant. What I actually wanted to say was … ___

  h What I meant was … ___

  i … can I put this straight? ___

  j The amount may seem …, but actually … ___

  k No, that's not right. ___

  l No, that's not exactly what I'm saying. ___

3 **Work with a partner and answer questions 1–3.**

  1 Which phrases in **2** are direct (**D**) and which are less direct (**L**)?

  2 Which words and structures are used to make the message less direct?

  3 When might you want to be less direct and when might you want to be more direct?

4 **Change the phrases in 1–5 to make them less direct using words from the list.**

  exactly   actually   really   sure   mean   quite

  1 That's not what I mean, I said … _____

  2 I didn't mean that. _____

  3 What do you mean? _____

  4 I don't know what you're talking about. _____

  5 No, that's not right. _____

  >> For extension and revision, go to **Useful phrases** on page 135.

5 **Work with a partner. Student A, make suggestions / complaints 1–4 and deal with any misunderstanding. Student B, misunderstand Student A. Change roles and repeat.**

  1 suggest new facilities for staff at your company (e.g. gym, canteen, TV room, etc.)

  2 suggest an idea for your partner's next holiday

  3 make a complaint about your partner's work

  4 suggest a task for your partner to do at work

  ⓘ » Interactive Workbook » **Exercises and Tests**

Culture question

- In your own language do you normally use direct or indirect language when informing someone they have misunderstood?

- How would you feel if someone corrected your English during a meeting?

- Would you be more direct in a meeting with native English speakers or with non-native English speakers? Why?

Michelin is one of the oldest tyre manufacturers in the world. As it is involved in what is considered an environmentally damaging industry, Michelin has developed an approach called 'Performance and Responsibility'. This concept allows the company to demonstrate that it is actively taking measures to reduce the industry's negative impact on the environment. It also has various projects throughout the world connected to its CSR programme.

Starting a CSR project
Background

Michelin's 'Green Gold' project

A small rubber project in north-eastern Brazil set up by Michelin has become a flagship for the French tyre giant's corporate social responsibility programme. With five rubber trees needed to produce one truck tyre, Michelin is an obvious target for those who claim that big business is using up natural resources too intensively. Although the company can't change the number of trees needed in the manufacturing process, it has initiated a successful project to offset the effects of its activities.

The Ouro Verde ('Green Gold') project in Bahia state is a 'marvellous human adventure', the late Edouard Michelin said at its inauguration. Having owned a 9,000-hectare site there for 20 years, the French firm considered closing the loss-making plantation and laying off the workers. Instead, it passed ownership to twelve local Michelin managers, who set up a cooperative with the backing of loans underwritten by the parent company. Far from laying off workers, 200 have been hired over the past two years.

Lionel Barré, the plantation director at Michelin, says that the initiative stands as 'an example of sustainable development in a poor region'. The last two years have seen a burst of activity: the cooperative has planted cocoa next to the rubber trees to diversify its output, recycled some of its revenue into providing facilities for its employees, and replanted parts of the depleted Atlantic rainforest in eastern Brazil, which contains 171 of Brazil's 202 endangered species.

Discussion

1 How could the local community benefit from this cooperative?

2 How could Michelin benefit from starting this kind of project?

3 Could there be any disadvantages for Michelin?

4 58▷ Listen to an interview with a Michelin director and compare your ideas.

Task

1 QP Plastics is a petrochemical company with a long history of manufacturing in Nigeria. The last few years have seen losses, but rather than closing the plant, QP Plastics wants to encourage locals to take it on as part of a CSR project. The company wants to retain a share of the business.

Work in groups. Read the facts and figures about Port Harcourt in Nigeria and discuss what kind of CSR project might benefit this region.

Location	Port Harcourt is located in southern Nigeria and has long been an important merchant port. Today it is at the centre of Nigeria's oil industry. Its exports include petroleum, coal, tin, palm products, cocoa, and groundnuts. Among the industries of the area are timber processing, car manufacturing, food and tobacco processing, and the manufacture of rubber, glass, metal, paper products, cement, petroleum products, paint, enamelware, bicycles, furniture, and soap.
Population	1,320,214
Literacy	57%
Education	two universities and several vocational colleges
Main industry	petroleum, but plastics and textiles are in decline
Property	Costs for industrial rents / office space are high.
Infrastructure	international airport, but the road system is very poor
Utilities (power and water supplies)	poor
Tax incentives	Pioneer companies located in economically disadvantaged areas are given a tax holiday period of five to seven years. Those involved in local raw material development qualify for additional concessions.

2 With reference to the Michelin example, discuss your ideas for a CSR project in Port Harcourt. During your discussion, try to answer questions 1–5.

  1 Will the government be involved in the project?
  2 Will you select a group of locals to help you set up the project?
  3 What do you hope to achieve with the project?
  4 What improvements can you contribute to the region?
  5 Can you foresee any problems with the project? If so, how can you avoid them?

3 A cost-benefit analysis will be needed to decide whether the project is feasible. Before this is possible, the project needs to be carefully planned. In your group, make notes on questions 1–2.

  1 What resources (financial, human, and physical) should be available in order for the project to take place?
  2 Think about both long-term and short-term strategy – what are the potential consequences of your decisions?

4 Using your notes from **2** and **3**, present your CSR project idea to another group. Do they have any further advice?

5 A dramatic turn of events has taken place. Turn to File 41 on page 145 and read the email. In your groups, discuss what you think your company should do. Consider these questions.

  1 Should you continue with the discussions about the project or should you withdraw?
  2 What would be the consequences of
     • continuing with the project?   • closing the plant?

The Expert View

In most parts of the world nowadays, companies are expected to contribute to good causes and community projects. In some places, this might now be considered part of a 'licence to operate' from society. Typically, the approach of companies has evolved from corporate philanthropy to more strategic, corporate community investment. The latter involves businesses supporting activities which maximize benefits to the business as well as to society. Business benefits may be building people (improving staff morale and skills) or building markets and reputation (increasing sales by linking the company with a social cause). Being a responsible business does not mean avoiding tough decisions (e.g. closing factories), but it does involve seeking ways to minimize any negative environmental and social impacts of these decisions.

Prof. David Grayson, CBE, Professor of Corporate Responsibility, Director of the Doughty Centre for Corporate Responsibility

Cranfield School of Management

Case study

10 | Leadership

Starting point

1 Think of examples of good leaders in different walks of life, e.g. politics, sport, business, the arts.

2 Can you learn good leadership skills, or are they something you are born with?

3 What is the difference between a *leader* and a *manager*?

4 In your view, what different qualities are needed to successfully lead
- a small team?
- a large organization?

Working with words | Talking about leadership styles

1 Work with a partner and discuss questions 1–2.
  1 What are the key characteristics of an effective leader?
  2 What differences might there be between leadership styles in established economies like those in Western Europe, Japan, and America, and emerging economies in Asia?

2 Read the text and compare your answers in 1.

What makes an effective leader?

Professor D Quinn Mills
Harvard Business School

Whether you are leading a team at work, captaining your local sports team, or in charge of a major company, your style of leadership is a critical factor in the success of your team. So what makes an effective leader? According to Professor D Quinn Mills of the Harvard Business School, research shows that there are certain preferred leadership qualities that are common to all cultures.

In general, people appreciate leaders who appear honest and trustworthy. However, **integrity** is a complex idea, often determined by national culture, and what is considered honest in one society is not necessarily so in another.

Conviction – a strong belief in what you are doing – is a characteristic of leaders in all cultures, but how it is displayed can vary widely. Demonstrating a whole-hearted **commitment** to the success of your team or project is possibly more overt in America than elsewhere. However, a **passionate** leader with energy and enthusiasm – someone who can energize and inspire their team to succeed – is an asset almost everywhere. Similarly, in most cultures it helps to be a good communicator, to be **people-focused** and have well-developed interpersonal skills.

The ability to make good decisions quickly is something most cultures see as important. However, being **decisive** means different things to different people. European and Japanese leaders are the most **collaborative** decision-makers, taking time to consult with colleagues and consider the options. This is typical of a more participative style of leadership. In contrast, Chinese leaders, for whom the typical role model is often the head of the family, are more likely to make decisions personally. This more autocratic approach tends to be typical of task-oriented, top-down leaders, where what counts is results – it is also frequent in American leaders.

Being **adaptable** is also an important quality; team leaders often need to be flexible in their response to changing circumstances. Similarly, the ability to delegate and to know when to be **hands-off** is also necessary.

There's evidence that being able to show **empathy** – to understand the feelings, needs, and motivation of others – is increasingly seen as a key trait of effective leadership in the United States and Europe, and will become more important in Asia as companies have to compete for managerial talent in a global market. Related to this, certain Asian cultures value leaders who are **self-aware** and **humble** – the ability to know yourself and accept your limitations is often a trait of the most effective leaders.

3 Which leadership qualities are these people talking about? Match the adjectives (*A*) or nouns (*N*) in **bold** in the text to quotes 1–12.

1 'I appreciate the way she isn't at all arrogant, even though she's so successful.' (*A*)
2 'Someone who isn't afraid to make difficult choices – who can weigh up a situation and commit to a course of action.' (*A*)
3 'He really understands us – he knows how we operate and what makes us tick.' (*N*)
4 'He knows his own mind and what he's capable of – I like that.' (*A*)
5 'My team are focused on the success of this project – they always give 100%.' (*N*)
6 'I love this business – it's my life and I want everyone to know how great it is!' (*A*)
7 'You have to believe totally in what you're doing – if you don't, you won't succeed.' (*N*)
8 'She's not afraid to change direction if the circumstances demand it, but she always thinks through the implications.' (*A*)
9 'People have to know that you are principled, that you mean what you say, and that they can trust you to do the right thing at the right time.' (*N*)
10 'I believe in involving everyone in the decision-making process.' (*A*)
11 'He never interferes unless we ask for his input – he just lets us get on with it.' (*A*)
12 'She's an excellent communicator – she gets on well with everyone.' (*A*)

4 Work with a partner. Turn to File 42 on page 146. Read the feedback from team members about their team leaders and describe the leadership styles. Then prepare a short verbal report on one of the team leaders to present to the class.

5 Work with a partner and discuss questions 1–2.

1 How would you describe the typical leadership style where you work or study? Is the style of leadership different at different levels of the organization?
2 How would you describe your own / a colleague's leadership style?

6 59, 60▷ Listen to two people talking about becoming a team leader and answer questions 1–2. Lydia works in a university research department, Bruce works for a major aircraft manufacturer.

1 What challenge did each new team leader face, and how did they approach it?
2 What do you think of the approach described by each speaker?

7 59, 60▷ Match 1–12 to a–l to make phrases from the audio, then listen to check which combinations were used. What other combinations are possible?

1	avoid	a	a sense of cohesion
2	be consistent	b	my authority
3	build	c	influence over
4	develop	d	them to work together
5	establish	e	individual achievement
6	establish	f	the temptation to micromanage
7	exert	g	confidence in them
8	generate	h	a culture of trust
9	get	i	a sense of team spirit and collaboration
10	instil	j	in my expectations and feedback
11	recognize	k	mutual respect
12	reinforce	l	my credibility

>> For more exercises, go to **Practice file 10** on page 120.

8 Work with a partner. Discuss what advice you would give in these situations.

1 A colleague has been offered a challenging team leadership role within their own department. This involves taking over an existing team who all know each other.
2 A team leader has to manage a large team involving people from a number of different professional areas and cultural backgrounds.

9 Work in small groups. Discuss how you would react to the challenge of a new leadership role. What would you be good at? What would you need to work on?

(i) >> Interactive Workbook >> **Glossary**

Culture question

1 What problems could arise at work when bringing teams together with leaders from different national cultures or different working cultures, and why?
2 Is it acceptable to challenge authority in your culture? Why/ Why not?

Context

Nordica is an American-owned financial services group in the Nordic and Baltic Sea region. It was created by the recent merger of several smaller independent banks in Norway, Sweden, Finland, and Denmark.

Currently 80% of its private customers and almost 100% of its business customers use Nordica's e-banking system. However, the technology within the group is not fully integrated, and the company has decided to upgrade its infrastructure with a single system that is fast, innovative, flexible, and cost-effective. An initial briefing document has been sent out to all departments. Local briefing meetings are now being held throughout the company to clarify the situation, ensure buy-in from staff, and deal with any concerns.

Agenda

Briefing meeting – E-banking system

Meeting location: southern Sweden

Attendees:
Jim Brolin, Group Corporate Account Manager, New York
Anna Kekkonen, Client Account Manager, Helsinki
Thomas Lindström, Client Account Manager, Gothenberg
Jessica Nielsen, Client Account Manager, Copenhagen

1 Information about project – Jim
2 Question and answer session
3 AOB

Meetings | Giving a briefing on change

1 **61 ▷ Listen to extracts from part 1 of the meeting and answer questions 1–3.**
1 What does Jim say are the main benefits of the proposed change?
2 Would you describe Jim's attitude to the proposed change as
   a mainly positive?   **b** mainly negative?   **c** neutral?
3 Which of the following techniques does Jim use to make the managers feel part of the change process?
   a says they are all individually important to the success of the change process
   b promises large bonuses if the process is successful
   c asks them to work as a team and suggests ways of working together
   d asks them to show commitment and leadership
   e warns them not to oppose the change
   f encourages consultation with their teams

2 **61 ▷ Listen again to part 1. Note down the phrases that Jim uses to do 1–3. Add any similar phrases you can think of.**
1 Announce decisions and distance himself from them:

2 Focus on the benefits of the proposed change:

3 Make the other client account managers feel involved:

3 **Work with a partner. You have to brief a group of colleagues on a potentially unpopular or problematic change that is going to take place within your organization. Choose one of the topics below, or use your own idea.**
• a budget cut
• a reorganization of staff into different groups
• a change to the reporting lines
• a change to a key system or working practice

A briefing document has already been sent round. Prepare a short introduction to the briefing meeting. Include steps 1–4.
1 Explain the change, and make it clear you are not responsible for the decision.
2 Focus on the positive benefits of the proposed change.
3 Make sure everyone in the meeting feels involved.
4 Present your introduction to the class.

4 **62 ▷ Listen to part 2 of the meeting and answer questions 1–2.**
1 What concerns do the three client account managers have?
2 How does Jim respond to their concerns? Is he dismissive or reassuring?

5 62▷ **Listen to part 2 again and complete these sentences.**

Jessica … it's something all of us are worried about. I understand the reasons for upgrading the system, that's clear, but ¹_____ the timing and its effect on my team. Will we have enough time to prepare properly? And will there be an increase in workload? ²_____ about this?

Jim Well, ³_____, but ⁴_____ the positive side. We've been given a deadline of the 30th of September, which is still more than three months away. ⁵_____, the switch over …

Thomas … You said you wanted us to work together, and I like the idea of regular meetings and sharing ideas, but ⁶_____ having to schedule and coordinate the training for my team. I don't really feel I have the expertise to do this. ⁷_____ we'll get the appropriate level of support?

Jim Of course. ⁸_____, but again ⁹_____. ¹⁰_____ that you will receive all the instructions and materials …

Thomas … I guess that should be OK. But ¹¹_____ the impact on customers. I mean, how do we ensure that we continue to provide a proper service? ¹²_____ that it will work?'

Anna That's a good point. And can we address the issue of costs and budgeting? I think the basic idea is good, but ¹³_____ the cost implications. I mean, whose money are we talking about here? ¹⁴_____ we won't be asked to contribute …

Jim Well, ¹⁵_____, of course. The core investment comes from central funding, obviously.

… I've been told that the costs need to be shared around. ¹⁶_____ the intention is to make everyone's lives easier and better – including yours. Anyway, the decision has already been made. I know it's not great, but come on, ¹⁷_____.

6 **Match phrases 1–17 in 5 to these categories.**

a Expressing concerns: _____
b Asking for assurances: _____
c Responding to concerns: _____
d Distancing speaker from information: _____

▶▶ For more exercises, go to **Practice file 10** on page 120.

7 **Work with a partner and discuss situations 1–3. Student A should express concerns and ask for assurances, and Student B should respond to the concerns and make a positive comment. Then change roles and repeat.**

Situation	Positive points
1 The company has announced a one-year freeze on recruitment.	It's only for one year and will keep spending down.
2 Your team's project deadline has been brought forward by one month, but there is no increase in resourcing.	The team is strong and will rise to the challenge. It will also allow the company to get ahead of the competition.
3 Your company plans to increase the number of management layers.	This will create more promotion opportunities.

8 **Work with a partner. Follow steps 1–2, then change roles and repeat.**

1 Student A, think of a change that has been / might be introduced in your company and explain it to your partner.

2 Student B, listen to the explanation of the change and make a list of concerns you would have if it happened in your company / department / industry.

9 **Use your lists from 8 and take turns to talk about your concerns and ask for assurances. Your partner should respond and should focus on any benefits.**

ⓘ ▶▶ Interactive Workbook ▶▶ **Email**

Key expressions

Giving information from other sources / distancing
A decision was taken …
It has been agreed that …
It is proposed that …
My understanding is …
Apparently …
As I understand it …

Focusing on positive benefits
What this will allow us to do is …
something we couldn't do before.
… it will be well worth …
In the longer term, the benefits are clear.
Another great thing about this development is …

Making people feel involved
You … are crucial to …
Each one of you has a key role to play in …
I'd like to see all of you … -ing
I would encourage all of you to …

Expressing concerns
I understand the reasons for …, but I'm slightly concerned about …
I like the idea of …, but I'm not very happy about …
I have some reservations / concerns about …

Responding to concerns
That's a valid point, but … I really don't see this as a problem.
I understand where you're coming from …
I understand your concerns, but I think we need to look at the positive side.
… let's give this a chance to work.

Asking for assurances
I wonder if you have any information about this?
Can you assure us / give us an assurance that …?
What assurances can you give us that …?
Are there any guarantees that …?

ⓘ ▶▶ Interactive Workbook
▶▶ **Phrasebank**

Language at work | Distancing and depersonalizing using the passive

1 **Look at sentences 1–8 from the meeting and <u>underline</u> the passive forms.**

1 OK, you're all aware that a decision was taken at last week's strategy meeting that affects all of us.
2 It has been agreed that we are going to combine our e-banking systems into a …
3 We've been given a deadline of the 30th of September.
4 The switch over to the new system will be coordinated centrally and you'll be briefed about it well in advance.
5 It is proposed that we hold a series of seminars for team leaders …
6 It's been suggested that the regional centres should contribute a certain amount of the training costs, on the basis that this will be recouped in increased business later on …
7 I've been told that the costs need to be shared around.
8 Anyway, the decision has already been made.

2 **Work with a partner. Look at the passive forms in sentences 1–8 in 1 and discuss these questions.**

1 In each sentence, what tense is the passive form in?
2 Why does the speaker use a passive form in each sentence? Consider these reasons (more than one may be possible for each sentence).
   a because the speaker wants to be more formal
   b because it's not important who is involved in the action
   c because the speaker doesn't know who is involved in the action
   d because the speaker wants to distance himself / herself from the action

3 **Look at sentences a–b in the table and answer these questions.**

1 Which active sentence has one extra word (an indirect object)?
2 What happens to this word in the passive sentence?
3 Is the following sentence possible? Why? Why not?
   I've been suggested that the costs need to be shared around.

Active	Passive
a My boss suggested that the costs need to be shared around.	It has been suggested that the costs need to be shared around.
b My boss told me that the costs need to be shared around.	I've been told that the costs need to be shared around.

>> For more information, go to **Language reference Unit 10** on page 132.

4 **Work with a partner. Look at the verb table and take turns to report the information in sentences 1–6 in the passive. Use the correct form of the verbs in *italics* and refer to your answers in 3 to help you if necessary.**

Verbs with the same pattern as *tell*	Verbs with the same pattern as *suggest*
inform, instruct, persuade	*agree, decide, propose*

1 Our new official deadline is the 31st of January. *inform*
2 Management think we should cut back on our use of freelance consultants. *agree*
3 The department will be restructured next year. *propose*
4 Head Office wants us to reduce our spending by 5%. *instruct*
5 Bonuses will be paid twice a year from now on. *decide*
6 We're going to take part in a new system trial. *persuade*

>> For more exercises, go to **Practice file 10** on page 121.

5 **Work with a partner. Turn to File 29 on page 142. Read the memo and decide how you would report this to colleagues, depersonalizing where necessary.**

Practically speaking | Expressing personal views

1 Work with a partner and answer questions 1–2.
   1 How easy do you find it to make people understand what you really think in English?
   2 Is it easy to get other people to tell you what *they* really think?

2 63▷ Listen to three conversations. For each one, say
   1 what the people are discussing
   2 where / when they might be having the conversation.

3 63▷ Listen again and complete sentences 1–9.
   Conversation 1
   1 But _____, I think there are still some things to sort out.
   2 And _____, I don't see how we can agree to something that we haven't
      even been consulted about.
   3 _____ I find that quite difficult to accept.

   Conversation 2
   4 It was challenging, yeah. But _____ I really enjoyed it.
   5 _____, I'm not particularly good at working in a big team.
   6 _____? It's fine, the job's good, but …

   Conversation 3
   7 Yeah, well … maybe. _____ I think that's down to their attitude.
   8 _____: you get out of these things what you put into them.
   9 Look, _____, if you expect something …

   ≫ For extension and revision, go to **Useful phrases** on page 135.

4 Work with a partner and answer questions 1–2.
   1 Look at your answers in **3**. What follows these phrases? Why might you use them?
   2 Turn to audio script **63▷** on page 164. What questions and phrases does speaker A
      use to encourage B to express their personal views?

**5 Work with a partner and have a conversation about situations 1–3. Take turns
   to be A and B (A and B are colleagues). Student A, encourage B to express their
   personal views. Student B, express your personal views.**
   1 You meet in a rest area while you are both are getting a coffee. B has been on
      a leadership training course – the content was useful, but the trainer was quite
      inexperienced and didn't seem to understand the participants' needs.
   2 You have both been in a briefing meeting, and leave together. Some proposals for new
      working practices have come down from senior management. The effect will be to
      increase everyone's workload, without any similar increase in resources.
   3 You meet over lunch in the staff restaurant. B has just sent his / her son on an
      adventure holiday with his school. It's the first time he's been away from home.

ⓘ ≫ Interactive Workbook ≫ **Exercises and Tests**

Key word | *even*

**Look at phrases 1–4 with *even*
and answer questions a–b.**
1 I don't see how we can agree to
   something that we haven't *even*
   been consulted about.
2 *Even* so, it must have been
   challenging at times?
3 What I'd really like to do is run
   my own operation – that would
   be *even* better.
4 *Even if* you aren't 100% sure, at
   least give it a try.

a In which sentence does the
   speaker use the word *even* to
   • emphasize that something has
     not happened?
   • emphasize a comparison?
b In which sentence can the
   phrase with *even* be replaced by
   • *nevertheless*?
   • *despite the fact that*?

Ryor

Ryor is an international cosmetics company based in Prague in the Czech Republic. It was founded in 1991 by Eva Štěpánková. Originally the company focused on manufacturing natural cosmetics for the professional industry (e.g. beauty salons). However, it soon started supplying the retail market too. Currently Ryor produces 63 products for the professional market and over 90 for the individual user. Recently it has diversified into the food market, selling speciality teas and natural nutrients. Ryor now has its own manufacturing facilities outside Prague which are equipped with an in-house laboratory and state-of-the-art technology. It has an annual turnover of an estimated six and a half million US dollars.

Eva Štěpánková wins 2006 Prague Leaders Magazine Woman of the Year award for Business

More than 500 guests attended the Women of the Year gala, an event where prominent Czech women are celebrated. Honours for 2006 were announced in five categories. Eva Štěpánková, owner of cosmetics company Ryor, was the recipient of the Business award in recognition of her life long achievements in the field of cosmetics.

Now a well-known brand, Ryor has come a long way since Štěpánková started it in 1991. She initially manufactured the products in her own flat, but since then she has built up a successful, multinational company. Ryor products are now being used by women in more than fifteen countries.

How a strong leader can steer a company to success

Eva Štěpánková is the founder of the successful international cosmetics company, Ryor. She is famous for her passionate leadership, and it is this approach that has driven her through hard times and made her company one of the most respected cosmetic firms in Europe. Here we look at how Štěpánková dealt with four situations the company faced.

1 Political change

Almost from the start Ryor was faced with a potentially make-or-break situation. The early bottles and labels were made in Slovakia, which at the time was part of a unified Czechoslovakia, but in 1992 Czechoslovakia was divided into two countries – Slovakia and the Czech Republic. This meant that the goods were suddenly subject to an import duty of 22%. Štěpánková had to be decisive. She realized she needed to be adaptable, so she moved the production of packaging back to Czech companies.

2 Finding the perfect design

One of Štěpánková's strengths is said to be her total commitment to achieving perfection. This was demonstrated during the process of creating the right 'look' for Ryor's products and packaging. A number of design companies put forward literally hundreds of potential designs, and all were rejected. Eventually a decision was reached and a contract signed. But even then, Štěpánková was not happy. Instead of going ahead, she had the courage to withdraw from the agreement and resume her search for the perfect design.

3 Room to grow

In 1996 another key decision had to be made. Štěpánková realized that the company had outgrown its production facilities in Prague. Ideally a purpose-built factory was needed, but the costs were prohibitive and interest rates at the time were unfavourable. Despite this, Štěpánková borrowed money and went ahead with the investment. She knew that the repayments would be high, but was also convinced that without the new facilities the company couldn't move forward.

4 Cash-flow crisis

Almost immediately, Ryor was faced with probably its most serious challenge. Major hypermarket chains were moving into the Czech Republic and were changing the way products were distributed, as well as driving down prices. Ryor's two major distributors folded, owing Ryor large amounts of money. Difficult decisions had to be made. 'They knew they were going to take a hit,' explains Jiri Kadlec, a Czech economist. 'They had a choice – they could either follow their distributors into liquidation or tough it out, go into debt, and try to turn it round.' Štěpánková had the conviction to keep going. She made changes to the cash-flow and distribution management, and although it took time, Ryor managed not only to survive, but to flourish in the new economic environment.

Discussion

1 What leadership skills did Eva Štěpánková display?

2 How did these skills help her overcome the problems the company faced?

3 The article doesn't mention Štěpánková's people management skills. Do you think it is possible to be so successful without having good people management skills?

Task

1 Read about Maximum Cocoa and its current situation.

> **Maximum Cocoa** is a small chocolate manufacturer based in the south of England. The chocolate is made using a simple, traditional process that avoids over-refining and captures the unique flavours of the world's best cocoa beans. The company has had moderate success, but is now in crisis. They have a serious cash-flow problem and are in danger of going bankrupt. Immediate action is needed and the following issues must be addressed:
> - costs of raw materials are escalating
> - profits are down due to stiff competition
> - rent for production facilities is expensive
> - salary demands in the south of England are high
> - staff are complaining that the production facilities are old and inadequate.

2 You need to make a difficult decision to help save the company. Work in groups of four. Students A and B, turn to File 43 on page 146 and read about issue 1. Students C and D, turn to File 05 on page 136 and read about issue 2. Each pair should follow steps 1–3.

  1 Discuss the issue and make a decision.

  2 Prepare a briefing to inform the staff of the decision you have made.

  3 Ensure that the briefing includes language to distance you and your partner from the decision.

3 Work in your groups of four and have two briefing meetings.
Meeting 1
Issue 1: The cost of cocoa beans

Students C and D are product and marketing managers who have invested a lot of time, energy, and creativity in building up the company's brand image based on the quality of the products.

  1 A and B, give the briefing and respond to any concerns.

  2 C and D, express concerns and ask for assurances.

Meeting 2
Issue 2: The cost of production facilities and salaries

Students A and B represent production staff who are unhappy about the facilities, but do not want to move and are concerned about losing their jobs.

  1 C and D, give the briefing and respond to any concerns.

  2 A and B, express concerns and ask for assurances.

The Expert View

'It's lonely at the top,' is a comment often made about being a leader. However, that statement ignores potential sources that would help a leader achieve effectiveness: the connections that can be made with subordinates, external advisors, and even competitors. These connections can give leaders access to views and ideas about the best way forward. History shows that the best leaders always sound out their decisions with trusted 'others', and even seek out adversaries who can indicate flaws in their ideas before they are put forward. Often when it appears that a leader has single-handedly taken some very tough decisions, the reality is that they were only taken after careful consultation with trusted 'others'.

Dr Donna Ladkin, Centre for Executive Learning and Leadership

Cranfield School of Management

Case study

11 | Values

Learning objectives in this unit
- Talking about values
- Reaching an agreement
- Using inversion for emphasis
- Raising a difficult point

Case study
- Developing ethically-responsible policies

Starting point

1 How would you define the term 'values'?

2 How important is it for a company to have values?

3 Would a company's values influence your decision to be an employee or a customer of that company?

Working with words | Talking about values

1 Look at these pictures of some global brands and discuss questions 1–2.

1 Which countries do they originate from?
2 Do you associate positive, negative, or neutral values with these brands? Why?

2 Read these values statements from two different companies.

1 Can you tell which of the companies in **1** they match? Why do you think so? Turn to File 45, page 146 for the answers.
2 What similarities or differences can you find between the two statements?
3 What do you think each company's statement says about the values of the culture it originates from?

Our values

We value integrity, honesty, openness, personal excellence, constructive self-criticism, continual self-improvement, and mutual respect. We are committed to our customers and partners and have a passion for technology. We take on big challenges, and pride ourselves on seeing them through. We hold ourselves accountable to our customers, shareholders, partners, and employees by honoring our commitments, providing results, and striving for the highest quality.

The five core values underpinning the way we do business are:

Integrity We must conduct our business fairly, with honesty and transparency. Everything we do must stand the test of public scrutiny.

Understanding We must be caring and show respect and compassion for our colleagues and customers around the world, and always work for the benefit of our country.

Excellence We must constantly strive to achieve the highest possible standards in our day-to-day work and in the quality of the goods and services we provide.

Unity We must work cohesively with our colleagues across the group and with our customers and partners around the world, building strong relationships based on tolerance, understanding, and mutual cooperation.

Responsibility We must continue to be responsible and sensitive to the countries, communities, and environments in which we work, always ensuring that what comes from the people goes back to the people many times over.

3 Match 1–8 to a–h, so that each sentence completes a verb phrase used in the statements in **2**.

1	We always conduct	**a**	sensitive to the needs of the communities we work with.
2	We have	**b**	our customers, colleagues, and suppliers.
3	We work	**c**	achieve the highest quality in everything we do.
4	We are committed to	**d**	cohesively with all our partners and colleagues.
5	We hold ourselves	**e**	our business with fairness and honesty.
6	We strive to	**f**	accountable to all our stakeholders.
7	We pride ourselves	**g**	a passion for innovation.
8	We continue to be	**h**	on our achievements in this field.

4 Work with a partner. Look again at the values in the statements in **2**. Discuss whether your company also has these values.

5 Work with a partner. Produce a values statement for a company from **1** or for another well-known organization. When you are happy with it, read it out and see if the rest of the group can guess the organization.

6 64▷ Listen to this discussion about a study of global attitudes to American brands and cultural values by the market research company NOP World and answer questions 1–3.
1 According to the study, why have global attitudes to America changed in recent years?
2 What does Carla say has been the effect on certain American brands?
3 What arguments does Doug make which challenge the results of the study?

7 Match these adverb + adjective combinations from the discussion to the statement that is closest in meaning.

potentially disastrous   profoundly worrying   relatively stable
appreciably more hostile   unexpectedly rapid   irretrievably damaging
significantly different   increasingly difficult

1 'It's going to get harder and harder.' _____
2 'Compared to earlier, the price hasn't changed much.' _____
3 'The variation between them is noticeable.' _____
4 'We didn't think it would change that quickly.' _____
5 'It could be a major problem and we can't ignore it.' _____
6 'I've noticed recently that they seem quite negative towards us.' _____
7 'We're really concerned about this problem.' _____
8 'We won't be able to reverse the effects of this.' _____

8 Look at your answers in **7** again. Could you replace any of the adverbs with *noticeably, comparatively, considerably,* or *surprisingly* and keep the same meaning?

>> For more practice go to **Practice file** 11 on page 122.

9 Work with a partner. Student A, turn to File 46 on page 146. Student B, turn to File 09 on page 137. Then follow steps 1–2.
1 Read the text and prepare to tell your partner about it.
2 Explain the situation to your partner – highlight the key problems, and say what it will mean for the company. Use these phrases if you wish.
   This is …   It has been …   It's going to be …   The situation is …   The customers are …

10 Work with a partner. Prepare a short statement about your company's values for a group of new employees. Include an explanation of why these values are important.

ⓘ >> Interactive Workbook >> **Glossary**

Context

Alanas Pharma Inc. is a cosmetics firm based near Barcelona, Spain. Its products have had a run of poor reviews in women's magazines, and it received some bad publicity in Germany and the Netherlands over its animal testing policies. It hopes to reverse this negative perception with its new range of skin creams – all organic and hypo-allergenic. The plan is to launch the range at an international cosmetics exhibition in Berlin in two months' time. The company has outsourced production to a factory in South Korea and is expecting the first batch of stock to be shipped to Berlin in time for the launch.

Negotiating | Reaching agreement

1 This email arrived last night from South Korea. What is the problem? What issues might this problem cause for the marketing managers, Laura and Andrew?

> Dear Laura and Andrew
>
> I am very sorry to say that we are having difficulties meeting your order. Please can we speak to discuss this? May I suggest a conference call with both of you, along with me and my logistics manager, Jin-Ho, at 8.30 a.m. tomorrow (Spanish time)?
>
> Kind regards
>
> Hyun-Ki
> Production Manager

2 65 ▷ Listen to the first part of the conference call. Work with a partner and discuss questions 1–3.
   1 What exactly is the problem at the factory?
   2 Who is more sympathetic about the problem, Laura or Andrew?
   3 What could happen to Alanas Pharma Inc. if the problem is not resolved?

3 Put phrases a–g from the first part of the conference call into these categories.
   1 Refusing to change plans: _____
   2 Accepting the need to change plans: _____
   3 Describing the current position: _____

   a … we are in a very difficult situation.
   b … let's try to find a way round this.
   c … this is beyond our control.
   d I'm afraid it is just not possible.
   e We are stuck with this situation.
   f I have to say no to …
   g … we have reached the point where we …

4 66▷ Listen to the second part of the call. Work with a partner and discuss questions 1–3.

   1 What suggestions are put forward?

   2 How do the others react to the suggestions?

   3 What solution would you have chosen?

5 66▷ Listen again and complete phrases 1–10.

   1 … that's _____ the question.

   2 … that _____ work.

   3 Would you _____ accepting delivery by the final day of the exhibition?

   4 That's not out of _____.

   5 … I refuse _____ on this.

   6 I have to _____ on this …

   7 Could you _____ with some samples of the product?

   8 We can't _____ that.

   9 What would you _____ a smaller run for us …?

   10 … I'd _____ to prioritize that.

6 Which phrases in **5** would be used by someone who

   a is trying to reach a compromise?

   b is not willing to compromise?

   c might be prepared to compromise?

   d knows that what he / she is offering is not really satisfactory?

7 67▷ Listen to the final part of the conference call. Do you think they have come to an acceptable agreement for all parties?

8 67▷ Listen again and note down the phrases they use to agree on a solution.

9 Work with a partner. Student A, turn to File 50 on page 148. Student B, turn to File 03 on page 136. Then follow steps 1–2.

   1 Have a discussion and agree on a solution, using the phrases from the *Key expressions*.

   2 Compare the solution you came to with other pairs in the class. Did the employee or the line manager benefit most from your solutions?

>> For more practice, go to **Practice file 11** on page 122.

10 Work with a partner. Think of a problem or a change you would like to make at work. Use an idea from the list or think of your own. Then follow steps 1–3.

- a pay rise
- a move to another office
- longer schedules
- more holiday days
- cooking facilities at work
- free parking

   1 Discuss with your partner how you want to present your proposal for change and think about what the effects will be on you / your colleagues / your work.

   2 Make brief notes about your proposal and then give them to another pair to analyse.

   3 Read the notes from another pair and think of some possible objections to their proposal.

11 Work together with the other pair. Take turns to discuss each other's proposal and negotiate a solution.

ⓘ >> Interactive Workbook >> **Email**

Key expressions

Stating the position
We are in a very difficult situation.
We have reached the point where we have no other option than to …
This is beyond our control.
We are stuck with this situation.

Initiating a negotiation
Could you make do with …?
What would you say to doing …?
Would you consider …?

Showing a willingness to negotiate
Let's try to find a way round this.
That's not out of the question.
I'd be willing to …

Being unwilling to negotiate
I have to say no to …
That's out of the question.
I'm afraid it is just not possible.
I refuse to budge on this.
I have to stay firm on this.
That just won't work.
We can't possibly …

Agreeing on a solution
Are we all agreed?
I'll go along with …
That sounds feasible.

ⓘ >> Interactive Workbook
>> **Phrasebank**

Culture question

Think about your negotiation style.

- How competitive are you during negotiations? Do you like to start with potentially unrealistic offers / expectations?

- Do you expect confrontation or do you try to avoid it?

- Do you prefer to base your arguments on logic or on emotions? Why?

- Do you think that negotiation style is connected to culture, to personality, or to both? Why? Can you think of some examples?

Language at work | Using inversion for emphasis

1 Compare the sentences labelled **A** with the alternatives from the negotiation labelled **B**, and answer questions 1–4.

1 What are the differences in form between the two alternatives?
2 Which sentence(s) begin(s) with a phrase followed by a verb + subject inversion?
3 Which sentence(s) is / are a conditional?
4 Why might you choose to use the **B** sentences rather than the **A** sentences?

A One of our contracts has just trebled their order and another new contract has just come in.	**B** Not only has one of our contracts just trebled their order, but another new contract has just come in.
A We have never suggested that we can be flexible on these dates.	**B** At no time have we suggested that we can be flexible on these dates.
A If I had been given more notice on these other jobs, this wouldn't have happened.	**B** Had I been given more notice on these other jobs, this wouldn't have happened.

>> For more information, go to **Language reference Unit 11** on page 132.

2 Read this notice and <u>underline</u> any sentences that include a verb inversion. Can you write these sentences in another way?

Memo

Notice to all staff – staff overtime

Following complaints about inconsistencies across departments in overtime procedure, it has been agreed that staff who work extra hours on their current projects are entitled to ask for time off in lieu. Not only are staff required to formally request this time off through their central administrators, they will also be expected to confirm the request with their line managers.

Under no circumstances will staff be paid overtime for working extra hours on their own projects. Were a member of staff to take on work outside their project team, this would be paid at a freelance rate agreed on between the member of staff and the manager of the outside team.

---

3 Rewrite these sentences using an inversion to add emphasis or formality.

1 We will never be willing to compromise our customer-care policy.
At no time _____.

2 If you joined the union, you would get free advice on this matter.
Were _____.

3 There is no situation in which we will negotiate a new deal.
Under _____.

4 We wouldn't have allowed this to happen if we had known about the consequences.
Had _____

5 You asked us to cut our costs *and* reduce our lead time.
Not only _____.

>> For more exercises, go to **Practice file 11** on page 123.

4 Some health and safety rules in your company have been ignored recently, resulting in injuries to staff. You need to make an announcement to remind staff of the rules and procedures. Work with a partner and create a formal statement using the phrases in **3**. Include some of the following issues.

- fire drills
- driving and cycling on site
- hot food and drink
- carrying heavy loads

Make your announcement to the rest of the class.

Practically speaking | Raising a difficult point

1 68▷ **Listen to five extracts from conversations at work and answer questions 1–2.**
1   In each case, what is the difficult point that is raised?
2   How does the person raising the point sound? How does the other person respond?

Key word | *mean*

Match phrases 1–5 with *mean* in *italics* to synonyms a–e.
1   *I don't mean* to sound rude.
2   *I mean, …* it's just that …
3   *You mean* I'm not smart enough?
4   It just seems *a bit mean* …
5   You haven't told us what these figures actually *mean*.

a   in other words
b   signify
c   I'm saying
d   a little ungenerous
e   it's not my intention

2 68▷ **Listen again and complete sentences 1–5.**
1   Look, _____, but could you try to be a bit quieter when …
2   OK, well … Look, _____. Please _____ _____, but … do you think it would be possible …
3   Look, _____ … I know you spent a lot of time on it … You see _____, it really needs a bit more work.
4   I'm not _____, but, well, I'm really delighted …
5   With _____, Thomas, _____ I don't think it's quite as simple as that … _____, there is still an enormous number of unanswered questions.

3 Rewrite statements 1–5 using phrases from **2** to make them less direct.
1   'Your design for the new brochure is rubbish. We're going to ask someone else to do a new version.'
2   'Your laugh is really loud and annoying. It disturbs everyone else in the office.'
3   'The price you've quoted for this job is ridiculously high. There's no way we can afford to pay this amount.'
4   'Your performance over the last year has been really poor. We're not going to increase your pay until you start improving.'
5   'Stop leaving your unwashed mugs around the office. They always go mouldy and they're disgusting!'

>> For extension and revision, go to **Useful phrases** on page 135.

4 **Work with a partner. Have a conversation about one of these situations. Take turns to raise the difficult point using an appropriate phrase.**
1   You share a small office. One of you constantly has meetings with other colleagues in the office. It's very difficult to work while this is happening.
2   You are in a meeting. One of your colleagues presents some facts and / or figures which you know are completely wrong.
3   One of your colleagues is taking a lot of time off work, officially because of stress, and this is increasing the workload and stress for the other team members.
4   Your colleague has produced some publicity material which doesn't match the brief they were given – you know they've worked hard on this, but it isn't right.

ⓘ » Interactive Workbook » **Exercises and Tests**

The CarbonNeutral Company

The CarbonNeutral Company (TCNC) was established over ten years ago and is the leading carbon offset and climate consulting business, with major clients including Barclays, BSkyB, Honda, and UBS. CarbonNeutral® is the company's registered mark, and is awarded when CO_2 emissions have been reduced to net zero. Since it broke new ground with the sale of carbon offsets in the mid-1990s, it has provided clients with a broad range of carbon offset and climate consulting services, helping them to measure, reduce, and offset their CO_2 emissions. With headquarters in London, and an international network of offices, it has over 300 business clients and 60,000 individual clients worldwide.

Glossary

carbon emissions = polluting carbon substances (e.g. CO_2) released into the atmosphere, mainly by burning fossil fuels
carbon offsetting = the practice of paying money towards projects that help the environment to try to cancel out the harmful effect of CO_2 emissions produced by a person's / company's activities
carbon footprint = a measure of the amount of CO_2 emitted by a person / company
carbon-neutral = when CO_2 emissions are counter-balanced by CO_2 reduction elsewhere, e.g. through planting trees

Developing ethically-responsible policies
Background

The **CarbonNeutral** Company

How can we help you achieve 'net zero CO_2'?
Through a mix of 'internal' and 'external' reductions. Internal reductions cover the CO_2 which is cut by changing processes, systems, and behaviour. External reductions (or 'carbon offsetting') are reductions that we make happen for you. For every one tonne of CO_2 produced, we arrange for an equivalent one tonne of CO_2 to be saved through a project somewhere else in the world. These projects include:
- Renewable energy: including solar, hydro, and wind as well as biomass and re-use of products like biogas.
- Resource conservation: including energy efficiency, methane recovery, and low-carbon fuel switches.
- Forestry: well-managed, long-term forestry which makes a real contribution to local communities and biodiversity.

Quality standards
We have developed a market-leading quality assurance programme. Our quality measures include:
- The CarbonNeutral® Protocol: This is the standard behind the CarbonNeutral brand mark. It incorporates international best practice and is a public and independently reviewed standard.
- Audit trail: Uniquely, we are the only company trading in carbon credits that commissions an independent third party to verify its carbon business. PWC reviews our operating system and verifies all aspects of our carbon management chain. This ensures, for example, against double counting.
- Guarantee of success: The CarbonNeutral Company guarantees every tonne of a carbon offset project.

Contact us today and join the carbon revolution!

Sky aims to become carbon-neutral

Perhaps Sky is not the first name that springs to mind when you think of fighting climate change. But over the last few years Sky has been committed to reducing its carbon footprint and becoming carbon-neutral.

The main method used to reduce its carbon footprint has been Sky's offsetting policy. Sky has worked with The CarbonNeutral Company to invest in quality offsetting programmes, including wind power projects in India and New Zealand.

Sky has also worked with TCNC to reduce carbon emissions. It has ensured that all its UK sites are supplied by renewable energy sources, it has renewed its company vehicle fleet to reduce CO_2 emissions, and introduced a 'switch it off' campaign to encourage employees to turn off electrical devices that are not being used.

The results speak for themselves. Sky offset 45,000 tonnes of CO_2 in 2006–2007 and is well on its way to meet the target of 225,000 tonnes by 2011.

Campaigners question offsetting policy

Green campaigners today labelled carbon emission offsetting policies 'an indulgence' and called on companies to start taking their responsibility to the environment seriously. Henry Shanklin, an environmental campaigner from Australia, said, 'Offsets give the polluter a passport to pollute. By buying offset credits the companies feel like they don't have to reduce their own emissions. They offer peace of mind, but not solutions. We would rather see people and companies change their behaviour and reduce their own emissions, rather than rely on others to offset them for them.'

Discussion

1 What do think is the best approach for companies aiming to reduce their emissions – carbon offsets or carbon emission reductions? Why?

2 To what extent do companies try to make commercial gains out of their environmental strategies?

3 Who do you think should take responsibility for tackling climate change – individuals, companies, or governments? Why?

Task

1 Read about Corutel and look at the sources of their carbon emissions.

Corutel's carbon emissions

Corutel is one of Europe's leading mobile phone companies, with 32 million customers in 23 countries. Given its position, Corutel is keen to set a good example of corporate responsibility and offset its carbon emissions. As a first step, Corutel measured its carbon footprint.

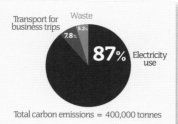

Transport for business trips 7.8%
Waste 5.2%
87% Electricity use

Total carbon emissions = 400,000 tonnes

2 The management team at Corutel have arranged a meeting with representatives from Carbon-lo, a green concultancy firm, to negotiate ways to help the company achieve its objectives. Work in groups of four.

Students A and B, you represent Corutel. Read your notes below and prepare to present the company's main principles in relation to its environmental strategy at the meeting.

Students C and D, you represent Carbon-lo. Turn to File 52 on page 148, read your notes, and prepare to present ideas that you think will help Corutel achieve its objectives.

What we want

- To be able to advertise our green credentials to our customers and investors.
- To use offsetting rather than emission reduction because one easy payment can be made per year and it will make it easier to budget for the environmental strategy.
- To have a company forest (as seen on Carbon-lo's website), but other offsetting projects will also be considered.

What we don't want

- An emission-reduction strategy wouldn't be effective. Saving energy shouldn't be a priority for staff as they are extremely busy and it shouldn't be their responsibility.
- A reduction in the amount of business trips is not possible. Allowing people from different countries to meet face-to-face is an important part of the company's development.
- Customers should not be included in this project because it is expected that they would want the company to accept responsibility for this and not pass it on to them.

3 Hold the meeting. Aim to negotiate a five-point action plan that will help the company achieve its objectives.

Turn to File 52 on page 148

The Expert View

There is now a heightened global awareness of the dangers of climate change. This has led to major banks and investment companies probing the carbon-reduction strategies of the businesses in which they invest. Additionally an increasing number of major companies are not only adopting carbon-reduction strategies themselves, but are also putting similar requirements on their supply chains. More individuals expect businesses they work for or trade with to implement carbon-reduction plans. Business as usual or cosmetic change will not suffice. Conversely, businesses embracing higher environmental standards may be able to save money, motivate talented staff who want to work for responsible companies, and create new business opportunities.

Prof. David Grayson, CBE, Professor of Corporate Responsibility, Director of the Doughty Centre for Corporate Responsibility
Cranfield School of Management

Case study

12 | Persuasion

Learning objectives in this unit
- Talking about how we are persuaded and influenced
- Selling an idea
- Using discourse markers
- Giving and responding to compliments

Case study
- Initiating an expansion programme

Starting point

1 Which of your decisions (both personal and work-related) are influenced by the following, and to what extent?
   - family members / friends / colleagues
   - media / advertising
   - politicians
   - celebrities
   - your boss
   - sales representatives
   - statistics

2 Are you easily persuaded? Give examples to explain why / why not.

Working with words | Talking about how we are persuaded and influenced

1 How does advertising manipulate what we think and the choices we make? Read the text and compare your answers.

Just how easily are you persuaded?

How many forms of advertising do you encounter on your journey to work every day? Can you remember any of the advertisements? Probably not, but somehow the images you see will make an impression, whether you are aware of it or not. Are we taken in by these messages? Of course we are, because it's the advertisers' job to generate demand for the product. But how do they do it? On a very simplistic level, advertising can be divided into three broad areas which identify how we are influenced.

1 **Need** Can you imagine a life without mobile phones? It wasn't actually that long ago (1992) when the Global System for Mobile communications (GSM) started, and less than 1% of people globally used a mobile phone. Clever marketing promoted the consumption of mobile phones by highlighting their usefulness and the 'necessity' of being reachable. Advertisers targeted our busy lifestyles and sold us a tool which made communication possible wherever we were. We didn't actually *need* mobile phones, but the need was created and the advertising was then tailored towards it. The mobile phone industry had taken off.

2 **Belonging** The images we are shown by advertisers tap into our fears of becoming an outsider. Two of the most basic human needs are love and a sense of belonging, so to show images of families and groups of people having fun together subconsciously plays on our emotions. This powerfully persuasive tool works especially well on young people. Take the soft drinks industry for example; the advertising tends to reinforce an association between young people and the product, appealing to young people's desire to be 'cool' and be part of the 'in' group. The product itself then becomes an icon for being 'in' and young people are keen to buy into this image.

3 **Esteem** As we get older, our urge to conform becomes less important and we are subconsciously attracted to things which gain us more respect or elevate our social status. Advertisers put across this message by using images which say 'if you buy this you'll be more successful, healthier, younger, a leader …', etc. Therefore, the person who has been holding out for recognition of his or her earning power may buy an expensive car. Often celebrities are selected to endorse a product because the target group aspires to live up to this person's image. Take the L'Oréal advertisements for expensive hair and beauty products; the celebrities may not all be young, but they look young and declare (in most languages), that it's 'because I'm worth it!'

2 Work with a partner. Think of your own examples of advertisements which target the areas of *need*, *belonging*, or *esteem* and discuss how they achieve this.

3 Make phrases with a verb from **A** and a preposition / noun phrase from **B**, then match them to definitions 1–13.

A	B	Definition
to reinforce	a demand for	1 to encourage people to buy something
to tailor	into	2 to promote a connection between two things
to promote	(sth) towards a need	3 to create the need for something
to generate	an association between	4 to adapt something to suit a requirement
to hold	across (message / idea)	5 to attract or interest someone or something
to appeal	into	6 to wait until you get what you want
to live	on (emotions)	7 to notice something and react to it
to play	up to	8 to use / exploit something for your own benefit
to be taken	up on	9 to be as good as someone expected
to buy	to	10 to believe in something
to pick	in by	11 to be persuaded to believe something that might not be true
to put	out for	12 to take advantage of someone's feelings
to tap	consumption of	13 to convey some information

4 Work with a partner. Turn to File 53 on page 148 and look at the advertisements. Discuss what each advertisement is trying to achieve using phrases from **3**.

5 69▷ Listen to an interview with Jacob McFarlane, a marketing specialist.
1 What does he say about how advertisers approach selling a product in the US?
2 How are Denmark, Russia, and China different?

6 Complete comments 1–8 using the following words / phrases from the listening.

materialistic   exploitative   consumer profile   USP
motivational   aspirational   status-anxiety   market penetration

1 'The way Sam is expected to take leave when he goes to trade conferences is awful. His company just takes advantage of him – it's so _____.'
2 'We need to think again – there's nothing at the moment to distinguish our product from the rest on the market. Can't you come up with an exciting _____?'
3 'Klara has a very _____ lifestyle. She's never satisfied with what she's got – she always wants to feel that she's moving onwards and upwards in her career and her life.'
4 'Jean-Noel is totally obsessed with money and possessions – he always wants to earn more so he can buy the latest designer products. He's incredibly _____.'
5 'We went to an external sales-training course last week. Absolutely fantastic! The trainer's approach was really _____ and I can't wait to try out his ideas.'
6 'How can we advertise this product when it's got such a high price tag? It won't be normal people we're targeting – only those who hate to feel they can't keep up with the neighbours and who have a high level of _____ _____.'
7 'I've just heard the competition is developing a similar product to our X1-11. That means we have to ensure _____ _____ is aggressive or we'll miss out.'
8 'The marketing of the new chocolate bar wasn't very successful. Surveys show the under-20s are buying it, but most potential customers aren't being reached. We'll have to analyse our _____ _____ again.'

›› For more exercises go to **Practice file 12** on page 124.

7 Discuss your company / a company you know well. How does it market itself? Is it effective? Would the marketing be effective in other cultures?

ⓘ ›› Interactive Workbook ›› **Glossary**

Business communication skills

Context

Ranjit Shetty, an entrepreneur based in Edinburgh, has a flourishing advertising company (AA Ads) which has focused on print media up to now. He has the opportunity to break into multimedia advertising after recruiting a colleague with expertise in this field. He has also secured financial backing, but Ranjit now has to sell his diversification concept to his key staff.

Presenting | Selling an idea

1 Work with a partner and discuss questions 1–2.
1 What are some of the reasons for a company to diversify?
2 How important is it to gain staff acceptance of new ideas and plans?

2 70–73 ▷ Listen to four extracts from Ranjit's presentation and answer questions 1–4.
1 What does Ranjit think will happen if the company doesn't diversify now?
2 What are the advantages of moving into multimedia advertising?
3 What steps will be taken to help the company achieve this?
4 Why does Ranjit think the company is in a strong position?

3 70–73 ▷ Listen to the four extracts again and answer questions 1–2.
1 Which of the following attitudes does Ranjit convey during the presentation?
- assertive
- pushy
- tentative
- upbeat
- enthusiastic
- insincere
2 Which of the following techniques does he use to convince the audience and keep their attention?
- invites audience members to speak
- addresses the audience directly
- asks the audience to do an activity
- uses visuals
- keeps a fast pace
- uses positive language / vocabulary
- plays music
- uses rhetorical questions
- uses word stress and intonation
- shocks the audience
- speaks slowly
- uses tripling (lists of three points)
- shouts at times
- speaks with enthusiasm

4 Match categories 1–5 in **A** to explanations a–e in **B**.

A	B
1 reinforcing the message	a saying why change is necessary
2 acknowledging different points of view	b making your beliefs absolutely clear
3 establishing the need for a change	c adding more information
4 asking for commitment	d dealing with counter-arguments
5 building the argument	e getting people on board

5 Match phrases a–j with categories 1–5 in **4**.

a Not only that. It's also essential that we … ____

b … having said that, it's important to remember … ____

c We're committed, we're motivated, and we believe in what we do. ____

d I know that, like me, you're concerned about where we're going. ____

e We could be missing out on a great opportunity if we don't … ____

f OK, that's the first benefit. Now, the second point … ____

g You could argue that …, but on balance … ____

h … *is* achievable. No question. ____

i Please give serious consideration to … ____

j I'm calling on you to … ____

6 Work with a partner. Look at the slides for this presentation and discuss which phrases from the *Key expressions* the speaker could use for each point. Then practise giving the presentation to each other.

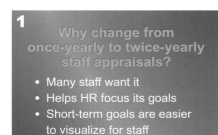

1
Why change from once-yearly to twice-yearly staff appraisals?
- Many staff want it
- Helps HR focus its goals
- Short-term goals are easier to visualize for staff

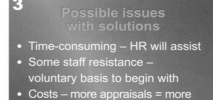

3
Possible issues with solutions
- Time-consuming – HR will assist
- Some staff resistance – voluntary basis to begin with
- Costs – more appraisals = more training? (not clear if this is true yet)

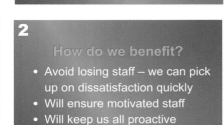

2
How do we benefit?
- Avoid losing staff – we can pick up on dissatisfaction quickly
- Will ensure motivated staff
- Will keep us all proactive

4
What next?
- Great staff – make them even better!
- HR will support us
- Help retain our best staff – give them what they want!

>> For more exercises go to **Practice file 12** on page 124.

7 Work with a partner. Think of an idea for your own department or company – it can either be completely new or one that has already been implemented. Prepare a mini-presentation to persuade your colleagues to adopt this. Find out if you have convinced them.

i >> Interactive Workbook >> **Email**

Key expressions

Establishing the need for a change
I know that, like me, you are concerned about …
What comes across from talking to you is …
It's become apparent that …
We could be missing out on a great opportunity if we don't …

Building the argument
We not only benefit from …, we also gain …
Not only that. It's also essential that we …
OK, that's the first benefit. Now, the second point …
In addition to that …

Acknowledging different points of view
Having said that, it's important to remember …
I accept that … but we have to recognize that … / put this into perspective …
You could argue that …, but on balance …

Reinforcing the message
So, as I said before, …
… is achievable. No question.
We're in an extremely strong position. Why? Because …
We're committed, we're motivated, and we believe in what we do.

Asking for commitment / concluding
I very much hope that …
Please give serious consideration to …
We can't afford to miss this opportunity …
I'm calling on you to …

i >> Interactive Workbook
       >> **Phrasebank**

Language at work | Discourse markers

1 74▷ **Listen to these extracts from the presentation and complete sentences 1–12.**

1 I've been doing some research into our position in the market and what opportunities are available to us, and _____, I'm excited.

2 I'm excited because what comes across from talking to you is your collective enthusiasm in what we do and your genuine wish for us to succeed. _____, without your support my plans won't be possible.

3 _____, things are going well now, but …

4 We could be missing out on a great opportunity if we don't diversify – _____, this won't be cheap and it won't be easy.

5 _____, I can't expect you to buy into this plan without some facts.

6 _____, studies show that most companies only invest a small percentage of their advertising budget in print media.

7 _____, most of our customers want agencies that offer a variety of advertising media – they want options.

8 _____, this information should ring alarm bells for us.

9 … we're third in our region for print media. _____, I'm not happy with that.

10 Ravi, our key account manager, actually comes from the field of online advertising so he's going to be our guru, _____.

11 Now, _____ before, we've secured external investment for our diversification plan and we've employed a consultant.

12 I accept that you may not like an outsider telling you what is the right thing to do, but we have to recognize that this person is an expert, and they may well see things, opportunities, that we might not. _____, he's on our side.

2 **Match the discourse markers in 1 to these categories. Note that some discourse markers could fit into more than one category.**

a Indicates how open the speaker is going to be: _____

b Connects information from before with something that will follow: _____

c Emphasizes how clear / fundamental the following point is: _____

d Indicates that words are used which don't have their normal meaning: _____

e Indicates change of topic: _____

▶▶ For more information, go to **Language reference Unit 12** on page 133.

3 **Work with a partner. Look again at the discourse markers in 1 and discuss questions 1–4.**

1 Do you usually notice discourse markers when listening to spoken English or when reading written English? Why?

2 Why do we use them?

3 Which do you currently use in your spoken English?

4 Which would you like to start using more often?

▶▶ For more exercises, go to **Practice file 12** on page 125.

4 **Think of some recent news. It could be one of the following.**

- company news
- national news
- international news
- competitor activity
- celebrity news
- personal news

Work with a partner. Take turns to talk about the news using discourse markers from 1.

Practically speaking | Giving and responding to compliments

1 **75**▷ **Listen to six conversation extracts and answer questions 1–3.**
  1 Which extracts include a compliment on someone's appearance? ____
  2 Which extracts include a compliment on someone's work / achievement? ____
  3 In which extracts does one or both speakers seem uncomfortable? ____

2 **75**▷ **Listen again and decide why the speakers might feel uncomfortable in some of the extracts.**

3 **Look at phrases 1–15 from the extracts in 1. Decide which are used to compliment someone (C) and which are responses to a compliment (R).**

  1 That was great.
  2 A very worthwhile meeting.
  3 Thanks.
  4 Thank you. I felt it went well.
  5 You're looking well.
  6 I like your …
  7 I thoroughly enjoyed your talk.
  8 It was very interesting.
  9 I don't know how you can say that, but thanks anyway.
  10 I'm glad you enjoyed it.
  11 Great design.
  12 I love …
  13 I was hoping it would be well received.
  14 Well done, you all did a great job.
  15 You have very nice …

  ▶▶ For extension and revision, go to **Useful phrases** on page 135.

4 **Work with a partner. Use phrases from 3 and have conversations 1–4. Avoid making your partner feel uncomfortable and respond to any compliments appropriately.**
  1 A You've just given a presentation.
     B Compliment your partner on his / her presentation.
  2 A Compliment your partner on his / her cake.
     B You've brought in a homemade cake for a colleague's birthday.
  3 A You've presented a new package design to your company.
     B Compliment your partner on his / her design.
  4 A Compliment your partner on his / her hair.
     B You have a new haircut.

  ⓘ ▶▶ Interactive Workbook ▶▶ **Exercises and Tests**

Key word | *kill*

Match the phrases in *italics* with *kill* to definitions a–f.

  1 I'm going to have to sit down, my feet *are killing me*.
  2 I heard he *made a killing* from selling doughnuts at the World Cup!
  3 … but don't tell Sandra – she'd *kill me* if she knew what I'd done!
  4 When I heard José wanted to become a singer I *killed myself laughing* – I mean, he's tone deaf!
  5 *It won't kill you* to admit we targeted the wrong market with that advert.
  6 John asked Abi about her new job, but she didn't get asked to second interview – it was a real *conversation killer*!

  a to make a lot of money from something
  b to laugh a lot about something
  c to be a lot of effort to do something
  d to be very angry about something
  e to hurt
  f to stop something abruptly

Culture question

  • How would you feel if someone complimented you on a) your general appearance, b) a specific part of your appearance – eyes, hair, etc., c) your belongings?
  • Do you know of any cultures where these types of compliments are not appropriate?
  • Does it depend how the compliment is made and who is making the compliment?

Company profile
FJR Immo

FJR Immo is a small international property company which has recently gone public. Its core business is buying and managing properties for the commercial sector. Its headquarters are in Belgium. It has already expanded into several international markets and has used local partners in these countries to ensure its success. FJR Immo now wants to initiate a gradual expansion programme into some of its new markets: China, Russia, and Brazil. The decision has been made to focus on Brazil first. It has already helped a few clients to find property there, and now FJR Immo considers it an important strategic step towards becoming more established in Brazil to open an office there.

Background

Property company seeks international expansion

Belgium-based FJR Immo is on the up. Having successfully conquered the German, Italian, UK, and Bulgarian markets, discussions are now in the pipeline for branching out into Brazil. FJR Immo is a relatively young company, but due to its clever strategy it has managed to become a key player in a highly competitive market.

Strategy
FJR Immo's strength lies in specializing in certain industry sectors, giving them the edge over the competition. At the moment their main client base lies with IT companies. By specializing in this way they now know exactly what IT companies' requirements are when looking for office space, and can give their local agents a very specific brief. FJR Immo also has a good track record in finding reliable and committed local agents who they work in partnership with – a rare commodity! By supporting them, providing them with international information about the property industry through newsletters, and offering yearly conferences, the agents feel well looked after and their results speak for themselves.

Communication
Expansion doesn't come cheap, but FJR Immo doesn't seem concerned by this. Henri Laurent, head of planning, is convinced the stakeholders will buy into the opportunities Brazil has to offer. 'Our stakeholders are involved in our business planning and kept informed of every strategic move we wish to make. Maintaining an open dialogue with them ensures we are all clear about the direction we're going in and why. If the stakeholders understand what we want to achieve, it's easier to move forward and make changes.'

Watch this space to see how FJR Immo's stakeholders affect the decision to enter the Brazilian market.

Discussion

1 How has FJR Immo tried to gain an advantage over its competitors?

2 Why might the stakeholders reject the expansion plan?

3 Would you consider expansion into a country such as Brazil a good idea? Give your reasons.

4 76▷ Listen to this phone call between two members of the strategic planning team and compare your answers to 2 and 3. What's the plan of action?

Task

1 **Work in groups of three.**

Student A, turn to File 55 on page 149 and read Michelle's email attachment.

Student B, turn to File 25 on page 141 and read Yves' fact file about Brazil.

Student C, turn to File 48 on page 147 and read Yves' research on doing business in Brazil.

Discuss FJR Immo's internal strengths and weaknesses and external opportunities and threats using information from your Files. Make notes during the discussion and work together to create a SWOT analysis of the company.

Strengths	Opportunities
Weaknesses	**Threats**

2 **You are on FJR Immo's committee for the expansion plan. You have to convince the stakeholders that this is a good idea. Prepare a presentation to 'sell' the idea to the stakeholders. Follow points 1–4 to help you.**

1 Decide what the implications for the company could be.

2 What USPs and skills does your company have to make the expansion a success?

3 Look at your KPIs: could they remain the same?

4 Look at your SWOT analysis. Are there any points that may be of concern to your stakeholders? How will you address these?

3 **Give your presentation to the rest of the class. When listening to presentations from other groups, you become the stakeholders and should decide how convincing each presentation is – would you agree to their expansion plans?**

The Expert View

When expanding your business into a new geographic market, it is vital to gain a solid understanding of the local customer market, the competitors, and relevant target market attributes including suppliers, government requirements, and legislation. Moreover, you need to correctly define the company's current financial, human, and technical resources. This will determine the best mode of market entry: exporting, licensing, joint venture, franchising, or direct investment. It should be noted that in an international business every single aspect of the business from contracts to packaging and payments has to have a local flavour. Subtle nuances can make a big difference! Serious planning and preparation can hence make entering foreign markets easier, faster, and much more successful.

Dr Stephanie Hussels, Lecturer in Entrepreneurship, Bettany Centre for Entrepreneurial Performance and Economics

Cranfield School of Management

Case study

Working with words

1 Complete these sentences with the verbs from the list. Change the form of the verb if necessary.

> build (x2)   process   form   manage   take
> read   keep (x2)   give   weigh up   work

1 Jens found it very difficult to _____ the situation at MMK – he couldn't understand what was going on at all.

2 If you want to _____ good relationships with clients from other cultures, you need to inform yourself about their customs and ways of doing things.

3 Before relocation, we _____ the pros and cons of staying in our own country or moving to a new location with lower costs.

4 I can't give you a final decision until I've _____ all the information you sent me.

5 I'll _____ my eyes open when I go to that meeting in Tokyo so I can learn more about office etiquette there.

6 Here in the south, we like to _____ our time to get to know people before we do business with them.

7 Some people _____ an opinion of a company based on first impressions, so the attitude and behaviour of reception staff is very important.

8 My six-month placement with ACI _____ me an insight into how business is conducted in India.

9 Erik will be managing a multicultural team so he'll need to _____ his intercultural skills.

10 Sanjit's move to the European office will _____ both ways – he'll learn about our culture and we'll get extra help with the project.

11 For me, the hardest part of doing business in a different culture is _____ unknowns – I don't like dealing with unfamiliar situations.

12 Petra _____ an open mind while she was investigating the cause of the communication breakdown – she wanted to talk to everyone before she reported to the CEO.

2 Replace the words / phrases in *italics* with the adjectives from the list. Make any changes that are necessary.

> out-of-the-way   outspoken   run-of-the-mill
> down to earth   unexpected   low-key
> up-and-coming   time-consuming   easy-going
> open-minded   tedious   self-assured

1 Sam is very *practical and sensible* _____, which helps us keep things in perspective when there are problems in the office.

2 DDM's new office building is attractive, but it's *quite difficult to get to* _____ and doesn't have good transport links.

3 I was *open and honest* _____ in my criticism of the plan and this offended my hosts.

4 I don't like to attract a lot of attention so my retirement party was *simple and not extravagant* _____.

5 The position they offered was not particularly interesting – in fact it was rather *ordinary* _____.

6 One of the most *surprising* _____ things was the number of times meetings were rescheduled at the last minute.

7 My manager has *a relaxed* _____ attitude towards timekeeping so I don't have to worry if I'm late for work.

8 This project is *taking a lot of time* _____, so hopefully the results will pay off.

9 We prefer to do business with companies that are *willing to listen to different ideas* _____ and not afraid to take risks.

10 Sometimes the fact that he is so *confident in himself* _____ does come across as arrogance.

11 They've just opened a new branch in an area of town that is *growing in popularity* _____.

12 Data entry is one of the more *boring and repetitive* _____ aspects of the job.

Business communication skills

1 Sonia and Luis are discussing Luis's visit to a potential site for the company. Choose the best answer from the words in *italics*.

Sonia How did you feel about the beach site?

Luis I've got to say that I'm not 100% [1]*agreed / convinced / decided.* I mean, it's beautiful. But it's more of a holiday resort than a business centre. There's too much of a holiday feeling – and it's not even especially close to the airport. All in all, it's going to be a bit more complicated than we [2]*anticipated / considered / proposed.*

Sonia I see. What about the potential pitfalls? What's your impression of the local workforce, for instance?

Luis Well, I [3]*shouldn't / wouldn't / didn't* go so far as to say that they don't speak English at all, but I did run into a couple of problems. [4]*I'm saying not / I'm not to say / I'm not saying* it's a bad thing that their French is better than their English, it's just that English will be a major factor as well, so I'm a bit [5]*aware / careful / wary* of that. I'll do more research if you want, but I can't promise [6]*nothing / something / anything.* I'm a bit reluctant to recommend the site at this stage.

Sonia What about the city-centre site?

Luis I [7]*ought to / 've got to / shall* say that I've never seen anywhere quite like it. I'm totally convinced by its potential, as it's really got everything you could ask for. I'm sure you'll agree that the local facilities are first class. There's also an old factory which I'm fully [8]*confident / assured / insured* we can acquire and refit.

Sonia I'm not sure whether the budget will stretch …

Luis That's not [9]*an explanation / a reason / a rationale* to delay. As you'll see from my projected figures, the price of the disused factory is a bargain! We [10]*can't / mustn't / don't* go wrong!

Sonia Then that shouldn't be a problem.

2 Correct the mistake in each sentence.

1 I'm not just 100% convinced – I mean, theoretically it's a good idea, but …

2 I'm fully sure that you'll agree to the proposal.

3 To be just, the whole matter could have been worse.

4 I collected from your report that he would not be coming.

5 I wouldn't go so much as to say that I think it is fantastic, but it certainly has potential.

6 From how I could see, there are already several established retail outlets.

3 Report these statements as indicated in brackets.

1 The meeting went much better than expected. (reporting a personal observation)

2 The trip did not go as planned and I had a lot of problems. (avoiding being negative)

3 The proposed site would be perfect for the company. (being persuasive)

4 The project is going fairly well. (reporting from another source)

Language at work

1 Choose the correct answer from the words in *italics* to complete these extracts from a company's strategy statement.

1 We *are growing / grow* our business by adapting what *makes / has made* our business a success in the UK in recent years to our other international markets.

2 We *have expanded / will have expanded* our Dutch operations with a move into retail banking. Initial figures *have been / were* very promising.

3 The fall in our share price *reflects / is reflecting* problems in the markets, and in the last year we *have continued / continue* to outperform the stock market overall.

4 Ian Opie *takes / will have taken* over as CEO on 1 March 2011, when Rita Flagstad *is stepping / has stepped* down after eight years in the job.

2 Read Xavier's notes for his conference presentation. Correct his use of tenses where necessary.

1 We are completing the second phase by the end of April next year.

2 We have originally hoped to commission Meyer for the redesign, but their books are full until 2012.

3 As the project nears completion, I'd like to thank all those who had been working on it and are here today.

4 I take questions at the end of this presentation, if you don't mind waiting till then.

5 I wanted to show a short video now, but there's seeming to be some kind of technical fault, so bear with me.

6 We will have sent these figures to you by email after the presentation, so don't worry about them now.

7 I'll now be handing over to Carla. She worked on this area of the project for the last six months.

8 Our sales have levelled off for some years, but now they're growing rapidly again.

9 That's a very good question. Actually, I thought about this in the taxi from the airport.

Working with words

1 Match 1–12 to a–l.

1 Although it may be difficult, it's important to stand ____

2 Always be aware of the most recent developments in your field so that you stay ____

3 Show your flexibility – don't cling ____

4 Be creative – show that you regularly come ____

5 If you're hoping for promotion, keep ____

6 My boss is great. She will always stick ____

7 I belong to a really supportive team. We all look ____

8 Make sure you prepare your arguments carefully so that they'll stand ____

9 Share success at work with your team. Don't hold ____

10 Employers value people who can use their initiative and get ____

11 Show that you are different – stand ____

12 You need to demonstrate your potential if you want to move ____

a up to close scrutiny from the management board.

b up with new ideas, and encourage innovation in others.

c out from the crowd and get noticed.

d up for what you believe is right and give your point of view.

e in with your superiors – their opinion of you is what counts.

f up for you, even if she doesn't agree with a decision you made.

g on to an idea stubbornly – if it doesn't stand up to scrutiny, just let it go.

h on to the next rung of the career ladder.

i ahead of the game by knowing more than your competitors.

j on to it just for yourself.

k on with their work without supervision.

l out for each other, even when we're under a lot of pressure.

2 Match the multiword verbs in **1** to these phrases with a similar meaning.

1 have an advantage ____

2 keep ____

3 continue with ____

4 take care of ____

5 defend ____

6 distinguish yourself from ____

7 be unwilling to let go of ____

8 progress to ____

9 be on good terms with ____

10 think of ____

11 support ____

12 remain valid ____

3 Choose the correct answer from the words in *italics*.

1 Sometimes it's important to *put / take / walk* a step backwards before you can move forward.

2 I don't want more responsibility so would prefer to *move / go / change* horizontally within the company.

3 It can often be far more interesting to *go along / lead / follow* less conventional paths than climb the promotional ladder.

4 *Broadening / Developing / Opening* your horizons and trying something new is always healthy.

5 Sometimes it takes time to *develop / work / grow* into your role and do your job well.

6 I want to do something that *aims / goes / takes* beyond the scope of my current position.

7 Doing a further training course should *place / put / post* you in a better position for promotion.

8 Inevitably, you will *come across / reach / find* a stage in life when you will welcome change and new challenges.

Business communication skills

1 Complete these phrases with the verbs from the list.

come in   like   get on to   come back   understand
get   suppose   think   mention   keen on   talk

1 So, let's ____ started. First, can we discuss …?

2 Perhaps you'd like to ____ us through some of the issues, John.

3 You probably won't ____ this idea, but I think we should do some more research before …

4 Would this be the right moment to ____ the contract details?

5 I'm sure you'll ____ the need to find the best possible candidate.

6 Can I suggest we ____ to this point about overtime later in the meeting?

7 I ____ so. But do you really ____ that will attract a better candidate?

8 I know you're not ____ Ana's suggestion, Matt, but we do need to consider it.

9　If I could just _____ here for a moment, Jan? How should we ensure …?

10　I'll _____ the subject of pay scales in a moment.

2　Match each phrase in 1 to these categories.

a　Involving people: _____

b　Disagreeing / Expressing reservation: _____

c　Managing the discussion: _____

d　Putting forward unpopular ideas: _____

e　Putting forward ideas you're confident about: _____

f　Asking permission to speak: _____

3　Correct the one mistake in each of these sentences.

1　Would you want to talk about that now, Sophie?

2　The obvious solution to this problem can be to advertise the position more widely.

3　The target of today's meeting is to draw up a short list of candidates.

4　It's interesting you had said that, because actually the opposite is true.

5　Could I only say something?

6　I'm not sure how your feelings are about this, but I think we need to review our recruitment policy.

7　But what makes you so true our company will benefit?

8　Given that Arturo does have much experience, wouldn't it be better to take on a contract worker?

4　Match the phrases in 3 to the categories in 2.

Language at work

1　Match 1–10 to a–j.

1　If the interview had gone better, ___

2　Even if the interview had gone better, ___

3　Unless you had got four years' experience, ___

4　You needn't have sent a CV – ___

5　My first boss could have given me more support – ___

6　If I'd been born into a very rich family, ___

7　Whether I'd gone to Harvard or Yale, ___

8　It would have been good ___

9　It's just as well ___

10　I still don't think that ___

a　my opportunities would have been similar.

b　your application form had all the relevant information.

c　I might have got the job.

d　if you'd told us about their offer.

e　we wouldn't have given you the senior post.

f　promotions at this level should be automatic.

g　that's my biggest criticism of him.

h　I probably wouldn't have got the job.

i　we were able to match their offer.

j　I don't think I would have had such drive.

2　Rewrite these sentences using conditionals, starting with the words given.

1　I didn't ask for a pay rise. I didn't get one.

Even if _____

2　The company didn't renew our season ticket. I couldn't go to the football game.

If _____

3　They got rid of the air conditioning. The office is unbearably hot.

If only _____

4　The airport staff called off their strike yesterday. I'm in Spain now.

If _____

3　Complete these sentences with words from the list.

would　　might　　should　　had　　have

1　Marketing _____ have let us see the promotional material before releasing it – it's terrible!

2　Perhaps you're right – I _____ have been a bit too direct.

3　I _____ have booked a taxi if I were you.

4　Jim might _____ finished earlier if the printer _____ been working.

5　I didn't realize you were so busy. You _____ have asked for my help.

6　I could _____ taken on some of your work – I had some free time last week.

7　If she _____ had the information last week she would have been able to include it in her presentation.

8　I can't find the receipts anywhere. I suppose it's possible that Rachel _____ have taken them from my desk so that she could process my expenses.

9　It _____ have been better if we had known about the delay to delivery sooner – we could have changed our plans, but it's too late now.

10　We _____ have bought that company when we had the chance. If we had, we'd be market leaders by now.

3 | Practice file

Working with words

1 Choose the best answer from the words in *italics*.

1 The new secretary is very *effective / efficient* – she works incredibly quickly and to an admirable degree of accuracy.

2 We're *accessing / entering* the final stage of the appraisal so all participants will need to *access / enter* key documents as quickly as possible.

3 She was given no *option / opportunity* but to accept the pay-off and leave at the end of the week.

4 The new CEO has completely *transformed / transferred* the working ethos in the company – employees are no longer apathetic and unmotivated.

5 Tests were *implemented / carried out* to confirm the seriousness of the diagnosis.

6 The change *procedure / process* is naturally a long one, which can be aided by having a set of *procedures / processes* in place.

7 A large, flexible team of staff provides the *means / ability* to offer a 24-hour service.

8 The group's main *purpose / meaning* is to oversee the implementation of the new management structure.

9 You don't necessarily have to jump around and be *energetic / dynamic* to make a good impression on an audience – but you really have to be *energetic / dynamic* if you want to keep their attention.

10 The security department has *put in place / installed* cameras everywhere – I even noticed one above the mirrors in the bathroom the other day.

2 Find the noun which does not collocate with each verb.

1	assess	progress / performance / targets / a situation
2	measure	progress / objections / success / performance
3	achieve	results / ideas / targets / success
4	generate	performance / ideas / enthusiasm / interest
5	anticipate	problems / objections / requests / productivity
6	facilitate	productivity / progress / change / objections
7	accommodate	needs / development / requirements / requests
8	exchange	information / potential difficulties / ideas / knowledge

3 Complete these sentences with the correct phrase from the list.

achieve good results	facilitate productivity
assess the situation	exchange ideas
accommodate the needs	anticipate objections
generate enthusiasm	measure the performance

1 It can be difficult to _____ of individual staff, but there are a lot of useful tools that use a rating scale of 1–10.

2 The marketing team met to _____ for a slogan for the new advertising campaign.

3 If you _____ to organizational change, you can prepare convincing arguments in response.

4 The investment in new machinery to streamline the production process should _____.

5 Staff morale has been low so the company has brought in a consultant to _____ and find out why.

6 We've introduced a new system of flexible hours to _____ of working parents.

7 Having a pleasant and comfortable working environment helps to _____ for the job.

8 He hopes to _____ in his accounting exam.

Business communication skills

1 Complete this presentation about flexible working and e-teams with the phrases from the list.

I said earlier	and this brings me	this is where
turning to	moving on	for example	I mean
just to fill you	I'd like to start	just to digress
something to think about	put it another way

… I'm going to talk about flexible working, and in particular e-teams. [1]_____ in on some of the background, research has shown that flexible working exists in 48% of companies with ten or more employees, and 61% of managers said that flexible working results in job satisfaction. It's [2]_____ and I'll return to this later …

[3]_____ by saying that a good communications policy is vital. The e-team operates on a 'dispersed' basis. To [4]_____, team members work in different locations and at different times. This means that synchronous communications need to be improved to take account of reduced face-to-face contact. By 'synchronous' [5]_____ meetings, telephone, video-conferencing. Asynchronous

communications – briefing notes, circulars, email, voicemail – need to be managed more carefully …

… OK, ⁶_____ to look at the customer dimension. Whatever the working arrangements, it's vital that the customer gets a quick response. So, ⁷_____, making the customer wait until a part-time member of staff is on duty, possibly several days later, is not acceptable. The vital information needs to be constantly available …

Now, ⁸_____ the issue of contacting staff members. As ⁹_____, the team is likely to be dispersed. The ideal is to have a 'seamless' telephone system. ¹⁰_____ people are integrated into the telephone network wherever they are.

¹¹_____ for a second – use of the telephone should be encouraged. Regular voice contact is important to avoid isolation.

¹²_____ to the last point – there's no substitute for getting everyone together on a regular basis. Make it fun, too …

2 Put the words in the right order to make phrases.

1 talk / divided / I've / into … / my / up

_____

2 I'll … / all / after / of / that / first / I'll …

_____

3 in / about / more / I'll / that / moment / say / a

_____

4 on / background … / to / fill / just / in / you / of / the / some

_____

5 are / now / know / with … / I / if / you / familiar / don't

_____

6 point / this / and / key / my / is

_____

7 now / I'll / any / happy / be / take / to / questions

_____

Language at work

1 Complete these sentences with the most appropriate future form of the verbs in brackets.

1 Sorry, Ali, I'm in a meeting right now.
   I _____ (call) you back in twenty minutes.

2 We _____ (roll) out the changes in our management structure over the next year.

3 The video link's down. Never mind, I _____ (give) the presentation on my own.

4 You _____ (listen) to me for over an hour by then, so at that point I _____ (take) any questions.

5 You _____ (learn) about your annual bonuses on 5 April, all being well.

6 Henry _____ (speak) to everyone in the room by the end of the evening, I think. He's such a networker.

7 Their shares _____ (yield) a decent dividend, given past form.

8 It _____ (be worth) finding out why they turned down the offer.

2 Rewrite these sentences using the words in brackets.

1 It's likely that the consultants will suggest merging the departments. (probably)

_____

2 I'm sure they'll deliver the stock in time. (almost certainly)

_____

3 The management will ask our opinion before making the changes. (bound)

_____

4 The tax changes might well turn investors away. (probable)

_____

5 I've got to go now, but I'll probably see you at the launch party later. (good chance)

_____

6 The training course probably won't be useful. (unlikely)

_____

7 We think the CEO will make an announcement at the dinner. (expected)

_____

8 They may need more identification than a credit card. (perhaps)

_____

Working with words

1 Match 1–12 to a–l.

1 It's advisable do some research and weigh ___

2 If you spread your investment across several companies, you minimize ___

3 We don't want to expose our customers ___

4 As a retailer we constantly have to try to anticipate changes ___

5 We've noticed that our staff find it difficult to accept ___

6 If we don't come up with a new concept we run the risk ___

7 Once we've launched the product it will be important to gauge ___

8 Insurance companies have to carefully evaluate ___

9 When scheduling a project, it helps to identify potential problems ___

10 His company went bankrupt because he failed to recognize ___

11 Before we invest in this new product we need to determine whether ___

12 Financial advisors analyse market conditions and trends to help them predict ___

a in consumer behaviour.

b the risks it was facing.

c how the markets react to it.

d which sectors will grow over the next few years.

e change, so we have to introduce new procedures carefully.

f of losing market share to our competitors.

g the risk of making a loss.

h there is a market for it.

i that could affect deadlines.

j to identity theft, so we have measures to safeguard customer data.

k risks to help them decide on their premium prices.

l up the potential gains and risks before investing in a company.

2 Complete these sentences. Use the answers to complete the crossword and find the hidden word.

1 He's such a _____ driver – he just doesn't seem to recognize danger and he puts everyone else at risk too.

2 He won't ever support my idea for this new concept – he's just really _____.

3 Lending so much money without any guarantee that it would be repaid wasn't exactly a _____ action.

4 Firing Piotr for acting without authorization was a pretty _____ decision – I think she regrets it now.

5 I tend to be quite _____ with my investments – I don't like anything that's too high-risk.

6 Expanding into new markets was a _____ step – I wasn't sure about it, but it seems to have worked.

7 It's _____ to think that you can use the company credit card for personal expenses without someone noticing.

8 If you want to be innovative, you simply can't be _____ because you have to be prepared to deal with unknowns and take a chance now and then.

```
1  R □ □ □ ▢ □ □
        2  O ▢ □  -  □ □ □ □ □ □ □
   3  P □ □ ▢ □ □
           4  R ▢ □ □
        5  C □ □ ▢ □ □ □
                 6  B ▢ □
           7  F ▢ □ □ □ □
8  R □ □ □ ▢ □  -  □ □ □ □
```

Business communication skills

1 Katja's team are organizing a company event. They are discussing the menus for the formal dinner. Complete their conversation with phrases from the list.

> could you let Torsten finish, please
> I'd be really interested to hear what you think about the printer issue
> I'm not fully convinced as yet
> we seem to have some sort of consensus …
> could you talk us through this
> you're saying that
> bring the conversation back to the agenda
> can I just check – we are now talking about
> maybe we're digressing a little

Katja I'd like to start with the menus. Torsten,

1 _____?

Torsten Yes. We've prepared the text for the menu and we've decided to use a company called Theta.

Wolfgang 2 _____ the printers we're going to use for the menus?

Torsten Yes, that's right. A couple of printers sent us some sample menus and I think Theta is the best. They've …

Elke 3 _____ Theta can offer the same level of quality as Schmidt's?

4 _____.

Katja Sorry, Elke. 5 _____?

Torsten Yes, well as I was saying, I chose Theta because they have the best prices and their design was great.

Wolfgang By the way, has anyone seen the new design of the company magazine – I think it looks terrible.

Katja ⁶_____.

Elke I totally agree with you, Wolfgang. I really don't understand why they changed it.

Katja If I could just ⁷_____. Wolfgang, ⁸_____.

Wolfgang Yes, well I agree with Torsten. Theta is offering the best deal, and although the quality is not quite as good as Schmidt's, it's still good enough.

Katja OK, well, ⁹_____.

2 They are now discussing entertainment. Choose the correct answer from the words in *italics*.

Wolfgang So, what's happening with the entertainment? We haven't discussed that at all yet.

Katja Maybe we can ¹*let / allow / ask* Elke answer that. She's been working on entertainment.

Elke Have you seen this brochure of party decorations? They look great. I think we should get some balloons and …

Katja That's interesting, Elke, but I think it's probably best ²*discussed / left / given* for another meeting. We don't have much time, so I'd like to prioritize entertainment.

Elke Sorry. Yes, er … we were thinking of hiring that Abba tribute band, but I'm having second ³*opinions / ideas / thoughts* about it now. Maybe the Beatles tribute band would be better.

Torsten With ⁴*regret / respect / regards* Elke, do we really believe that those kinds of bands are a good idea at such a sophisticated evening event?

Wolfgang Do we need any live music at all?

Elke Well, I've started to wonder that. Maybe we don't …

Katja I'm not sure this ⁵*gets / leaves / is getting* us anywhere. The decision has already been made that we'll have live music, so can we try and make a decision on this? Can I just ask everyone ⁶*to conclude / to sum up / to tell* their views on this?

Wolfgang OK, well I still have serious ⁷*reservations / considerations / observations* about having a tribute band. If we must have live music, I would prefer a jazz band or a string quartet.

Torsten I totally agree.

Elke Well, I suppose I could look into that.

Katja So am I right ⁸*about / with / in* saying that the general opinion is we'll go with either jazz or classical?

Elke Yes – I think so.

Katja Good. I'd like to ⁹*draw / say / manage* things to a close now, so …

Language at work

1 Rewrite these pairs of sentences using *it, this,* or *that*. Sometimes more than one answer is possible.

Example: *We've booked you a videoconferencing room. The videoconferencing room will be ready from 3.00 p.m.*
→ *It will be ready from 3.00 p.m.*

1 **A** Didn't we meet at the Jakarta conference in 1999?

 B Yes, the Jakarta conference was one of the most useful conferences I've been to.
 _____

2 Aleph's submitting his evaluation by email. His evaluation should be very helpful, I think.
 _____

3 We need to minimize the chances of a downturn. A downturn would be disastrous.
 _____

4 We need to minimize the chances of a downturn. Minimizing the chances of a downturn is just good business practice.
 _____

5 The auditors are arriving tomorrow. What's worrying me is: … _____

6 **A** My problem is understanding all the jargon.

 B Understanding all the jargon is my problem, too.
 _____

2 Complete this presentation with *it, this,* or *that*. Sometimes more than one answer is possible.

'We can't say exactly what will happen next year. ¹_____ would make our jobs much less interesting, anyway! But there are some predictions we can make fairly confidently. ²_____ is why I've called the meeting today. ³_____ will have three parts. Firstly, we'll carry out a review of our performance last year. ⁴_____ will help us identify the current trends in the market, and our strengths and weaknesses. Next will be a "blue skies" session. ⁵_____ will involve us splitting into groups of six.'

3 Look back at your answers in 2 and decide what they refer to. Choose the correct answer from the options below.

1 **a** next year
 b being able to say exactly what will happen next year

2 **a** the fact that there are some predictions
 b the fact that we can be fairly confident

3 **a** the meeting   **b** today

4 **a** our performance   **b** the review

5 **a** the session   **b** splitting into groups of six

Working with words

1 **Complete these sentences with the best option a–c.**

1 My skill in languages was viewed _____ by the rest of the team.
   a helpfully   b clearly   c positively

2 We've spent a lot of time together this month because we've been working _____ on the Remdon account.
   a tightly   b closely   c directly

3 I didn't receive the same pay rise as my colleagues so I thought I'd been treated _____.
   a unfairly   b illegally   c thoughtlessly

4 You have to tread very _____ with Simon as he is easily upset when there is a problem.
   a easily   b thoroughly   c carefully

5 It's quite hard working with Jenna. She doesn't express herself very _____ so I don't always understand what she means.
   a obviously   b clearly   c noticeably

6 When there's a crisis in the office, Clare has the ability to consider the facts and look at things _____.
   a objectively   b evenly   c exactly

7 My boss pushes us _____ to meet deadlines and achieve the results he wants.
   a heavily   b forcefully   c hard

8 Ideally, we want someone who can come up with good ideas and communicate them _____ to the rest of the team.
   a completely   b effectively   c thoroughly

2 **Choose the correct answer from the verbs in *italics* and the prepositions in bold.**

1 Admittedly, there are certain tasks that I tend to not *spend / pay / save* attention **in / to** because I find them boring.

2 Part of my job is making sure that the team *keeps / obeys / goes* **at / to** the budget.

3 I like to *follow / steer / guide* clear **in / of** arguments at work as I prefer a calm environment.

4 I'm afraid your work has *dropped / gone / fallen* short **of / to** the standards the company expects.

5 Technical people are often able to *point / focus / aim* **with / on** solutions in a systematic way.

6 I don't know how to *cope / make / control* **with / at** this situation so I'm going to ask my boss for help.

3 **Rewrite the sentences in 2 using these verbs in place of the multiword verbs.**

achieve   neglect   pinpoint   handle   avoid   meet

1 _____
2 _____
3 _____
4 _____
5 _____
6 _____

Business communication skills

1 **Put these words in the right order to make phrases.**

1 how ... / don't / just / understand / I

   _____

2 try / and / we / look / avoid / any ... / can ?

   _____

3 propose / with / you / how / deal / issue / do / we / this ?

   _____

4 try / and / facts / we / on / can / focused / the / stay ?

   _____

5 real / is ... / the / here / issue

   _____

6 say / you / what / to / do / trying / I'm / understand ?

   _____

7 I / mean / but .../ what / you / see

   _____

8 get / here / not / to / try / personal / let's

   _____

9 I've / make / correctly / I / sure / can / just / this / understood ?

   _____

10 you / if / aware ... / don't / are / know / I ?

   _____

2 Complete these sentences with the phrases from the list.

> we try and avoid   you be happy   a bit worried
> not happy with   I be right in thinking   prepared to
> what you mean   just don't understand
> if you are aware   be more than happy

1 I don't know _____, but the reason the situation arose in Sales was that the brochures were late.

2 Would _____ that no one bothered to tell the HR department?

3 I _____ how we let the complaint get so far.

4 I'm _____ delay the campaign if we can sort out the problem with the printers.

5 Would _____ to meet with a mediator?

6 I'm _____ about what is going on in the new factory.

7 I see _____, but surely we need to do something about this now?

8 I'd _____ to look into a compromise.

9 Look, can _____ any unpleasantness – we're all adults after all.

10 I'm really _____ the way this has been dealt with.

Language at work

1 Rewrite the underlined sections of these sentences to change the emphasis, starting with the words given.

1 He didn't contribute to the meeting until the end.
   Only at _____

2 She didn't even answer my main question.
   My _____

3 I like her as a person, but I can't stand her lack of professionalism.
   It's _____

4 Ben isn't very well-qualified, but his boundless enthusiasm is impressive.
   What's _____

5 Zoe is the best listener in our meetings.
   The person _____

6 It's matters like that which you need to inform me of.
   It's absolutely vital _____

7 I value creativity above anything else.
   Creativity _____

8 I don't like his constant need to make stupid jokes.
   It's _____

2 Correct these sentences.

1 We were very indeed impressed with all the proposals.
   _____

2 Team players like Martine are very essential to any business.
   _____

3 She's so just close to being an excellent manager, if only she'd listen more.
   _____

4 Not only the report is a month late, but also I now find it's full of mistakes.
   _____

5 Mo is completely good at a few things, but she's not an all-rounder.
   _____

6 It was annoying was their lack of punctuality.
   _____

7 What like I best about my job is the variety.
   _____

8 Never I have seen such an appalling presentation.
   _____

9 Why which is I decided to get in touch with you.
   _____

10 The person is chairing tomorrow's meeting is Xavier.
   _____

11 Reason why I'm saying this is to be constructive.
   _____

12 It's someone from HR she is on the phone.
   _____

Working with words

1 Complete this text with the verbs from the list.

get   try   hit   think   look   fall
figure   get   bounce   run

Six tips for creative thinking

- Creativity often needs peace, so ¹_____ out ways of getting some quiet time for yourself. Or have an 'away day' with colleagues to ²_____ around ideas together.

- To come up with new and unusual ideas, you need to ³_____ outside the box. Be open to new perspectives. ⁴_____ beyond your beliefs and usual ways of doing things.

- Writing down your ideas and thoughts will help the creative process. The more ideas you have, the greater the chance you might ⁵_____ on a few good ones.

- Take risks! Expect that some ideas will fail or ⁶_____ by the wayside. See them as experiments rather than mistakes then ⁷_____ back on track and come up with new solutions.

- Be curious. Ask a lot of questions. Challenge existing methods and ⁸_____ out different things.

- The end result of a creative idea needs a lot of hard work. So don't give up when you ⁹_____ into problems or when projects fail to ¹⁰_____ off the ground.

2 Match 1–10 to a–j.

1 In the service sector, quality is a measure of what the customer perceives, which shifts ____

2 From this point of view, employees are the most important part of a business, an idea which is causing quite ____

3 To serve customers better, employees are encouraged to pursue ____

4 Good managers know how far to tolerate ____

5 In fact, staff retention is now seen as the key driver to boosting ____

6 On the other hand, quality control measures such as Six Sigma demand ____

7 ... who sometimes criticize it for imposing ____

8 Nevertheless, strict measures are needed to control ____

9 ... otherwise they can significantly cut into ____

10 In the end, both innovation and control are needed to successfully outperform ____

a costs and prevent overheads from spiralling out of control ...

b ideas to achieve the best results for clients.

c the emphasis from the product per se to the product and the employee.

d precision in measuring, which may be unsuitable for many companies ...

e the competition and maintain a competitive edge.

f mistakes and see them as part of the innovation process – they also budget for learning costs.

g targets which bear little relation to good service for the client.

h a stir among traditional, number-crunching managers.

i the bottom line and reduce profits.

j earnings in service-oriented companies where employees need the freedom to choose how they serve.

Business communication skills

1 Put these words in the right order to make brainstorming phrases.

1 work / would / not / how / I'm / sure / how / but / practice / this / in / about ... ?

_____

2 I / have / be / possible / would / it / thought / would / to ...

_____

3 you / work / think / what / that / makes / would ?

_____

4 could / about / we / it / thinking / even ...

_____

5 you / would / like / on / expand / to / that ?

_____

6 that / just / in / that / I / well / thought / way ...

_____

7 certainly / thinking / it's / about / worth

_____

8 we / shouldn't / be / more / thinking / about ... ?

_____

9 the / lines / thinking / I / was / along / of ...

_____

2 Complete this problem-solving brainstorm with appropriate phrases using the key words in brackets.

A So we've got to make significant changes or face receivership.

B ¹_____ (consider) poaching market share?

C I don't see how that helps. Increasing market share doesn't necessarily help the bottom line.

B So, where does that leave us?

C ²_____ (supposing) ignore market share and our competition …

B ³_____ (sorry / saying) that we don't bother selling anything?

C Not exactly. I mean, let's look at ourselves rather than outside.

A Oh, I see, ⁴_____ (thinking) that we should be trying to reduce our costs rather than increase our revenues. Am I right?

C Well, for example, we could look at which of our customers actually make us money.

B Erm … all of them?

A Well, that's probably not quite true. But actually, ⁵_____ (bad idea). We could even drop those clients who don't make us enough of a margin!

B ⁶_____ (concerned) how that would look.

C I think it would be fine. By focusing on those clients who generate the most profits and selling to similar clients, we can increase revenues and profits without expanding the infrastructure or fixed costs. ⁷_____ (consider).

3 Correct these sentences.

1 I'm a bit worried over the deadline – I don't think we can make it.

2 I'd be more of happy to help out – just let me know what you'd like me to do.

3 I just won't be able giving my full attention to this project, if I still have to complete all these administrative tasks.

4 Let's try not to get personalized here – it's not just one person's fault that this has been such a disaster.

5 The real issue is here that management simply aren't aware of the resourcing problems we've been having.

Language at work

1 Complete this email with words from the list.

quite (x2) rather little all absolutely
just actually even only

Hi Jack

I'm writing from Milan, where I'm at ¹_____ a good conference on technologies in business. It's all been ²_____ interesting so far, although I'm getting a ³_____ tired – I've ⁴_____ been having about four hours' sleep a night, because I keep bumping into old colleagues and going for meals and drinks with them. Talking of meals, the food here is ⁵_____ wonderful. ⁶_____ the most basic things are ⁷_____ spectacular. And the wine's not ⁸_____ that bad either. I've ⁹_____ got back from lunch, ¹⁰_____. Anyway, I needed to ask you …

2 Complete this conversation with a suitable adverb / adverbial phrase.

A That was ¹_____ a useful meeting, wasn't it?

B Yes, although I'm not ²_____ convinced about the brainstorming.

A To be ³_____, I'm not either. I found that part of the day ⁴_____ tiresome, ⁵_____.

B Yes. Nick couldn't ⁶_____ keep his eyes open!

A Well, yes, his attention did seem to wander, but ⁷_____ towards the end – for most of the meeting he was concentrating.

B Of ⁸_____, and even if we didn't get a clear outcome, it was useful ⁹_____ to be thinking about all those issues together.

A Yes, I don't ¹⁰_____ think it would have been possible to reach any firm decisions today, do you?

B No, I suppose not. And I have to say, it was ¹¹_____ the most productive meeting of that kind we've had on this project so far.

Working with words

1 Complete these sentences with phrases from the list.

> shared vision performance management
> personal development plans structural change
> employee participation skills deficit
> collective aspiration paradigm shift

1 'We left the company and started our own business together. We knew it would work because we had a _____ of what we wanted to achieve.'

2 'The company was completely reorganized after those management consultants came in – a radical _____ was implemented.'

3 'In the next year, carrying out our business in an ethical way is both a _____ and a mutual responsibility for us all.'

4 'I would like to encourage _____ in all departmental decisions.'

5 'We need to have more control over staff progression, so we need to start taking _____ more seriously and I think we should introduce formalized _____ for each member of staff.'

6 'There was a real _____ in the team when Gareth left and Jens was appointed team leader. Everyone suddenly became far more target-orientated and enthusiastic. Sales went up dramatically.'

7 'Where are all the competent IT specialists? There seems to be a real _____ in this area!'

2 Correct the mistakes in this conversation.

Andrew Why haven't they put salaries up by 8% over the board? Why is it just management level that get that?

Tiago That's what always happens. You need to get in the reality world and realize that this is just the way it is.

Andrew I know, but I think this decision is actually counter-productive with the long run. Some staff might leave. It will cost a lot to recruit new staff.

Tiago True, but they'll always defend these types of decisions. They'll argue that management deserve bigger pay rises because they're the ones who have to think about the huge picture and make decisions.

3 Complete these sentences. Use the answers to complete the crossword.

Across

3 We wanted a more _____ structure so we gave a lot of decision-making power to the regional offices.

6 I don't think the CEO and the board should continue to alter strategy. Any changes should come from the people who are actually doing the work – it should be a _____ approach.

8 I planned and implemented my own learning programme – it was completely _____.

Down

1 When looking for a job, you can't just have a _____ cover letter – you should adapt the letter for each job that you apply for.

2 Head Office decide which training courses should be made available to staff, so I guess you'd say that training is _____.

4 We can offer _____ language training – we'll teach you exactly what you need for your role.

5 A few of your team are unhappy about your traditional management style and I think you need to develop a more inclusive and less _____ approach.

7 Franchises use a _____ business model that is then adapted to meet local markets.

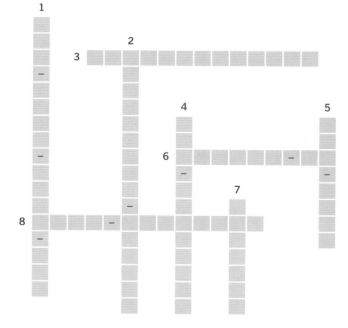

Business communication skills

1 Put the words in *italics* in the right order to create a conversation.

Gerhard Hi, Nicole. I'm calling to discuss the recent delivery problems we've been having.

Nicole Oh, hi, Gerhard. I've heard there have been a few delivery issues with recently. ¹*problems / the / Could / were? / what / you / exactly / clarify*
_____

Gerhard Yeah, sure. Basically it's White Route Logistics, they just don't seem able to deliver on time any more.

Nicole ²*mean / you / Do / that* the other logistics companies we use aren't causing any of the problems?

Gerhard Well, not exactly. ³*is / I'm / saying / What*
_____ that it's mainly an issue with White Route Logistics, but we have also had a couple of problems with Utome.

Nicole ⁴*logistics / of / What / name / other / again? / was / the / company / the*
_____

Gerhard Utome.

Nicole Oh, yes. That's right. ⁵*That / Have / notice? / Hans / you / handed / that / his / has / reminds / in / me. / heard* _____ He's been headhunted by that web company, Utopia.

Gerhard Really? I knew he wasn't particularly happy. ⁶*about / way, / By / talking / the*
_____ people leaving, have you heard about Helga?

Nicole No. What's happened?

Gerhard Apparently, she's taking early retirement. ⁷*That's / of / digression. / a / bit / sorry. / a / Anyway,*
_____

Nicole ⁸*main / back / issue. / to / Let's / get / the*
_____

2 Choose the correct answer from the words in *italics*.

1 **A** Can I speak to Rachel Warner, please?

 B Did you *ask / said / say* Rachel Ward?

2 I'm not quite clear *with / about / at* your last suggestion.

3 Could you run it *by / through / along* me again?

4 Could I ask you to spell *it / with / out* some details?

5 No, it's *bad / not / problem* that we don't have the resources. We don't have the time to do this.

6 Just a *second / little / thought*. It may not be entirely relevant, but have you noticed how tired David looks?

7 Actually, it *doesn't / won't / isn't* matter – it's a bit off topic right now.

Language at work

1 Use Joanna's 'to do' list to make sentences using 'the future in the past'. Use the past continuous, *would, was to, was supposed to*, as well as *was going to*.

Tuesday: To do

1 finish working on Kelner case (too busy)

2 meeting: Sue, her office, 10.00 a.m. (she was off sick)

3 meeting & lunch, Hungarian rep, 12.30 p.m. (his plane was delayed, didn't arrive till 3.00 p.m.)

4 file corporate credit card expenses (couldn't find receipts)

5 book flights for Atlanta conference (website kept crashing)

6 meet Sarah at Café Carlucci for after-work drink (closed, went to Spangio's instead)

7 check bank account – salary will go in today (I was wrong – will have to wait until tomorrow!)

1 _____
2 _____
3 _____
4 _____
5 _____
6 _____
7 _____

2 Rewrite these sentences using a participle clause.

Example: Because I had worked on similar projects before, I was made team leader on this one. ➡ *Having worked on similar projects before, I was made team leader on this one.*

1 We were faced with a financial crisis, so we cut 50 jobs.
_____

2 Because of the new interest rates, I think now is a good time to borrow some money.
_____

3 After I had retired, I decided to rethink my life.
_____

4 Since I didn't understand what to do, I asked for help.
_____

5 Because he knows what to do in situations like this, Paddy stayed calm throughout the meeting.
_____

Working with words

1 Complete the text with the verbs from the list and an appropriate preposition. Change the form of the verb if necessary.

have   make   see   gain   take   feel

Name: Allan Reed
Job: Researcher, Biotechnology, GTT

What inspired your interest in biotechnology and working for GTT?
I've always had a passion for science, but what brought me to GTT was knowing that the work I'd do would ¹_____ a difference _____ people's lives.

What do you like about working for GTT?
The people, the research, the culture, the whole environment! The company has ²_____ recognition, and awards, _____ its overall performance as a company and its workplace culture. It offers an environment that supports both team work and individual initiative – so I
³_____ a say _____ the research I want to do. I
⁴_____ part _____ an incredibly talented team of people who ⁵_____ pride _____ the products they produce.

People are very supportive of each other, and the benefits that the company offers are so generous that I don't
⁶_____ a future _____ myself anywhere else.

2 Choose the correct answer from the verbs in *italics* and the prepositions in **bold**.

1 Often the first wave of a new technology product doesn't *match* / *live* **on to** / **up to** your expectations, so you feel disappointed.

2 Feeling as if I'm being *put* / *set* **with** / **to** the test often helps me to perform better.

3 In customer service you are continually responding to requests, so *deciding* / *thinking* **from** / **on** your feet is a key skill.

4 At DPF, we *rely* / *believe* **in** / **of** the need to invest in people to make the company stronger.

5 Chances don't always come to us, we need to *seek* / *find* **out** / **for** opportunities ourselves.

6 Listening is fundamental in *making* / *building* **on** / **up** rapport with people.

7 In intercultural situations it's important to *use* / *benefit* **with** / **from** the diversity of opinion offered by different cultures.

8 The secret of success is to offset the need to work with *striving* / *reaching* **at** / **for** a healthy work-life balance.

3 Complete the sentences with the words from the list.

willingness   ability   recognition   desire

1 Sam is desperate for _____ so you have to give him constant praise for his work.

2 Berthe is always happy to do overtime, which shows her _____ to take on extra work as necessary.

3 Kit demonstrated his _____ to keep to a schedule when the project finished on time.

4 Marc shows a _____ to excel at his job – he's won 'employee of the month' twice!

Business communication skills

1 Complete this impromptu presentation with the phrases from the list.

a good point   have to admit that
I think you should be aware   it would be a good idea if I
I'll get back to you   we are at the moment
the first thing is   just like to outline   remember exactly

Anton Could you run through the opportunities for students at DHN?

Caro OK. Where ¹_____ is, we've just finished putting together the introductory programmes for students – there are two programmes where students can learn the business from the inside out. I'd ²_____ the main features of these. And perhaps
³_____ touched on the main opportunities for graduates. So …
⁴_____, our Intern Programme gives hands-on experience during the summer vacation. We look for candidates with good leadership and communication skills.

Anton Does it matter what year of their degree they're on?

Caro That's ⁵_____. They need to have completed their second year of study.

Anton Do they need to be studying a specific degree?

Caro I can't ⁶_____, but most opportunities are for students in business and technical fields. OK, next point. We also run a Co-op Programme – with alternate school / work semesters – which helps students gain experience and try out ideas from the classroom.

Anton Great …

Caro And ⁷_____ that for students whose home is at least 40 miles from the work location, we provide an accommodation allowance at the beginning of each work term.

Anton What about academic grades? Are you only looking for high achievers?

Caro Well, principally we look for people who can work well with others. I ⁸_____ grades are important, obviously. Let me check the exact requirements and ⁹_____.

2 Correct the mistake in each sentence.

1 I like to be able to tell you more, but unfortunately …

_____

2 You're quite right, we are need to address this question.

_____

3 I don't have the exactly figures, but what if I summarize?

_____

4 I think really this is an important point.

_____

5 I can check double if you like?

_____

6 I think that's covering everything.

_____

7 You'll appreciate that I still have need to run that by the board.

_____

Language at work

1 Put the words in *italics* in the right order to form questions.

1 A *say / would / many / you / you / weaknesses / have*
   _____?
   B I have some, but I always try to overcome them.

2 A *position / like / know / I'd / you / attracted / what / this / to / to* _____?
   B Well, the company's reputation is really good and I'd love to have the opportunity to work for you.

3 A *you / you / your / 're / are / present / unhappy / job / not / in* _____?
   B Not at all, no, but I'm ready for new challenges.

4 A *looking / you / what / are / for / salary*
   _____?
   B My current salary is about €40,000 a year, so …

5 A *you / us / questions / have / ask / must / to / some*
   _____?
   B Yes, I do have several questions for you. Firstly, is career progression seen as important here?

2 Choose the most appropriate answer to continue these conversations / presentations.

1 Is our employees' happiness important to us?
   a (*same speaker*) Yes, it's of absolutely paramount importance.
   b (*new speaker*) Yes, it's of absolutely paramount importance.

2 Can I just check whether you feel valued at work?
   a Yes, you can. I don't, really.
   b In general, yes I do, mainly because I'm in a supportive team.

3 Why do you think the company has such a high staff turnover?
   a I'm not sure – that's something we're trying to address.
   b Not a clue. What do you reckon?

4 Will the union ask for a higher pay settlement this year?
   a When have they ever not?
   b Probably. And what will we do then?

5 And employees' productivity is the best it could be?
   a Well, these things can always be improved, but it's not far off.
   b No.

6 Do you know how many sick days the average employee took off in 2009?
   a 2.3.
   b I don't know. I'd imagine somewhere between 2 and 5.

7 Are you with me so far?
   a (*new speaker*) Of course we are.
   b (*same speaker*) Good. Moving on, then. This next slide shows …

8 How can I put this?
   a You're fired.
   b Basically, as you know we are having severe problems in terms of resources, and …

9 And how about childcare?
   a (*same speaker*) Are there any plans to introduce a crèche?
   b (*new speaker*) Well, how about it?

3 Find an example from the sentences in 2 for each of the following.

a a rhetorical question ____
b an embedded question ____
c a question to check the listeners are paying attention ____
d one question used to introduce another question ____
e a statement used as a question ____

Working with words

1 Match 1–8 to a–h.

1 As we planned the project, we discussed how our resources ____

2 The public were asked if it was important to them how our company was ____

3 The project was over budget and it was clear that resources had been seriously ____

4 The project leader resigned after allegations that he had squandered ____

5 If the CSR programme is to work, there needs to be careful consideration which resources should ____

6 The company was criticized for its waste, so a committee was set up to establish how best to ____

7 The newspaper article questioned whether our resources were ____

8 Financially, the company was in difficulties, so consultants looked at ways ____

a mismanaged.

b of maximizing resources.

c optimize resources.

d being put to good use.

e utilizing its resources.

f resources.

g would be best allocated.

h be deployed.

2 Complete sentences 1–7 with words from the list.

> corporate accountability   track record
> assets   bottom line   knowledge base

1 I really believe in the importance of _____ _____ – companies have to show some kind of responsibility for their own actions.

2 I don't think we can rely on Piet to manage the project successfully. Do you remember the disaster with the last project? He doesn't have a great _____ for this kind of thing.

3 We've invested a lot of money in training and we're now seeing the benefits – we've built up an excellent _____ within the company.

4 Our company owns a lot of land and this is one of our most secure _____.

5 When you work for an insurance company, you know that natural disasters can have a really negative effect on the _____ of the company.

3 Complete this email with phrases from the list.

> short-term profit   drain on resources
> return on investment   market value
> cost-benefit analysis   long-term viability
> competitive advantage   quantifiable data

To: a.santos@bhi.com
From: v.kierly@bhi.com
Subject: In-house CSR project / PR position

Hi Alex

We've discussed the CSR proposal and these are our suggestions and concerns.

Before any scheme is chosen, a detailed 1_____ has to be carried out to ensure the project won't be a 2_____ and finances. In order to get the shareholders on our side we have to be able to show immediate results – they'll want to see some 3_____ from this project. This will be easier if projections show a good 4_____, say within a three-year period. Our report needs to include 5_____ – the shareholders will expect to see some facts and figures.

From a PR point of view, the CSR issue is one we must address as it will boost our overall 6_____. As this particular project is our first, we must check its 7_____ carefully, so that we can be sure of a positive effect on our reputation in the future. We're not aware of any similar projects by our competitors, so potentially this could give us a real 8_____.

Let me know when you would be available for a follow-up meeting about this.

Regards

Verena

Business communication skills

1 Tara and Amal are discussing strategy and the resources available to them. Choose the correct answer to complete their conversation.

Tara So our aim is to improve our reputation. 1____ we need to focus on improving more than just our product.

Amal Exactly – we can't just focus on one area. 2____, which means addressing everything that affects our image.

Tara Right. We could start with our physical resources. Look at the state of our offices – they're old and run down.

Amal So you think we should find new premises? That could be really expensive.

Tara Good point. 3____

Amal No, I don't think we could.

Tara Then maybe it would be best to update and renovate our current offices.

Amal Possibly, but remember – ⁴___ for this improvement programme – we should think about other issues too. People, for example. We need to retain our best staff members and try to attract new people.

Tara Yes, but ⁵___ attract the best people if we can't even offer them a modern office to work in.

Amal Maybe you're right. So ⁶___ our staffing problems could disappear.

Tara Well, I think it would help.

Amal I think so too. ⁷___ – we'll start looking into the costs of redecorating and modernizing the offices.

Tara That sounds like a good idea. But before we go ahead with that, ⁸___?

Amal Yes – what about our actual processes …?

1 a We have a number of options,
   b Looking at it from a long-term perspective,

2 a I think we need to look at the bigger picture
   b We have to bear in mind the long-term viability

3 a I think our options are quite clear here.
   b Realistically, would we be able to finance this strategy?

4 a we have a number of options
   b we're in a really strong position

5 a provided we
   b there's no point in trying to

6 a I'm not sure that would work,
   b assuming we decided to renovate the offices,

7 a Right. So we're decided.
   b I'm not sure that would work.

8 a how would it work if we continued tomorrow?
   b are there any other points to consider?

2 Put the words in *italics* in the right order to complete these sentences.

1 Let's be positive – *we / work / provided / together / all*
   _____, we can still meet our deadline.

2 Well, *hold / we / assuming / decided / to*
   _____ the next team meeting in Brussels, we could also take the opportunity to look at some office buildings to rent next year.

3 It seems manageable, but we *long-term / mind / have / bear / in / viability / to / the*
   _____ of this project.

4 Look, *going / no / we / meeting / don't / with / there's / ahead / point / this / if*
   _____ have any of the key decision-makers here today.

Language at work

1 Match 1–10 to a–j.

1 If we appear to have green credentials, ___
2 If I remembered to copy you in on the email, ___
3 If we raise dividends, ___
4 We'll be able to minimize damage ___
5 In their culture, if you're introduced to someone, ___
6 We may lose market share ___
7 If everyone turned off their computer at night, ___
8 If we don't start providing incentives, ___
9 If I had taken the job at Kurwenal, ___
10 If he's been at work all night, ___

a you should have got it some time yesterday.
b you shake hands with them.
c providing you stick to the measures I've put in place.
d we would save the equivalent of two directors' salaries.
e ethically-minded customers are more likely to buy our products.
f I would never have met my wife.
g we keep shareholders happy.
h no one will want to move to the new offices.
i his concentration probably won't be 100%.
j if Kirput and Sinderzy merge.

2 Correct these sentences using the clues in brackets.

1 If I know Chris's email address, I'd give it to you. (I don't know it.) _____

2 If we disagreed, we say so. (This is how it worked in my last job.) _____

3 If John turns up on time, I am amazed. (It's very unlikely.)
   _____

4 If we hadn't changed suppliers, we wouldn't had so many outstanding orders. (We have a lot of them.)
   _____

5 If the directors have had a pay rise last year when we had our bonuses cancelled, a lot of people would have left the company. (The directors didn't have a pay rise and people didn't leave.)
   _____

6 If they would offer you the job, would you take it? (It might happen.) _____

Working with words

1 **Complete the puzzle using these clues. Find the hidden word (clue = a bad leader may do this).**

1 If you have this, you are totally dedicated to what you are doing.

2 Able to make decisions.

3 If you have this, you believe completely in what you do.

4 Knowing your capabilities and your limitations.

5 Interested in, and good with, people.

6 Modest, not arrogant.

7 Working together and involving everyone.

8 Letting people do their work without interfering.

9 Flexible, willing to adjust to different situations.

10 If you have this, people believe you are honest.

11 Understanding other people's feelings.

12 If you are this, you feel very strongly about something.

```
C
D
      C
S   -
   P           -
   H
C
   H       -
   A
I
      E
P
```

2 **Complete this advice for someone taking on a team-leadership role with the words / phrases from the list.**

avoid   be consistent in   credibility   culture of trust
establish   generate   influence   instil   recognize
reinforces   sense of cohesion   work together

'Be especially careful at the beginning. You won't
1_____ your authority as a team leader by
being too heavy-handed. Your team need to accept that you
have the right to lead them. And you certainly won't
2_____ confidence in your team by being
too hands-on – they may see that as a sign that you don't
trust them. So at all costs, 3_____ the
temptation to micromanage.'

'Your team need to know you can do the job, so it's
important to establish your 4_____ right
from the start. You're unlikely to be able to exert any
5_____ over people if they don't believe in
you. Show them that you recognize their professionalism,
and they're more likely to see you in the same way – in

other words, make an effort to 6_____
mutual respect.'

'You have to get them to 7_____. If they're
suspicious of each other, or too competitive, that has to
change, so try and build a 8_____ between
the individual team members. It takes time, but it's worth
it. Getting them to collaborate on projects can work, or
sharing responsibility for key tasks – anything to bring
individuals closer together and develop a
9_____ within the team. This enables the
team to work "as one".'

'People need to know where they stand. It's important
to 10_____ your expectations and your
feedback – so treat everyone the same. Always
11_____ individual achievement when
it's appropriate to do so. But also acknowledge successes
that are a team effort – any manager that does this
12_____ a sense of team spirit.'

Business communication skills

1 **Complete this briefing with phrases from the list.**

the benefits are clear   as I understand
another great thing about this change is
you and your teams are crucial to
has a key role to play in   it has been agreed that
I would encourage all of you to
it will be well worth the inconvenience
apparently, the decision was taken
what this will allow us to do is   my understanding

'As you may have heard, 1_____
from 1st January, the activities of all the European offices
will now be independently managed from Brussels rather
than reporting directly to New York.
2_____ at yesterday's meeting
of the new senior management team, and obviously it
affects all of us. 3_____
it, although the initiative came from Head Office, it has been
welcomed by all the regional offices.

Now, firstly, 4_____ to offer a
faster and more tailored service to all our European customers.
5_____ that we will
have complete independence, and the freedom to develop
our own ways of operating that are right for our market.

Now, there is likely to be some restructuring on a local
level, but 6_____ is
that there will be no job losses. Even if a few people do have
to relocate, 7_____
to have so much more control over our destiny. And long-
term, 8_____: more
freedom, more opportunities, more rewards.

Obviously ⁹_____ the success of this strategy. It's up to you to seize the opportunity and to make it work. As I see it, each one of you ¹⁰_____ ensuring that the transition is as smooth as possible. It is proposed that we hold an initial planning meeting next week, so ¹¹_____ consult with your teams and come up with some initial ideas for this.'

2 Write spoken extracts from two meetings using the notes. Use as many phrases from the list as possible.

> I like the idea of …, but I'm not very happy about …
> That's a valid point, but …   My understanding is …
> Let's give this a chance to work.
> I have some concerns / reservations about …
> Are there any guarantees that …?
> Can you assure us / give us an assurance that …?
> I understand where you're coming from.

Reduction in departmental training budgets

SH has some reservations about the proposed changes. He understands the need to be more cost-effective, and make departments more accountable. However, he's worried that the essential training needs of individuals and small teams will not be met due to increased competition for a limited budget.

CJ recognizes SH's concern, but it will now be the responsibility of individual departments to decide how the money is spent – not the HR Department. At the moment, departments have to spend a certain proportion on job-specific training, IT skills, and language training, but in future, they will be free to choose their own priorities.

1 **SH:** This is something I wanted to bring up. _____

_____

_____

_____

CJ: Well, of course, _____

_____

_____

_____

Language at work

1 Rewrite these sentences with passive forms of the tenses / verbs in brackets. The underlined words are not relevant in the passive sentence.

1 Shops were selling five of our products every minute in 2008. (past continuous)

_____

2 We asked him to email us details, but he didn't get back in touch with us. (perfect -ing form, start the sentence with the -ing form)

_____

3 Immigration will interview you before they allow you to register for work here. (will + present simple)

_____

4 Someone might have sent the flowers yesterday. (might + perfect)

_____

5 Someone selected me. It was a great honour. (perfect infinitive, start the sentence with to)

_____

6 An employee had been processing your order, but then the whole system crashed. (past perfect continuous)

_____

7 Someone is going to write a formal reply to address your complaints. (going to)

_____

8 We have received 15,000 orders – a staggering number. (present perfect)

_____

2 Choose the correct answer from the words in *italics*.

By the end of the year, the third quarter's losses ¹*had more than made up for / had been more than made up for* by final quarter gains. This ²*put / was put* us back on target for a strong year-end performance, and indeed, when our annual figures ³*published / were published*, they ⁴*showed / were showed* a year of record profits.

These profits ⁵*divided / were divided* as follows: 50% ⁶*reinvested / was reinvested* in the business, we ⁷*paid out / were paid* out 20% as bonuses to employees, and the remaining 30% ⁸*went / was gone* into dividends for shareholders. Our dividend ⁹*raised / was raised* to 8%, the highest rate for some years.

¹⁰*Looking / being looked* towards the future, we're delighted ¹¹*to have invited / to have been invited to put in / to be put in* a proposal for the competition ¹²*to build / to be built* a major new skyscraper in London. ¹³*Having voted / Having been voted* Britain's most innovative architecture firm for the third year in a row, ¹⁴*we anticipate / are anticipated* success in this.

Working with words

1 Rewrite these extracts from company values statements using the phrases from the list. Make any changes in form that are necessary.

> continue to be sensitive to   work cohesively with
> strive to achieve   conduct our business
> hold ourselves accountable to   pride ourselves on
> are committed to   have a passion for

1 'In this day and age, it's really important for us to carry out our operations with openness and integrity.'

_____

2 'We take great satisfaction from the fact that our engineers personally oversee the construction of each vehicle, from start to finish.'

_____

3 'It's extremely important for us to maintain our awareness of the needs of people in the communities where we conduct our business operations.'

_____

4 'We want everyone to know that we care about and make an effort to meet the needs of our employees as well as our customers and stakeholders.'

_____

5 'We take our responsibility to all our stakeholders very seriously, no matter who they are or where they are.'

_____

6 'We are excited by new concepts and new solutions – technical innovation is what we really care about.'

_____

7 'In everything we do, we always work our hardest to ensure we reach the highest possible standards.'

_____

8 'We recognize the need for unity and cooperation with our colleagues in other industries.'

_____

2 Underline the adverb in _italics_ that can't be used in each sentence.

1 A rise in interest rates at this stage would be _comparatively / potentially / significantly_ disastrous.

2 Although expected, the negative figures for the last quarter are _potentially / profoundly / surprisingly_ worrying.

3 Fortunately, demand has remained _comparatively / irretrievably / relatively_ stable.

4 The growth in demand for new hybrid cars has been _potentially / relatively / unexpectedly_ rapid.

5 Since the negative publicity over the recent share issue, media reports have become _appreciably / noticeably / relatively_ more hostile.

6 Even if the allegations aren't true, their effect is _comparatively / irretrievably / potentially_ damaging for the company.

7 Disposable income across the population as a whole is _irretrievably / noticeably / significantly_ different from even a year ago.

8 It's a fact that we are now finding it _potentially / increasingly / relatively_ difficult to find skilled workers prepared to work for these wages.

Business communication skills

1 A company is thinking of relocating its offices. The Managing Director is meeting a union representative to discuss the impact on staff. Complete their conversation with words or phrases from the list.

> possibly   say to   out   beyond
> stuck   firm   way round

Union representative So, we're all extremely worried. I would urge you to consider redeveloping the current site.

Managing Director Yes, I can understand your concern, but the decision is ¹_____ our control. We need to assume the move is going ahead and plan accordingly.

Union representative Well, if we really are ²_____ with this situation, then I want to make sure that the employees get a guarantee that they will be looked after.

Managing Director We can guarantee that most members of staff will be invited to move to the new site.

Union representative OK, but we can't ³_____ expect all staff members to move. They have family ties and partners with jobs here.

Managing Director Obviously, there will be some severance pay for those who leave us.

Union representative Well, yes, of course there will. But not everyone wants to leave the company.

Managing Director So they come with us to the new location. Simple as that.

Union representative No, it's not as simple as that. I have to stay ⁴_____ on this. We need to think about alternatives for the ones who can't move. What would you ⁵_____ offering people the option of working from home?

Managing Director That's not ⁶_____ of the question, but it wouldn't work with every job.

Union representative OK, but I don't think it's good enough to offer people a couple of months' salary and no further job prospects. We need to find a ⁷_____ this …

2 Choose the correct answer from the words in *italics*.

1 We have *arrived / got / reached* the point *which / where / when* we have no other option but to withdraw our custom.

2 Would you consider *of employing / employing / to employ* some extra staff for the project?

3 No, I'm afraid it is *not just / just not* possible.

4 Unfortunately, management is refusing to *change / budge / adapt* on this.

5 I'll go *along / willing / agree* with that.

6 We are *with / at / in* a very difficult situation right now.

7 Could we make *out / do / up* with a smaller order for now? I don't think we have enough cash to make our usual order.

8 I *had / can / would* be willing to offer a discount of 5%, if you ordered a minimum of 100 units.

9 I'm afraid I have *to say / to answer / to give* no to this contract – the price is just too high.

3 Correct the mistakes in this conversation.

A I can't understand why you're being so negative about this. We're in a very much difficult situation, and we really need to work together on this.

B I know, but this idea about job-sharing won't just work. It's not an effective use of time or resources. Would you consider re-allocate jobs and redefine roles instead?

A Well, I'd be willing hearing your suggestions, but I have to say no to redefine roles. People do the jobs they are skilled in doing. If we change that we'd need to start retraining, which is a further drain on resources.

B No, I agree that that's outside of the question, but what I meant was, reformulating job descriptions so that everybody is clear on where their job starts and ends.

A Hmm. I suppose that feasible. Do we all agreed that we need think about more fixed job descriptions?

Language at work

1 Rewrite the sentences so that the meaning is the same, using an inversion and the words or phrases in brackets.

1 Eric didn't get your email. And he didn't get your voicemail message either. (neither)

_____

2 I don't know how often she's away from her desk. And I don't care, really. (nor)

_____

3 It's not often that so many strong applicants have applied for a post with us. (seldom)

_____

4 Visitors must never go beyond reception without a pass. (under no circumstances)

_____

5 It's the first time that I've seen such a wonderful production. (never)

_____

6 I won't be satisfied until we're the market leader. (not until)

_____

7 They offer a very generous pension scheme. And they also offer flexitime. (not only)

_____

8 We've never failed to live up to our core values of decency, innovation, and trust. (at no time)

_____

2 Rewrite sentences 1–5 from this value statement. Use the words and phrases and an inversion. See the example.

Example:

1 *At PAFO Organics, not only are we committed to providing the best-tasting produce, we're also inspired to source the most ethical food available.*

only by   rarely   ~~not only~~   nor
under no circumstances

---

¹At PAFO Organics we are committed to providing the best-tasting produce and we're also inspired to source the most ethical food available. ²We won't accept food that hasn't been created with sustainability of resources in mind, under any circumstances. ³And we won't allow our food to travel thousands of miles unnecessarily.

We're passionate about sourcing the finest-tasting ingredients on offer. ⁴We can only do this by testing our produce regularly. ⁵But we don't often have to change suppliers; most of the small farmers who provide our vegetables are skilled agriculturists – many of them have won regional and national awards.

---

2 _____

3 _____

4 _____

5 _____

Working with words

1 Replace the phrases in *italics* in this email with a phrase from the list.

> generate a demand   play on   tailor
> reinforce an association   promote the consumption of

Dear Sylee

Here's an update on the advertising campaign for the new drink. Our discussions have led us to believe we have to *create the need* ¹_____ for our product amongst 14 to 21-year-olds. By showing young people with the product we can *strengthen the connection* ²_____ between them, and promote the idea that if you drink our product, you'll be 'in' with the trendy crowd. We know that young people do anything they can to avoid being an outsider, and we can *take advantage of* ³_____ their insecurities and fears about this.

We're really pleased with the work that CHMedia has done so far and they're now going to *adapt* ⁴_____ our usual slogan towards our new target group. It's an exciting project and one that will definitely *encourage people to purchase* ⁵_____ our beverages.

Let me know if you have any questions. I've attached the first drafts.

Bea

2 Complete these sentences with the correct preposition.

1 The message we want to put _____ is one of 'belonging'.

2 We're hoping to appeal _____ the younger market.

3 We want young professionals to buy _____ the lifestyle that we portray.

4 We think our target customers will be easily taken _____ by the idea that owning our product will improve their social status.

5 The advertising agency have picked _____ on several potential problems with our proposed logo and slogan.

6 The first draft of the advert didn't really live _____ to our expectations.

7 I think we need to hold _____ for a much improved second draft of the advert – we can wait for another two months, so we should push for what we want.

8 The economy is in trouble and people are trying to cut their spending, so I think we should tap _____ this by pushing our low-price 'value' products.

3 Choose the correct answer from the words in *italics*.

1 We all want to work hard for Suzy, she's a good leader and really *aspirational / motivational*.

2 Jens has a lot of ambition, and he's very *aspirational / materialistic* – he wants our team to win the sales team of the year award!

3 With this new product we're hoping for rapid *USP / market penetration* ahead of the competition.

4 It's well-known that they expect their employees to reach impossible deadlines, even if it means working through the night. I think that's really *exploitative / materialistic* and they have to change their policies if they want to improve their reputation.

5 Helen is very worried about what her neighbours think of her new car. If she's not careful she'll start suffering from *materialistic / status-anxiety*.

6 The product is selling extremely well because it has a *USP / consumer profile* that no competitor could match.

7 Kids these days always want new gadgets and are never satisfied – we were never so *materialistic / exploitative* when we were young.

8 We've studied purchasing trends and have drawn up some very accurate *consumer profiles / market penetration*.

Business communication skills

1 Complete this presentation with phrases from the list.

> second point   strong position   having said
> become apparent   very much   is achievable
> comes across   because we   first benefit
> serious consideration

'So, we're here today to discuss change. It has ¹_____ that although you all know change is inevitable, you don't want to face up to it. Also, what ²_____ from talking to many of you is your reluctance to embrace the changes. I'd like to reassure you that this can only be a positive move. Let's look at the plus points; by changing our internal structure we can optimize our skills and strengths …

… OK, that's the ³_____. Now, the ⁴_____ – if we become more efficient, it'll be easier to meet customer demand. But ⁵_____ that, it's important to remember to stay focused and not overreach ourselves. Our goal here is to gain market share. I believe a 5% increase by the end of the year ⁶_____. No question. Through hard work and determination we'll succeed. In fact, we're in an extremely ⁷_____. Why? ⁸_____ have both the knowledge and the resources. I ⁹_____ hope that you'll support me in this. Please give ¹⁰_____ not only to the company's future, but your future. Change does make sense.'

2 Match 1–6 to a–f.

1 I know that, like me, ____

2 Not only that, it's ____

3 We're committed, we're motivated, ____

4 You could argue that we're taking a risk, ____

5 I'm calling ____

6 We could be missing out on ____

a and we believe in what we do.

b on you to support this change.

c you are concerned about the future of the company.

d a great opportunity if we don't pursue this.

e but on balance it will be worse if we don't act now.

f also essential that we put the necessary finances in place to fund this.

Language at work

1 Choose the correct answer from the words in *italics*.

Jason

Time's running out for the in-house magazine! ¹*Basically / Mind you*, the editorial team have had enough of waiting for articles and have started writing them themselves. It's ²*obviously / anyway* been forgotten that they have real jobs to do too! ³*Of course / Anyway*, could you send whatever you've collected? ⁴*After all / So to speak*, anything is better than nothing at all.

⁵*Quite honestly / Admittedly*, I don't know why they don't scale it down to publishing it twice a year. We discussed this a few months ago but no one seemed very keen. ⁶*As a matter of fact / Obviously*, when Henri left the meeting he was so upset! ⁷*Quite honestly / Admittedly*, someone said they found the themes he suggested for articles boring!

Have you heard, Ivica's abandoning us, ⁸*mind you / so to speak*? She's taking a year off to travel. She says if she doesn't do it now she never will. ⁹*As I was saying / Mind you*, I don't blame her. Her department's changed so much since the shake-up. ¹⁰*Of course / After all*, she didn't say that was the reason for leaving, but we all think it is. ¹¹*Basically / To tell you the truth*, I'd think of travelling the world if I worked for her boss!

Tanya

2 Complete this conversation with the correct answer from the options in 1–10.

A Look, James – we're really having problems here. ¹_____, I think we should cancel our stand at the Mumbai conference.

B ²_____, that seems like a bit of a radical solution – I'm really not sure about it.

A I know what you mean, but ³_____, we're just not going to be ready to put together a decent stand by May.

B ⁴_____, I'm still not convinced. ⁵_____, all of our most important customers will be expecting us to have a big presence there.

A Yes, but our stand is going to look terrible. ⁶_____, that's not going to give our company a very good image in the industry. ⁷_____, I think we should consider other methods of promotion and avoid the conference – we could print extra copies of our catalogue and advertising posters, for example.

B OK – those are good ideas, and ⁸_____ that would be the easier option, but I really think we should do those in addition to having the stand. If we all work really hard I'm sure we can get it ready in time for Mumbai.

A I really don't think having the stand will be possible. ⁹_____, if we could get more people involved in the preparation it might be possible, I suppose. ¹⁰_____ we need to sort this out immediately. Could you find out if we would be able to expand the team?

1	a Of course	b	If you ask me
2	a Quite honestly	b	Mind you
3	a after all	b	as I was saying
4	a As a matter of fact	b	To tell you the truth
5	a After all	b	So to speak
6	a Obviously	b	Anyway
7	a Of course	b	Basically
8	a admittedly	b	so to speak
9	a Mind you	b	As a matter of fact
10	a So to speak	b	Anyway

Unit 1 | Tenses

Present simple

Use the present simple

1 to talk about general facts, states, and situations
*The purpose of business **is** to make a profit.*

2 to talk about regular or repeated actions, or permanent situations
*Jack **works** for Nissan.*

3 to talk about timetabled future events
*The meeting **starts** at 10.00.*

Present continuous

Use the present continuous

1 to talk about an action in progress at the time of speaking / writing
*I'm **trying** to get through to Jon Berks.*

2 to talk about a very current activity, taking place around the time of speaking
*They **are pushing** the area for development.*

3 to talk about fixed plans or arrangements in the future
*I **am meeting** the management committee on Friday.*

Watch out! Don't forget that stative verbs are not commonly used in the continuous form. Here are some examples: *like, love, hate, want, need, know, suppose, understand, remember, seem.*

Present perfect simple

Use the present perfect simple

1 to talk about actions which finished recently and for which there is a present result
Recent action: *The IT guys **have changed** all the PCs and access codes.*
Result: New PCs and access codes.

2 to talk about actions that started in the past and are still going on
*Silvio **has worked** for us since he left school.*

3 to talk about experiences in your life or events in history
*I've never **been** to Bahrain.*

Present perfect continuous

Use the present perfect continuous to talk about a recently completed action. The focus is on the activity, not the result.
*The IT guys **have been changing** all the PCs and access codes.*
(Implication: There are still wires and tools lying around showing that they have only just finished.)

Past simple

Use the past simple

1 to talk about past actions which are over at the time of speaking
*I **heard** from the locals that there were several interesting sites.*

2 to talk about past states
*I **lived** in Haringey when I worked in the City.*

Past continuous

Use the past continuous to talk about being in the middle of a past action – there is likely to be an interruption (in the past simple) in the sentence.
*Everything **was going** really smoothly, when Wu **took** over the project.*

Past perfect

Use the past perfect to put events in the past in sequence. The past perfect indicates that the action it refers to happened before a reference to the past simple.
*I **had heard** from the locals that there **were** several interesting sites.*

Past perfect continuous

Use the past perfect continuous to refer to an action in progress before something else happened.
*He was the one **who had been working** on the project, but his boss was the one who got all the credit.*

Should

1 Use *should* + infinitive to recommend something strongly.
*You **should try** that vegetarian restaurant on the river.*

2 Use *should* + perfect infinitive to talk about a lost opportunity.
*You **should have gone** this morning – it was quite an interesting meeting.*

3 Use *could / should* + infinitive to predict.
*It **could / should turn out** to be quite an interesting conference.*

Future forms

1 Use *will* + infinitive to make on-the-spot decisions.
*We'll **have to** point out the training need to the client.*

2 Use *be going to* + infinitive when we are talking about an action we have already given some thought to.
*We're **going to have to** point out the training need to the client.*

3 Use the future continuous to talk about something that will be in progress at a particular time in the future.
*I **will be writing** everything up later this week.*

4 Use the future perfect to refer to events which finish before a given time.
*I **will have finished** by the end of the next financial year.*

》 For more on the future, see **Language reference Unit 3** on page 127.

Unit 2 | Expressing attitudes to the past

Third conditional

1 Use the third conditional to talk about past situations that did not happen.
*If you **had chased up** the reference, you **would have known** not to employ him.*

2 Note that only the situation in the clause with *had* (the *if*-clause) must be in the past. The other situation can be past, present, or future: something that did not happen, or is not happening, or will not happen, but which is seen to be linked with the situation in the *if*-clause.
*If I **had got** the job at Chelco, I **would have been made** redundant when the company folded. (past situation, past result)*
*If I **had got** that job, I **would have been able to** afford to buy property by now. (past situation, present result)*
*If I **had got** that job, I **would have been able to** retire in two years' time. (past situation, future result)*

3 The result clause usually has *would*, but we can use *might* instead for a less likely result, and *could* to express possibility.

> If we **had reduced** prices, more people **might have bought** our products. (= would perhaps)
>
> If you'**d told** me before about the operation, I **could have arranged** cover for you. (= it would have been possible for me to arrange cover for you)

4 Informally, we can use *'d* as a short form of *had* in the *if*-clause, and as a short form of *would* in the result clause.

> I'**d have** phoned if I'**d known**.

5 We often use the third conditional to express regret, or to analyse past actions (especially for criticisms).

> If I **had sold** my shares in May, I **would have made** a good profit.

6 When the past situation is negative, the effect is sometimes to congratulate ourselves or others for the actions they took. This can also happen with past situations that are not grammatically negative, but which are seen as undesirable.

> If you **hadn't warned** us about that supplier, we **would have had** serious problems. Thank you so much!
>
> If we **had followed** the consultant's advice, **we'd have** probably **gone** bankrupt. (It's a good thing we didn't!)

>> For more information on conditionals, see **Language reference Unit 9** on page 131.

Perfect modals

1 The **bolded** result clause in this third conditional sentence would make sense on its own. This section of the sentence is a perfect modal (a modal verb followed by a perfect infinitive).

> If we had invested in Northern Rock, **we would have lost nearly everything**.

This pattern is especially useful to talk about our likely actions if we were in the situation described.

> **I would have told** my manager straight away, rather than hiding everything.

2 We can also use *could, might, should, ought to,* and *needn't* followed by perfect infinitives (perfect modals) to talk about things that did not happen in the past. Notice that *should* and *ought to* often express irritation and criticism, and that *might* and *could* also do this in many contexts.

> You **could have told** me you'd be late.
>
> I **might have known** the distributors would let us down.
>
> They **should have consulted** me about the cancellation.
>
> They **ought to have warned** us about the strike.
>
> You **needn't have sent** flowers – but they're lovely.

Other ways of expressing condition

1 There are several other words we can use instead of *if* in the *if*-clause of a third conditional sentence.

> **If** we had invested in Northern Rock, we would have lost nearly everything.
>
> **Suppose / Supposing** we had invested in Northern Rock …
>
> **Imagine if** we had invested in Northern Rock …

2 Use *if only* to emphasize regrets and wishes.

> **If only** we hadn't relocated, we'd be sitting on €1 million of real estate by now.

3 We can use *even if* to talk about an unreal past situation, but to say that it would make no difference to the situation in the result clause.

> **Even if** we had kept to our schedules, the manufacturers probably wouldn't have kept to theirs.

4 Note that we do not usually use *unless* with the same meaning as *if not* in third conditionals, but we can use it with the meaning *except if*.

> I wouldn't have employed him, **unless** he had had exceptional references. (I didn't employ him.)

5 We can use *whether* when we are talking about two or more past situations that would have had the same result.

> **Whether** we had given the job to Hogg, Curtis, Xama, or Kzenksy, they would have had a difficult task ahead.

Unit 3 | Speculating about future changes

Will / shall or going to

In many sentences and situations, either *will* or *going to* is possible. However, in general use *will*

1 to make predictions based on experience

> We've changed the job description so more people **will** apply.

2 to give or ask for information about the future

> When **will** we need to be ready?

3 to make future promises, requests, and threats

> **Will** you give me a hand?

4 to make spontaneous decisions (at the time of speaking)

> You're running late? OK, well, I'**ll** start the presentation without you.

5 Note that for offers and suggestions, we use *will* in positive and negative sentences, but *shall* in questions.

> **Shall** we have a quick drink before dinner?

Use *going to*

6 to make predictions based on our current feelings and thoughts

> I'm **going to** get angry in a minute.

7 to talk or ask about plans or intentions

> Sue's **going to** attend the Milan conference in June.

8 to talk about decisions that have already been made

> I'm **going to** give Ed a written warning, no matter what he says.

9 Note that we also use the present continuous for arrangements.

> Jeremy's **attending** the conference in Berlin in May.

Future continuous, future perfect, and future perfect continuous

1 Use the future continuous (*will* + *be* + *-ing* form) to say that something will be in progress at a time in the future. The focus is on the future actions, rather than their result.

> This time next year, I'**ll be playing** golf on afternoons like this.

2 Note that *going to* + *be* + *-ing* form is also possible, especially for plans and intentions.

> We're **going to be experimenting** with Internet campaigns from next March.

3 Use the future perfect (*will* + *have* + past participle) to say that something will be finished at a time in the future.

> Our end of year figures **will have come out** by the time of our next meeting.

4 Use the future perfect continuous (*will* + *have* + *been* + *-ing* form) to stress the continuation of an action, seen from a later time in the future.

> Our companies **will have been working** together for ten years in May – we should plan a celebration.

Certainty and the future

1 Several modals can be used to make predictions about change in the future, with different degrees of certainty.

> The recession in Spain **might / could / will** affect sales across Europe.

2 With similar meaning, *will* + adverbial (negative: adverbial + *won't*) is possible.

> The Spanish recession **will perhaps** affect pan-European sales.
> The euro's strength **probably won't** continue beyond June.

We can also use a range of adjectives

3 with structures like *be … to …*

> The Spanish recession **is (un)likely / expected / certain / bound to** affect sales across Europe.

4 with structures like *it's … that … will …*

> **It's (un)likely / probable / certain that** the Spanish recession **will** affect sales across Europe.

Note that not all these adjectives can be used with both structures. For example, we can say *bound to*, but not *bound that*, and *probable that*, but not *probable to*.

We can also use adverbs of degree (*quite, very, really,* etc.) with most of these structures, to add emphasis or distance.

> The Spanish recession is **quite** likely to affect sales across Europe.

Unit 4 | Pronouns *it, this,* and *that*

Referring backwards

It, this, and *that* can be used to refer back to something that has just been mentioned.

All three words can refer back to a person or thing, a situation, or a thought / idea / proposition, etc.

> He said the greater the risk, the greater the potential reward. **This** might well be true.
> Here's our prototype. **It** gives a pretty good idea of what we hope to make.
> John was arguing for cuts in the R&D budget. **That's** the last thing we need.

Emphasis

1 *It* is used for neutral reference: as a simple way of continuing the discussion, without giving special emphasis to the information being referred to.

> There's also a subsidised canteen. **It's** OK, but no better than in most companies.

2 *This* and *that* are more often used to add emphasis to the information: they draw our attention to what has just been said.

> And we have a gym exclusively for staff. **That's** one of the best things about working here.

3 *This* in particular is used when there is something new or especially relevant about the information introduced.

> Finally, there's our final salary pension scheme. **This** has been praised throughout the industry.

Reference

1 In sentences where several things are mentioned, *it* is usually used to refer to the main topic, whereas *this / that* more often refer to the last topic mentioned.

> There's a meeting in the Kennedy Suite. **It's** very important and could go on for hours. (it = the meeting)
> There's a meeting in the Kennedy Suite. **That's** on the third floor, by the lifts. (that = the Kennedy Suite)

2 Generally, *this* refers to things that are near to us (in space, in time, or conceptually – thought of as close and relevant); *that* refers to things we think of as more distant.

> Carlos asked about the depreciation of the dollar. **This** will affect us all, he said.
> Carlos asked about the depreciation of the euro. **That** was unlikely in the foreseeable future, Kate answered.

He, she, they, these, those

1 When we are referring to a person mentioned in the previous sentence, *he* or *she* is used in the same way as *it*.

> Heather was the first of the candidates to be interviewed. **She** was very impressive.

2 When the information referred to has a plural form, *they* is used instead of *it*, *these* instead of *this*, and *those* instead of *that*.

> We discussed several options during the brainstorming sessions. **They** were all considered impractical, though.
> We discussed several options during the brainstorming sessions. **These** were quite good fun, by the way, but hard work.

New information

This can refer forward to new information. We do not use *that* or *it* in this way.

> Craig isn't a great team player. **This** is his main problem, though – his lack of creativity. (refers forward to the new information about his lack of creativity)
> Craig isn't a great team player. **That's** his main problem. (refers back to the information about the fact that he is not a great team player)

Even when *this* is used to refer to old information, there is always a sense that what we are going to say about it is new.

Unit 5 | Adding emphasis

Adverbs of degree

1 Adverbs of degree can add emphasis to most adjectives and adverbs. These include: *very, really, extremely, so, just so, very … indeed*.

> It was **just so** short-sighted of them to risk upsetting our Japanese distributors.

2 Some adjectives and adverbs are ungradable: they express extreme qualities such as perfection. With these words we use adverbs such as *completely, absolutely, utterly* (not *very*).

> It's **absolutely** vital that you inform me of things like that. (Not: ~~It's very vital that you inform me of things like that.~~)

>> For more information on adverbs of degree, see **Language reference Unit 6** on page 129.

Fronting

1 In most active sentences, the subject of the verb comes first. However, we can alter the word order to place the information we want to emphasize at the beginning of the sentence. This is call 'fronting'.

> *I liked the conference hall, but I thought the accommodation was awful.* → ***The conference hall** I liked. **The accommodation** I thought was awful.*

2 Note that subject and verb / auxiliary are inverted after negative expressions, after *only,* and after participles.

> ***Rarely have I** seen such a confident presentation.*
> ***Only in Japan can you** get fish as fresh as this.*
> ***Included** in the contract **was a** job description.*

It-clefts

Form

it + *be* + emphasized language + relative clause

Use

To focus our attention on a noun phrase or adverbial.

> *It was <u>the finance director</u> who suggested freezing recruitment.*
> *It was <u>earlier this morning</u> that she phoned me.*

What-clefts

Form

what + noun phrase / clause + *be* + emphasized language

Use

To move our attention to the end of the sentence.

> ***What** he does is <u>assess proposals</u>.*
> ***What** I want is <u>an evening off</u>.*

Other phrases

We can also use phrases such as *the person / people who / that, the place where, the reason why, the thing that* to add emphasis.

> <u>Tom</u> *is **the person that** you need to speak to.*
> ***The place where** our 2012 conference will be held is <u>Brighton</u>.*
> ***The thing that** annoys me most is that <u>no one contacted us</u> about the problem.*

Unit 6 | Adverbs
Adverbs of degree

1 Many adverbs of degree are used to qualify the gradable adjective or adverb they precede, e.g. *quite, rather, pretty, fairly, a bit, a little,* and, especially in American English, *somewhat.*

> *The figures were **quite** promising.*
> *He suggested, **rather** stupidly, that we forget about the deadlines.*

2 We can use most of these words with adjective + noun combinations. Note the word order with *quite.*

> *It was **a rather tedious speech**.*
> *It was **quite a good party**. (Not: It was a quite good party.)*

3 We can also use an adverb of degree with *not,* e.g. *not very, not really, not absolutely.* We can also say *not at all.*

> *I'm **not very / not at all** concerned about the canteen's closure.*

4 Note that *not really* can mean both *not very* and *not, in fact.* The word stress (see the <u>underlined</u> words in the examples) in the sentence helps to convey the different meanings.

> *I'm **not really** <u>angry</u> about her resignation, just disappointed. (not angry, in fact)*
> *He wasn't <u>really</u> angry, but he raised his voice. (a bit angry)*

5 When the adverb comes before *not,* the meaning is different.

> *I'm **not absolutely** convinced. (less than 100%)*
> *I'm **absolutely not** convinced. (0%)*

Note that putting the adverb before *not* isn't possible with *very.*

> *I'm not **very** happy with this situation.(Not: I'm very not happy with this situation.)*

Focus adverbs

1 The adverbs *even, just,* and *only* focus our attention on one part of a sentence. They usually come before a main verb, but after an auxiliary or *be.*

> *Exetica **only** had better results than us in May. (not in June, etc.)*
> *I **just** don't understand why team A didn't complete the first away day task. (I really don't understand)*
> *Jo couldn't **even** remember all the details. (a criticism of Jo)*

2 If these adverbs refer to a noun phrase then they come before it, and the meaning is changed.

> ***Only** Exetica had better results than us in May. (no other company)*
> *I don't understand why team A didn't complete **just** the first away day task. (they managed to complete all the others)*
> *I don't understand why **just** team A didn't complete the first away day task. (all the other teams managed to do it)*
> ***Even** Jo couldn't remember all the details. (Jo is expected to be good at remembering and the fact that she couldn't indicates that there were a lot of details.)*

Functional adverbials

Adverbials are often used to refine the message conveyed by the sentence, without altering the meaning of any individual words. For example, they can be used

1 to soften negative reactions

> ***Unfortunately**, I can't agree with you. (also: regrettably, sadly)*

2 to provide a link to what someone else has said

> ***Of course**, you're right about that, but … (also: no doubt, obviously, evidently, certainly)*

3 to move the subject of conversation / writing onto a different area

> ***Frankly**, I'd prefer not to discuss that … (also: to be honest, honestly, actually)*

Unit 7 | Participle clauses | Future in the past
Participle clauses

1 An adverbial clause begins with a conjunction (e.g. *because, when, after*) and gives extra information about the main topic in a sentence.

> ***When I travel by train**, I prefer to sit by the window.*

Often it is possible to use a clause with a present participle instead. This is called a participle clause.

> ***Travelling** by train, I prefer to sit by the window.*

2 We can use most conjunctions before the participle. An exception is *because*.

> *After travelling by train, I needed some fresh air. (Not: ~~Because travelling by train, I allowed plenty of time.~~)*

3 Usually, we use the present participle (verb + -*ing*) for present and recent situations, in place of the present simple / continuous / perfect, and past simple / continuous.

> *Since **living** in Dubai, I've learnt to cope with hot weather. (= since I have lived …)*
>
> ***Learning** English, I often wrote difficult words on post-it notes. (= when I was learning … / learnt …)*

4 *Having* + past participle is used in place of the past perfect (for a past action before another past action).

> ***Having decided** to hire Fatima Mattar, we made her a job offer. (= after we had decided)*

5 We can use a passive participle in place of a passive adverbial structure.

> ***Offered** the job, I wasn't sure whether to accept it. (= when I had been offered the job)*

6 Note also *given*, which has a meaning similar to *because* + *be*.

> ***Given** his reluctance to accept criticism, you'll have to be careful how you word the letter. (= because he is reluctant …)*

Future in the past

Was going to

1 We can use *was going to* to talk about the future from a point of view in the past: to talk about things that were planned, or former intentions.

> *I **was going to** visit our Alicante office too, but my plane was delayed.*

2 It is the intention that is in the past and has changed. The time the plan / intention refers to can be in the future.

> ***Tomorrow** we **were going to** go to the races, but the course has been flooded.*

3 The time the plan / intention refers to can also be in the past.

> ***Yesterday** I **was going to** have my appraisal, but my boss was ill.*

4 This structure is often used to explain why something did not happen, to make excuses, to explain changes to plans, to give background to our current intentions / thoughts.

> *Hi, John. I **was going to** call you today, but I totally forgot.*
>
> *We **were going to** have the meeting in the café, but it was too noisy.*
>
> *I **was going to** invite Denis out to dinner tonight. Do you think it's a good idea?*

5 We can also use perfect tenses with *going to*, for different perspectives in the past.

> *She's **been going to** visit this office for ages – I don't think she ever will.*
>
> *They **had been going to** make me redundant, if I hadn't taken early retirement.*

Other structures

A number of other structures are also possible.

1 The past continuous can be used for former arrangements (just as we would use the present continuous for a current arrangement).

> *I **was meeting** their sales rep at 3.00 p.m., but he's just cancelled. (Compare with: I'm meeting their sales rep at 3.00 p.m.)*

2 *Was to / were to* is possible, as the past form of *be to*, particularly to talk in a formal style about past plans and arrangements.

> *We **were to** launch the product at the International Spring Convention. Unfortunately there were delays beyond our control.*

Unit 8 | Using questions

Yes / no questions

Yes / no questions are questions that could be answered *yes* or *no*. They usually begin with an auxiliary verb or *be*, followed by the subject. It is usually impolite to reply with just *yes* or *no*. Extra words are necessary for politeness, and often giving extra, more detailed information is appropriate.

> ***Is this** the best solution? ~ **Yes**, after detailed research we're convinced that it is.*

Wh- questions

Wh- questions ask for specific information about people, places, etc., and begin with *what, where, when, why, how, which, how many*, etc., followed by inversion of subject and auxiliary (note the position of *did* and *you* in the example below).

> ***Where did you** study for your MBA? ~ In Stanford. Why do you ask?*

Indirect questions and modals in questions

1 In indirect questions, the question that asks for information is contained ('embedded') within another question or a statement. Note that, unlike with standard questions, there is no inversion of subject and auxiliary.

> *I'd like to know **how many days annual leave you offer**.*

2 Modal verbs are also used to make a question less direct.

> ***Would** you say that you're a team player? (Rather than: Are you a team player?)*
>
> ***May** I ask if you'd be likely to accept the job?*
>
> ***Could** I check whether you've signed in with security?*

Other ways of asking questions

1 A statement can sometimes have the function of a question. In writing, this is shown by a question mark (?). In speaking, there is a rise in intonation.

> ***And you trained as a lawyer before moving into banking?** ~ Yes, that's right.*

2 Particularly in speech, we can sometimes use parts of statements to similar effect.

> ***And your other interests?** ~ I like football and tennis.*

Question tags

1 We can follow a statement with a question tag (inverted subject and auxiliary / *do* / *be*), to check or confirm information, or check that the person we are talking to agrees with or is following us. Usually a positive statement has a negative tag, and vice versa.

> *They said they'd arrive around 9.00 p.m., **didn't they**?*
>
> *It's probably best if we deal with that later, **don't you think**?*

2 Note that it is possible to have a positive tag after a positive statement, to express a reaction to something you have just heard, for example.

*And you're happy with that decision, **are you**?*

Functions of questions

Beyond asking for information, questions can have a range of functions. We can use them

1 to check that the audience is following / understands

It's not, is it, a question of threats, but of opportunities, do you see?

2 to set up / introduce a subject which you then explain

What are our objectives for the coming year? Well, first of all, we hope to …

3 to give yourself time to think, or to give the audience a pause in concentration

And then, erm, how can I put this? Well, we have decided that …

4 to challenge what someone has said

And you really believe that these measures will have an effect, do you?
~ Well, they should certainly help relieve the pressure in the short term.

5 to lead someone towards a specific point of view

That may not be a good thing, surely?
Don't you agree that it's better to wait?

Unit 9 | Conditionals
Form

These are the main conditional forms.

Type	Situation	Result
zero	*If* + present	present
	If you hand in work late,	*you make a bad impression.*
first	*If* + present	*will* + infinitive
	If we lose the contract,	*we'll be in trouble.*
second	*If* + past tense	*would* + infinitive
	If we lost the contract,	*my job would be on the line.*
third	*If* + past perfect	*would have* + infinitive
	If we'd got the contract,	*we would have made a lot of money.*

Zero conditionals

1 Use zero conditionals when the relationship between the situation and result is always true or always the same; there is no element of chance or doubt.

*If we **hit** our targets, we **get** a bonus.*

2 We can also use two past tenses, to talk about something that always used to be true.

*We **got** time off in lieu if we **worked** weekends.*

3 Informally, we can use this structure where a first conditional would be more appropriate in a formal situation.

*If we **lose** the contract, we're in trouble.*

First conditional

1 Use the first conditional when a situation is very likely to have the result given.

*If you **arrive** late, you'**ll miss** the first part of the meeting.*

2 The present continuous and present perfect are possible in the *if*-clause.

*If Jenny'**s working** on this project, she'll learn a lot of useful stuff.*
*If Amit'**s broken** his leg, you'll have to give the presentation.*

3 Other modal expressions such as *can, may, be going to* are possible in the result clause.

*If we don't gain market share, we **may** be in a sticky situation.*
*I'**m going to** change distributors if Kikibo don't get their act together.*

Second conditional

1 Use the second conditional when a situation is hypothetical or imagined.

*If taxes **rose**, we **would consider** relocating.*

2 The second conditional is also useful to make suggestions, offers, warnings, etc. more distant and polite.

*If you **arrived** at meetings on time, we'**d get** much more done.*

3 *Might* and *could* are also possible in the result clause.

*We **could** save hundreds of hours if we adopted the new system.*

Mixed conditionals

1 It is possible to use the *if*-clause of a second conditional (*if* + past simple) with the result clause of a third conditional (*would* + perfect infinitive). This is an example of a mixed conditional.

*If you **cared** more about your work, you **would have been promoted** years ago.*

Note that here we are talking about a general hypothetical situation, with an imagined past result.

2 More often we use the *if*-clause of a third conditional (*if* + past perfect) with the result clause of a second conditional (*would* + present / continuous infinitive).

*If I **had got** the job, I **would earn** €100,000 by now. (would + present infinitive)*
*If I **had got** the job, I **would be commuting** for four hours a day. (would + continuous infinitive)*

Note that here we are imagining something that didn't happen in the past, with a present result.

▶▶ For more information on the third conditional, see **Language reference Unit 2** on page 126.

Passives

Passive forms are possible in all types of conditional sentence, in either clause.

*If the contract **is lost**, we'll be in trouble.*
*If we adopted the new system, hundreds of hours **could be saved**.*

Other words instead of *if*

1 In many conditional sentences, *when* can replace *if*. This makes a situation sound more likely. The same is true of *every time*.

***When** we hit our targets, we get a bonus.*
***Every time** we hit our targets, we get a bonus.*

2 In zero, first, and second conditionals, we can use *unless* to mean 'except if' or 'if not'.

> **Unless** *we keep our contract with Zimiercz, we'll be without a Polish partner company.*

3 Participles such as *providing, provided, assuming,* and *supposing,* and phrases such as *on the condition that* and *as long as,* can also replace *if.*

> **Providing** *the building goes well, our new offices will be ready in May 2012.*
>
> **As long as** *the pound stays strong, our projections will be realistic.*

Unit 10 | The passive

Forms

1 In all tenses (simple, continuous, or perfect) we form the passive with *be* in the appropriate tense + past participle.

> *Mistakes* **were being made.** *(past continuous)*
>
> *Eight applications* **have been received.** *(present perfect)*

2 Passive modals are also possible in simple, continuous, or perfect forms.

> *Forms* **may be filled in** *with black ink, or typed.*
>
> *The computer network* **must be being updated** *– I can't access it.*
>
> *Your timesheet* **should have been received** *by now.*

Semi-modals (e.g. *have to, be going to*) follow the same rules.

> *You're* **going to be offered** *a position in the Frankfurt office.*

3 A passive infinitive is *to be* + past participle. A passive perfect infinitive is *to have been* + past participle.

> *I'm delighted* **to be offered** *the post, but unfortunately I must decline.*
>
> *I'm delighted* **to have been offered** *the post, but unfortunately I must decline.*

4 A passive -*ing* form is *being* + past participle. A passive perfect -*ing* form is *having been* + past participle.

> **Being asked** *to leave the company wasn't pleasant.*
>
> **Having been offered** *three options, Jim chose the cheapest.*

5 The object of an active sentence becomes the subject of a passive sentence. If a verb has two objects, either object can become the subject.

> *Someone at the door gave us a handout.*
>
> <u>We</u> **were given** *a handout.*
>
> <u>A handout</u> **was given** *to us.*

Verbs that do not take an object (e.g. *go, come, fall*) cannot be made passive.

> *Profits fell last year. (Not: ~~Profits were fallen last year.~~)*

Use

1 We use the passive to focus attention on the action mentioned, or on the object of the action (the person or thing affected by it). We do not know who does the action, or it isn't important.

> *The office* **has been redecorated.** *It looks so much better than before!*

2 Using the passive helps create an impersonal style. This is often appropriate in formal English, for example in business letters and reports, where a personal style would not be appropriate.

> *Results for the first quarter* **were published** *on 6 April, and were strong.*

3 The passive is a useful way of adding distance between an action and those doing it, for example, when giving people bad news.

> *Regrettably, redundancies* **will have to be made.** *Some of those sitting here* **will be affected.** *(Compare: I'll have to make redundancies. It will affect some of you.)*

4 In discourse, we often choose to use the passive if it provides a better link with the sentence before. In these cases, we can say who does the action using *by.*

> *We asked for ways to improve customer relations. Making changes to our complaints procedure* **was suggested by** *several respondents.*

Passive reporting

1 We use the passive with reporting verbs when we don't know, or would prefer not to say, whose words we are reporting – for example, if their identity is confidential or sensitive.

> **I've been asked** *to write you a reference.*

2 In the active sentence below, *Carol* is an indirect object.

> *Jim told* **Carol** *the likely result of the restructuring.*

The indirect object becomes the subject of a passive sentence.

> **Carol** *was told the likely result of the restructuring.*

Some reporting verbs do not take an indirect object, so cannot form passives in this way. These include: *agree, allege, announce, argue, claim, decide, predict, report, say, state,* and *suggest.* Instead, we use them in a structure with an empty subject: *it* + *be* + past participle + *that.*

> **It was alleged that** *you stole money from the company.*

Unit 11 | Inversion

Questions

The most common uses of inversion word order are in questions and short answers.

1 In inversion word order, the auxiliary comes before the subject.

> **Have you** *got any paperclips? ~ No. ~ Neither* **have I.**

2 *Do / does* is used as an auxiliary with simple-tense verbs.

> **Does Chris** *like the new receptionist?*

3 Ordinary verbs *be* and *have* and modal auxiliaries do not require *do.*

> **Was I** *the best candidate?*
>
> **Can you** *help us?*

As well as in questions, inversion is used in a variety of structures, often rather formally.

Negative expressions

1 Inversion is used after the negative words *neither* and *nor,* and after phrases with *not* and *no.*

> **In no way do I** *accept their conclusions.* **Neither do I** *think the report should be circulated.*
>
> **Not without careful thought am I** *writing this letter.* **Nor is it** *without having consulted several of my closest associates.*

2 We also use inversion after adverbs such as *seldom, rarely, scarcely, hardly (ever), little* that restrict the meaning / reference of the verb that follows.

> **Rarely have I** *been to such a well-organized product launch.*
>
> **Little did we** *know that she had accepted a position with our rivals.*

Only

When *only* is used with time expressions or prepositional phrases, the verb that follows is inverted.

*Only before 30 September **can you** hand in a non-calculated tax return.*

*Only by travelling overland **can you** really appreciate a country.*

Participles

When participles are moved to the front position, inversion takes place in formal English.

*Waiting for us in his office **was my boss**.*

Conditionals

Instead of saying *if I had, if she was*, etc., we can use inversion. Note that *was* becomes *were*.

Had the minister *announced the tax increases more openly, he would have faced a storm of criticism.*

Had I *been told about the dress code, I wouldn't have felt such a fool.*

Were she *to be fired, she'd probably sue.*

We can use the inverted structure *should* + subject as another way of expressing condition.

Should we *require further information, we will contact you again. (= If we require …)*

These forms are especially common with passive structures.

Unit 12 | Discourse markers

Truthfulness

1 *Honestly* and *frankly* are used to claim that the speaker is telling the truth. Often they introduce criticism or negative remarks. *Quite* adds emphasis to both words.

Frankly, *I didn't like the venue.*

Quite honestly, *I thought your comments were ill-judged.*

2 *To tell you the truth* and *to be honest* have a similar function.

To tell you the truth, *I didn't enjoy the conference.*

To be honest, *the meeting was a complete waste of time.*

Strengthening arguments

All of the following discourse markers stress the importance of the point that follows.

1 We can use *in fact, as a matter of fact*, and *after all* to suggest that an opinion is not personal, but is based on evidence.

As a matter of fact, *house prices fell by 2.5% last month.*

2 We can use *if you ask me* and *I must say* to suggest that it is personal.

If you ask me, *the government is to blame for ruining the economy.*

3 We can use *clearly, of course, naturally, obviously, undoubtedly*, and *after all* to suggest that what will follow is not controversial or will not be questioned.

Clearly, *the next two years will be critical for the future of the economy.*

Concession

1 We can use *admittedly, to be sure, it's true that*, to acknowledge that someone has made a good point before disagreeing with them, or to concede a negative point before making a different point. The sentence that follows often begins with *but* or *however*.

Admittedly, *the result could have been better.* **However**, *we retained our position as market leader.*

2 We can concede that someone else has a point before making our own point, to make our own point sound stronger or more carefully thought out. To do this, *admittedly, to be sure*, and *it's true that … but / however* are possible.

A *We're in danger of missing the deadline.*

B **It's true that** *we're dealing with an incredibly large workload at the moment, **but** I know that we can meet this deadline.*

Discourse patterns

Some discourse markers draw attention to the discourse itself – the pattern of what is said.

1 We can use the following to rephrase or paraphrase an argument: *as I was saying, as it were, I mean, if you like, so to speak, that's to say, to put it another way, well.*

*Your holiday could cause a real problem for … **well, I mean**, we need to amend the schedules, really.*

2 We can use the following to link to a new topic: *now, anyway, mind you, moving on, actually, indeed.*

*So, that's the plan for the next two months. **Anyway**, didn't you want to ask me about the sales figures?*

3 We can use the following to return to a previous topic: *anyway, as I was saying.*

*The contract was signed yesterday and … oh, David, you've decided to join us! **Anyway, as I was saying**, the contract has just been signed and …*

4 We can use the following to introduce a conclusion: *so, anyway, basically, in conclusion, to sum up.*

*That was what my report uncovered, so **basically**, we have to consolidate our product list over the next year.*

Acknowledging non-literal meanings

Some discourse markers show that language is being used in a way that is different from its usual, literal meaning: *so to speak, as it were, if you will / like.*

A *George seems quite volatile.*

B *Yeah, he's a bomb waiting to go off, **so to speak**.*

1 | Introducing yourself to a group

Saying who you are
Hi, my name's X. I'm from the Y office.
As most of you will know, I'm ...
For those of you who don't know me already, I am ...

Talking about your role
I'm accountable for ...
My responsibilities include ...
I'm empowered to ... and have the task of ...
Lately I've been concentrating on ...
Basically, my role is to coordinate ..., making sure ...
This entails ...
I'm responsible for ...

Giving your reasons for being there
What's the point of me being here today?
I hope to share some of my ideas with you.
I'm here today to ...

Updating people on achievements / activities
I'm pleased to say that ...
I've now managed to ...
I'd like to point out that over the years, I have been continually ...
We've had a great few years.
You'll be happy to know that ...

Talking about your aspirations
And I can see ways of further improving ...
We want to help out ...
I guess I'm ready to take on board ...
I can't wait to share our expertise with you and to help you ...

2 | Getting your point across

Reformulating
Yes, sorry, let me rephrase that ...
In other words, ...
To put it another way, ...

Clarifying what is meant
What I'm saying is that ...
I was actually referring to ...
What I mean by ... is ...
To clarify, I'm saying that ...

Illustrating or offering to illustrate a point
Would it help if I gave you an example?
Well, if you look at ... you'll see ...

Summarizing
The fact of the matter is ...
But the point I'm trying to make is ...
Basically, ...
To summarize, ...

3 | Showing understanding

Showing you understand the problem
I know what you mean.
No, it hasn't, has it?
I hear what you're saying ...
I can see where you're coming from.
I totally understand.

Explaining why you understand
It's quite hectic over here, too.
I know this is a tricky time for a lot of you.
I had a similar problem at ...
That happened to me, too.

Offering practical solutions
It might be worth ... -ing ...
I still think you should ...
You might want to ...
What about ... -ing?
Have you tried ... -ing?

4 | Establishing rapport

Recalling past events in common
It must be two years or more since we last met?
Wasn't it at that conference in ...?
Oh, yes, ... – it was really beautiful.
Do you remember that ...?

Paying a compliment
You're looking well.
You look great – have you been on holiday?

Asking a follow-up question
And are you still enjoying it? Really?
And what do you think of it?

Asking about someone's journey
How was the journey?
Was the journey OK?
How was the flight?
Did you get here OK?

Showing knowledge about a person you have just met
It's X, isn't it? I've seen your picture on the website.
You're not the X who ..., are you?
And anyway, X, I've heard quite a lot about you, too. You ..., didn't you?

Giving a brief summary of your recent history
Well, I'd been working in ... for five years when ...
So I've been in ... for the last ..., in a luxury apartment overlooking ...

Echoing the other person to encourage them to say more
A I have had a few ups and downs.
B Ups and downs?

A I've just been on a business trip to Budapest.
B Budapest?

Picking up on a key word to extend the conversation
A ... but the job's pretty challenging.
B ... Challenging in what way?

A I'm not sure about Jack. I find him a bit distant.
B Distant in what way?

Joking about yourself
I may be old, but you can't get rid of me that easily.

Being modest about achievements
Well, it wasn't just me. There was a whole team involved.
Oh, it was nothing.
I couldn't have done it without the team.

5 | Responding to feedback

Responding to positive feedback
Thanks for your support – it's good to know I'm on the right track.
Thanks, though I have to admit, I got the idea from ...
Thanks. I'm glad you liked it.

Taking on board negative feedback
I'm sorry, I didn't realize – thanks for pointing that out.
Oh, I see. Well it seems a pity to ..., but maybe you're right.
Oh, really? Why do you think that?
So how do you think I could improve it?
OK, I'll see if I can improve it.
Actually, I'm very happy to have some honest feedback. I'll just keep working on it.

Challenging negative feedback
Look, you're entitled to your opinion, but ...
I see what you're saying, but ...
To be honest, I just don't have time to ...
Fair enough, but it's a bit late now.

No, I'm sorry. I don't see what you're getting at.
I'm not sure I agree with you.
I'd like a second opinion on this, if you don't mind.

6 | Using vague language

Something about …, I think!
… you've put me on the spot there.
I'm not quite sure now.
I seem to remember …
… something like that, in any case.
I'm sure I would have done.
I'm trying to think …
I'd say you're on the right track.
… it's the kind of thing …
It just needs a bit more …
You know, … and so on.
Something along those lines …
Yes, … something like that.
No, not really.
It's difficult to explain, really …
It almost had a hint of …
It was kind of …
… you know, that sort of thing.
… a bit like that, but not quite as …
It was a bit … oh, I don't know.

7 | Expressing dissatisfaction

I have to admit, I'm not getting much out of it.
It's doing my head in!
It's really testing my patience.
I think I've reached my limit.
It hasn't lived up to expectations so far.
I have to say, I was expecting something a bit more …
It's just not up to scratch.
To be frank, I'm not very happy with …
I can't really see the point of … -ing.
To be honest, I'm finding it a bit frustrating that …
I just don't think this is the best use of my time.
This is ridiculous.
This is just not good enough.

8 | Dealing with difficult questions

Admitting ignorance
I'm afraid I don't know any more than you do.
Sorry, I don't know what you mean.
I'm afraid I'm not up to speed on …

Refusing to answer
I'm sorry, but I can't answer that.
I would prefer not to talk about it.
I'm afraid I can't disclose that information – it's confidential.

Avoiding the question
Well, it's not that straightforward.
It's hard to say at the moment.
I can't really comment.

Distancing yourself from the question
I'm afraid I'm really not in a position to talk about that.
It's not for me to say.
It's nothing to do with me.

9 | Dealing with misunderstandings

Saying you haven't understood
I don't know what you're talking about.
What do you mean?
I don't get it.

Responding to a misunderstanding
I didn't mean that.
Sorry if I didn't make that clear.
No, you've got it wrong.
I was thinking more along the lines of …
That's not really what I meant – what I actually wanted to say was …
What I meant was …
Can I put this straight?
It may seem …, but actually …
No, that's not right.
No, that's not exactly what I'm saying.

10 | Expressing personal views

Encouraging someone to express personal views
So what did you think of …?
Such as?
You're not in favour of …, then?
I was interested in what you said earlier about …
What did you like about it in particular?
It must have been …?
How does it feel to …?
You were saying earlier that …
I heard …
What do you mean?
So …?
What are your thoughts on …?
I'd like to know what you think about it.

Expressing personal views
To be honest with you, …
Personally speaking, …
I have to say …
To tell you the truth, …
To be perfectly honest, …
Honestly?
Personally, I think …
I look at it like this: …
My attitude is …

11 | Raising a difficult point

I don't mean to sound rude, but …
This is a bit delicate.
Please don't take offence.
Please don't take this the wrong way.
You see, the thing is, …
I'm not quite sure how to put this.
With respect, …
I have to say that …
The fact is, …
Don't be offended, but …
I'm sorry to have to say this, but …

12 | Giving and responding to compliments

Complimenting
That was great.
A very worthwhile meeting / discussion.
You're looking well.
I like your …
I thoroughly enjoyed that.
It was very interesting.
Great design.
I love …
Well done, you did a great job.
You have very nice …
That was brilliant.
I saw your … and I thought it was excellent.

Responding
Thanks.
Thank you. I felt it went well.
Thanks for the feedback.
I don't know how you can say that, but thanks anyway.
I was hoping it'd be well received.
Glad you enjoyed it.
I'm glad you liked it.

File 01 | Unit 1

Business communication skills, Exercise 4, page 9

Student B

Contrary to expectations, this country is being surprisingly slow to awaken investors' interest. The cost of production in this country is lower than in a lot of other European states, and the number of skilled workers is high and constantly improving. The infrastructure is adequate to deal with the predicted volume of traffic, but if some serious action is not taken soon in terms of offering incentives for investment, then the potential will not be met.

File 02 | Unit 1

Business communication skills, Exercise 9, page 9

1 You have just returned from a market research trip overseas. Report back to your team on
   - what you learnt about the local market
   - how well the market is doing generally
   - how your new product line is being received
   - the presence of the competition.

2 You are behind schedule on a project. Your boss has just called you into his / her office. Fill him / her in on
   - the status quo (current situation)
   - the reasons for the delay
   - how you are going to catch up in the future
   - whose fault the delay is.

3 You work for a football club. You have just been to a press conference where it was announced that the coach is resigning. Report back to the team on
   - his motives
   - his plans for the future
   - his experience of working at the club
   - some negative comments about some of the players
   - where the football club goes from here (what you intend to do about finding a new coach).

File 03 | Unit 11

Business communication skills, Exercise 9, page 89

Student B
Manager
You are Student A's line manager. You have a very close-knit team and you feel that it is important for team spirit and for productivity to have regular chats and face-to-face updates. You also feel it is essential for this team spirit that everyone on the team is treated the same.

Student A has a request. Discuss the possibilities of this request. State your position, try to negotiate some terms with A, and come to an agreement.

File 04 | Unit 1

Case study, Task, Exercise 2, page 13
Group B

Edinburgh, UK

- 'Buzzing' cultural city attracting a large number of tourists all year round, and particularly in August for the Edinburgh festival.
- Wide variety of food-related venues / styles, e.g. fabulous seafood, cafés, tea rooms, quality restaurants, pubs.
- Clients are usually well entertained by their Edinburgh hosts, taken out for lunch in a restaurant or pub, or to a restaurant in the evening.
- Language: English is the first language spoken by most Scottish people.
- Economy is focused on the service sector, especially tourism, financial services, and banking.
- Very compact city, making it easy to get around on foot.
- Some established competition, e.g. historic taverns or ghost walking tours and visits to the farmers' market, but most Scottish food-related tours seemed to be focused on castles in the Highlands.

File 05 | Unit 10

Case study, Task, Exercise 2, page 85
Students C and D
Issue 2: The cost of production facilities and salaries
The rent for the production facilities is much more expensive than in other parts of the country. The facilities are also ageing and run down, and staff are not happy about their working conditions. Salaries are also relatively high.

You have to cut costs and you have two options with approximately the same cost-saving benefits. Decide which option to take.

- move to more modern production facilities in Wales – the rent will be cheaper and the cost of living is lower, so salary expectations of staff will also be lower
- modernize the current facilities and cut the number of employees by making some people redundant

When preparing your briefing, be aware that this decision will not be popular with the staff because they will either have to move and take a pay cut, or face the possibility of losing their job.

File 06 | Unit 2

Business communication skills, Exercise 9, page 17

Student B

Item 1
- limit employees to one coffee a day
- increase price of coffee
- other ideas?

Item 2
- issue everyone with a company mobile
- hold a daily team meeting first thing in the morning
- other ideas?

Item 3
- set up closely-monitored e-learning programmes
- allocate x number of hours for study in working time
- other ideas?

Item 4
- pay employees a bonus for keeping days absent to a minimum
- allow employees greater flexibility so they can work from home if they choose
- other ideas?

File 07 | Unit 8

Business communication skills, Exercise 6, page 65

Context: You are researching customer reactions to your new product.

- You don't have as much quantifiable data as you'd originally planned, but will submit the final report by the agreed deadline.
- You are making good progress, but can't give exact figures now – still processing the feedback.
- You need to wait for more questionnaires to come back before finishing the report.

Key points you intend to cover

- give an overview of responses to the product so far
- explain some of the difficulties involved
- talk about 'effective questionnaires'

File 08 | Unit 2

Practically speaking, Exercise 4, page 19

Student A

Monthly reports

You would like everybody's report to be handed in one week earlier than originally planned.

Sales figures

Official figures have not yet been released, but you believe your group did particularly well.

File 09 | Unit 11

Working with words, Exercise 9, page 87

Student B

Company Y fact file

- makes laptop and desktop computers for home and business use
- is highly successful, with a reputation for quality and reliability
- advertises its laptops as robust enough to be taken anywhere, using the slogan 'Ready to go whenever you are'

Company Y laptops a health hazard!

A laptop fire on an intercontinental flight caused panic amongst passengers. Fortunately, the cabin crew were able to extinguish the fire, but it's still unclear why this happened. This isn't the first time that a laptop from Company Y has caught fire. There have been several other reports of laptops exploding or bursting into flames without warning. One destroyed a truck in America, while another caused a huge fire in a family home in Britain. As a result of the latest incident, several airlines have now banned passengers from travelling with laptops made by Company Y. According to the company, the fault lies with the batteries, which are made and supplied by another company.

Company Y's situation following the news article

- Company Y issued a statement publicly blaming their supplier for the problem.
- Despite the statement, sales of their laptops are falling, and an increasing number of corporate customers are cancelling their contracts.
- To limit the damage, the directors have agreed to replace any laptops that have been destroyed, and have recalled all recently sold laptops for free battery replacement.

File 10 | Unit 4

Business communication skills, Exercise 1, page 32

Guidelines for participating in a teleconference

1 Before the call starts, familiarize yourself with the agenda.
2 During the call itself, enunciate clearly, be concise, and try to avoid making long speeches or talking over other people.
3 It's often a good idea to identify yourself each time you come back into the conversation – otherwise people can quickly get confused about who's speaking.
4 When you want to ask a question, nominate the person you want to respond.
5 If no one else is doing it, offer occasional brief recaps. Paraphrase or summarize what has been said – it's a good way to help people focus and you can check if you have really understood.
6 Stay on topic, keep to the agenda, and encourage everyone else to do the same.

File 11 | Unit 4

Business communication skills, Exercise 7, page 33

Background

You are regional managers for Farmview, a manufacturer of dairy products. Farmview has recently launched a new, very strongly flavoured blue cheese. Despite a positive reaction to its taste, the cheese hasn't been selling well and it has been agreed that the name 'Old Mouldy' (which was intended to be humorous) has probably been putting customers off. A teleconference has been arranged to decide on a new name and marketing strategy.

Preparation

1 Each person in the group should think of their own suggestion for a new name and some reasons why it should be used.
2 Prepare to do at least three of the following during the teleconference.
   • digress
   • check your understanding
   • express doubts
   • nominate another person to say something
   • intervene to ensure a speaker doesn't dominate
   • interrupt in order to take over the topic

Agenda

1 Introductions
2 Each participant to suggest a new name with reasons
3 Reach agreement on new name

File 12 | Unit 4

Case study, Task, Exercise 3, page 37

Pair A

America still likes it hot!

Recent reports have confirmed that there has been no slow-down in America's love affair with spicy food. A recent survey found that sales of the hottest varieties of frozen meals went up by more than 20% in the last two years. In addition, most varieties of hot cook-in sauces and spicy condiments have also shown remarkable growth. A spokesman for a major supermarket in Florida explained, 'We are becoming more and more familiar with hot foods. Most consumers want to keep trying something a little bit spicier each time.' However, in comparison with Europe, where Indian and Thai foods are very popular, the most popular spicy food in the States is still Mexican.

Food fears

After a number of widely publicized health scares, it seems that America may be falling out of love with highly-processed foods. The recent scandals surrounding adulterated imported toothpaste and pet food have had a dramatic knock-on effect. This has led to a sharp decline in sales of imported microwaveable ready-meals, even though they weren't associated with the problems. At the same time, America is becoming increasingly nervous about additives and fat levels. New research shows that consumers are going out of their way to avoid unnatural colourings and preservatives in their food – and there is growing awareness of (and even legislation on) the so-called 'bad fats'. Following an intense media focus on these issues, the American consumer is now looking much more closely at food labels.

Spice yourself up for a long life

Scientists report that Indian food is very good for you. Because the cuisine is based around using fresh vegetables, an Indian meal is full of anti-oxidants which are natural fighters of illness. More than that, some of the ingredients, such as the spice turmeric, may even protect against heart disease, Alzheimer's, arthritis, and perhaps even cancer. Although these claims have yet to be proven, there is a lot of anecdotal evidence. For example, statistics show that Alzheimer's is four times less common in India than in the USA. And there are reports that rats who had been fed turmeric completely avoided problems associated with arthritis.

File 13 | Unit 9

Language at work, Exercise 5, page 74

YP fitness studio yearly review meeting

Last year

1 **Past action / inaction and past results**
- invest in new equipment → able to increase membership fee
- failed to develop competitive January special offer → lost potential customers to competition

2 **Past action / inaction and present results**
- failed to address HR crisis and recruit new personal trainers → only three personal trainers – all overworked, several customers on waiting lists
- developed partnership with local school → overweight teenagers now following fitness programme

Next year

3 **Suggestions / predictions for next year plus results**
- develop new membership packages → increase number of members
- start more initiatives with teenagers → improve gym reputation and get new young members
- employ more trainers → more personal programmes for customers and more profit
- renovate pool area → improve reputation, increase swimming prices

File 14 | Unit 1

Case study, Task, Exercise 2, page 13

Group C

Vancouver, Canada

- The commercial and cultural heart of Canada's West Coast, and a major convention and tourist destination.
- Attracts national and international tourists (particularly from the Far East).
- A major port. One of the most vibrant economies in Canada, particularly in the areas of technology, tourism, financial services, film production, education, and natural resources.
- Diverse ethnic communities have a strong influence on the restaurants which cater for every taste and budget, and there is also a varied programme of cultural events.
- Lots of pathways along the shoreline connecting up Vancouver's distinctive neighbourhoods. Spectacular coastal and mountain scenery.
- Lots of organized tours to Vancouver's surrounding outdoor attractions, including gourmet barbecue lunches on a remote beach, or seaside restaurant meals. Also combined tours, flexibility, and personalization offered.

File 15 | Unit 5

Working with words, Exercise 10, page 39

Project outline 1

1 **Task / project**
International charity football match organized by two top teams and a charity promoting peace in an area of conflict.

2 **Colleagues / team mates**
Very varied, from the club president (who expects VIP treatment), to the charity volunteers.

3 **Schedules / pressure**
Deadline is fixed and non-negotiable because of the match timetable. Player availability is also a factor.

4 **Issues / problems**
The television scheduling – due to time zone differences, finding a good local kick-off time is problematic.

5 **Confrontation / fairness**
Differing attitudes to time is causing conflict. The culture of the charity is 'inclusive', so much consideration is given to finding a satisfactory solution for everyone.

Project outline 2

1 **Task / project**
A fashion show based in a luxury boutique to promote the new collection (especially the top-end jewellery).

2 **Colleagues / team mates**
Models
Shop staff
Caterers
Lighting / sound crew
Security staff
Head Office staff

3 **Schedules / pressure**
The date and time of the show are published and invitations sent to the top 1,000 customers in the boutique's database. The new collection must be launched on time.

4 **Issues / problems**
There are health and safety issues regarding the maximum number of people who can be in the boutique at any time.

5 **Confrontation / fairness**
It's a challenge to manage a team made up of people from different companies and areas of expertise, who all come to the project with their own personal needs and agendas. The models are notoriously unreliable and temperamental.

File 16 | Unit 2

Practically speaking, Exercise 4, page 19

Student B

The competition

The competition have been very active recently – you saw a number of very good presentations at the conference last week.

Travel budget

This has been greatly reduced this year, so only employees in senior positions are able to travel overseas.

File 17 | Unit 5

Business communication skills, Exercise 10, page 41

Student A
Situation 1
You are working on a project with very tight deadlines. You are expecting a piece of work from Student B tomorrow. Check with Student B that she / he will deliver on time. (The work is already a week late.)

Situation 2
You share an office with Student B and Student C. The office has to be manned constantly so you can't go out at the same time, even for a few minutes. Think of a very important reason which means you have to be somewhere else at 2.30 p.m. tomorrow. Student B will be on annual leave. Talk to Student C and see if she / he can look after the office for you while you are away from your desk.

Situation 3
You work in a team with Student B and Student C. The project you are all working on is seriously delayed because Student C is refusing to accept work from Student B, claiming it is of poor quality. Student B claims she / he followed the brief. Try to help them find a solution so that the project can continue to move forward.

File 18 | Unit 2

Business communication skills, Exercise 9, page 17

Student C

Item 1
- change opening hours
- close down the cafeteria
- other ideas?

Item 2
- employ more administrative staff
- improve communication by sending staff on a training course
- other ideas?

Item 3
- give employees the choice of which courses they take part in
- make sure certain training courses are completed before employees get promoted
- other ideas?

Item 4
- set up team-based pay so the onus is on the employees to make sure that everyone is there
- give employees greater flexibility in the hours worked
- other ideas?

File 19 | Unit 9

Business communication skills, Exercise 6, page 73

Students C and D

You support these original proposals from Floralope.

1 Investing in training for all staff on the new system is essential.

2 Using cash in the bank to invest in the system is necessary.

3 Going ahead with the new system as soon as the cost-benefit analysis has been done.

Discuss the advantages of these original proposals. Think about how the company's performance or reputation will be affected.

File 20 | Unit 5

Language at work, Exercise 5, page 42

Student A

Agenda

1 Unfocused meetings
Team members have a tendency to go off track and not to focus on the agenda.

2 Team members with different working styles
It's a new team, bringing together people from different departments who don't normally work together.

3 Lack of communication outside team meetings
Instructions often lack clarity.

File 21 | Unit 2

Case study, Task, Exercise 1, page 21

Group A

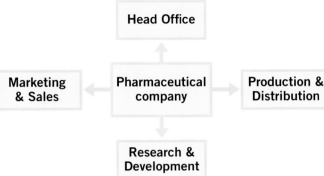

Due to the rapid expansion HR have employed staff on a short-term needs basis. They have had to give particular attention to
- R&D roles (e.g. research scientists)
- Head Office roles (e.g. legal, financial, HR, secretarial, IT).

Commercial roles (e.g. medical reps) and production / distribution roles (e.g. production operatives, supervisors) will become more important once the company has developed more commercially-viable products. This means that the Marketing, Sales, and Production departments are not yet fully resourced.

File 22 | Unit 5

Practically speaking, Exercise 5, page 43

Student A

1 Give feedback to Student B on her / his report.
  The report your colleague wrote was incomplete. You are particularly concerned about the summary. Most of the summary doesn't link with the findings of the report. However, you thought the report was well presented and the findings that are included are very interesting.

2 Student B is going to give you some feedback.
  Your boss wants to talk to you. You think it is about the mistakes you made in the database management.

File 23 | Unit 6

Business communication skills, Exercise 5, page 49

Students A and B

Choose two of these ideas to discuss in the meeting.
- Introduce a yearly summer ball for staff, with free food, wine, and entertainment.
- Provide in-house gym facilities with showers.
- Offer staff a 'work at home' option.
- Install in-house 'nap machines' to allow staff to power-sleep for 20 minutes when necessary.

Discuss the advantages of the ideas and how they would work. Think of possible disadvantages and prepare a counter-argument.

File 24 | Unit 5

Case study, Task, Exercise 2, page 45

Student A

Head of Finance

You've just joined the company and your main objective is to increase profitability.

Your suggestions
- Lose the 'all-for-one' principle – the company is too big now for this to work.
- Create more of a hierarchical structure – several competitors are succeeding with this kind of structure and it may allow you to cut back on staff and save money.
- Servers should just get on with their jobs – they should serve customers as quickly and efficiently as possible and leave the 'ideas' to management.

Ideas that you do not support
- You do not support a continued lack of clarity in roles. Managers should manage and servers should serve.
- You do not want to spend more company profits on expensive Christmas parties or food-tasting days.

File 25 | Unit 12

Case study, Task, Exercise 1, page 101

Student B

Fact file: Brazil

Country size: 8.5 million square kilometres, fifth largest country in world

Population: 180 million

Economic factors
- Property price returns of 20% per annum in some locations.
- Good currency exchange rates, making it cheap for foreign investors.
- President's progressive policies have brought many improvements to Brazil, including a decrease in inflation to an all-time low of 5.7%.
- Active encouragement of and incentives for foreign investment – you can own 100% of land and property.
- Cost of living at only 20% of that in the UK / Europe, while property maintenance costs are extremely low.
- Increase in manufacturing industries relocating to Brazil and boosting the economy.
- Expected to be self-sufficient in oil reserves within the next year.
- Brazil believed by some economists to be amongst the leading economies of the future, along with Russia, India, and China.

File 26 | Unit 5

Case study, Task, Exercise 2, page 45

Student C
Server

You've been at the company for two years. You've been chosen to represent all servers at this meeting. The main objective for servers is to re-establish a good relationship with management and make the job fun again.

Your suggestions
- Outlet managers should help out with serving again to re-establish a good team atmosphere.
- More time should be allowed for servers to go on training courses to improve their skills.
- Have meetings where servers can discuss their ideas for new sandwiches and improved processes.

Ideas that you do not support
- You have heard rumours that team-building events like the food-tasting days and the parties might be cancelled. You do not support this, as these events are fun and help to improve teamwork. They're one of the reasons that people enjoy working for the company.
- You do not support any ideas that may result in job losses or pay cuts.

File 27 | Unit 5

Language at work, Exercise 5, page 42

Student C

Agenda

1 Unfocused meetings
   Not all team members attend team meetings – without regular updates, it's difficult to work out what stage the project has reached.

2 Team members with different working styles
   Some team members appear to be competing against each other.

3 Lack of communication outside team meetings
   It's not clear who is responsible for what.

File 28 | Unit 1

Case study, Task, Exercise 2, page 13

Group A

Beijing, China

- International city undergoing rapid change, with new office blocks, hotels, and commercial plazas springing up.
- Wide variety of food-related venues / styles, e.g. street markets offering local snacks, tea houses, 'Red Mansion' banquets, and imperial food. The city's restaurant scene still not as vibrant as Shanghai's, though.
- The city is spread out, which means you may have to catch a taxi home, rather than taking a walk after eating out.
- Language: Mandarin. There was a huge drive for people in the service industries to improve their English for the 2008 Olympics.
- A lot of well-established competition – most hotels offer tours. Caters for domestic and international tourism. Walking tours available with English-speaking guides.

File 29 | Unit 10

Language at work, Exercise 5, page 82

Memo

3.1 Job shadowing initiative

From: Senior Management Team
To: all group heads – Juan C, Chris T, Anastasia G, Bruno R, Robert C, Suzanna H, Tim J, Andy W

Decision
We have approved a job-shadowing scheme within the division.

Objective
To foster cooperation and teamwork by helping staff to better understand what their colleagues do on a daily basis, and the demands of job roles outside their own discipline.

Departments involved: Finance, Operations, Marketing, Sales, Production, Customer Service, Logistics, Research & Development

Requirements
All members of staff at team leader grade and below will have to spend a minimum of four half-days (by the end of next month) shadowing a colleague in an appropriate department. We want all individuals to
- set up and schedule their own shadowing programme
- report back on and evaluate their experiences
- agree with their line manager what changes to make to their work as a result of their participation in the scheme.

We will not allow extra time for work you don't complete within this period. We expect that staff will cover for absent colleagues.

File 30 | Unit 6

Practically speaking, Exercise 3, page 51

Student B
Situation 1

Student A will ask you for some tips on how to organize a tour and presentation of your company to a group of graduates. You organized the same event last year. You can remember the day in general, but you have trouble recalling the details.

- Started with a tour of the building – lasted all morning?
- Short lunch break – sandwich lunch in meeting room, or fast food in staff canteen?
- Afternoon – talk by representative from each department. Introducing different job types?
- Finished with question and answer session?

Situation 2

In order for the MD to authorize the new project you are working on, you need to present a written proposal with Student A. You have written the first draft. Ask Student A for feedback before writing the second draft. Ask questions if you feel you need more detail from Student A.

File 31 | Unit 6

Case study, Task, Exercise 2, page 53

Post-1990s – the downturn begins

- A split in the management team led to Adam Crees gaining full control of the company in 2001. Against advice he decided to diversify and to invest in developing a model for the luxury market, competing with Porsche, Aston Martin, and Maserati. This led to the launch of the Adamo Tera in 2004.
- The Tera was not well received and failed to compete in its class on performance, quality, and price. However, the push toward diversification continued, and in 2006 and 2007 Adamo launched the Tera 2 and the Bos.
- Production became increasingly automated, leading to the company having more managers than workers, many of whom had been with Adamo since the start and knew little about running a large company.
- Increased competitor activity meant that the luxury car market became flooded with high-quality models. Adamo's costs spiralled while its revenues began to fall.
- The poor reputation of the Tera and Bos models has had a negative impact on the AV1 and the Capra – customers are turning away from these models and sales have plummeted.
- A slowing global economy has accelerated the recent downturn in sales with Adamo expecting a fall in revenue of at least 25% on the previous year.

File 32 | Unit 7

Working with words, Exercise 10, page 55
Company 1
- no formalized training approach – training needs of each department are extremely varied, so this would be too complicated
- no in-house training – only learning from more experienced employees whilst doing the job
- money for external training available, but only given in response to a direct request from an employee

Company 2
- structured and formalized training approach
- senior management decide what kind of training courses are made available
- employees in first year of employment must complete two courses designed for their particular job – this is decided by the line managers
- employees in the second year of employment must complete two more general courses related to the company (e.g. product presentations, business processes, etc.) – this is decided by the line managers and employees during appraisals
- employees must complete two training courses per year after their second year

File 33 | Unit 7

Case study, Task, Exercise 2, page 61

Student B

Suggested action

1 Continue recruiting in UK, but use psychometric testing to help find people with the right attitude and who will learn skills quickly. Why?
   - Although it will be expensive to employ a qualified practitioner to manage the tests, the company will have more control over the recruitment process.
   - It will enable the company to find people who can grow within company and make it easier to develop training to meet their needs.
2 Introduce an extensive training programme, including specific job-related and company-specific training in-house, along with generic external courses. Why?
   - Although this will be expensive, it will be worth it in the long-term – employees will gain skills specific to their job as well as a wider understanding of the company as a whole.
   - External courses will also enable them to increase self-awareness and develop their general business skills.
   - The government is likely to make such training schemes compulsory in a few years, so starting it now will put the company in a strong position.

File 34 | Unit 8

Working with words, Exercise 10, page 63

Company profiles

Company A

A is a multinational with offices in every major city in EMEA (Europe, Middle East, and Africa). A's core business is accountancy and auditing, but they have a small up-and-coming consultancy division which is gaining a lot of recognition. There is a rigid hierarchical structure and clear career path.

Company B

B is an SME (small and medium-sized enterprise) specializing in the provision of office supplies. They operate only within national borders, although some of their suppliers are found abroad. B values flexibility and rewards loyalty above all.

Company C

C is a franchise business which focuses on cleaning (commercial and domestic) and disaster-recovery services. It is a rapidly expanding business, although at the moment it has relatively few full-time employees. The master franchisee holds the licence for many further related brands which have not yet been exploited in your market. The master franchisee's Head Office is also based in your city.

Company D

D is a family business managed and owned by a husband and wife. Their core business is software development and they have made a name for themselves in the industry for their cutting-edge programming. Both the husband and wife also teach IT courses at the local university as well as an online master's degree in programming. There are three other employees.

File 35 | Unit 2

Case study, Task, Exercise 1, page 21

Group B

- Establish a system to find the right people to develop in order to fill existing and emerging roles in the company.
- Invest in training – e.g. how to conduct career development interviews.
- Invest in an IT programme for monitoring employees' career progression and to help managers to select the right 'internal' candidate.
- Establish a process to ensure that career development is a shared process between employee and employer.
- Establish a set list of questions that all managers ask in performance / career review interviews.
- Write role profiles for existing and emerging positions.
- Write achievement-orientated career plans and make them clear to employees from the outset.
- Other ideas?

File 36 | Unit 5

Business communication skills, Exercise 10, page 41

Student B

Situation 1

You are working on a project with very tight deadlines. You are supposed to hand over a piece of work to Student A tomorrow. You need a few more days. You've been ill and you also think the deadlines weren't very realistic. Student A is going to ask you about progress.

Situation 2

You share an office with Student A and Student C. The office has to be manned constantly so you can't go out at the same time, even for a few minutes. Student A and Student C both want some time away from the office tomorrow afternoon. Help them to reach an agreement. (You can't man the office for them, as you are on holiday tomorrow.)

Situation 3

You work in a team with Student B and Student C. Student C is refusing to accept work you have carried out. You don't want to do the work again because it would delay the whole project, and anyway, you carried out the work according to Student C's brief.

File 37 | Unit 8

Practically speaking, Exercise 4, page 67

Student B

1 You've just come out of a meeting where the suggestion was made to cut the budget on Student A's project and to push back the schedule date, because priorities have changed. Respond to Student A's difficult questions by
   - avoiding the question
   - distancing yourself from the situation.

2 You've heard from colleagues that your department is going to be restructured within the next year. Find out from Student A
   - who is ultimately responsible for the plan
   - if it would mean any redundancies.

File 38 | Unit 9

Business communication skills, Exercise 6, page 73

Students A and B

You support these alternative suggestions from the Dutch parent company.

1 Replacing some of the older staff with more IT-literate staff.

2 Raising capital by selling off some unused property and getting a bank loan.

3 Delaying the decision for six months until more information has been gathered by
- reviewing return on investment for a new IT system
- analysing the company in comparison to the competition
- conducting a customer satisfaction survey.

Discuss the advantages of these new suggestions. Think about how the company's performance or reputation will be affected.

File 39 | Unit 5

Practically speaking, Exercise 5, page 43

Student B

1 Student A is going to give you some feedback on your report. You spent a lot of time preparing the report. With the deadline approaching you asked a colleague to help you with the summary, but the report is still yours.

2 Give feedback to Student B about a recent project.
Your want to congratulate Student B on the success of a recent database project which she / he was managing. You also want to mention concerns about difficulties one team member had with working long hours on the project.

File 40 | Unit 5

Language at work, Exercise 5, page 42

Student B

Agenda

1 Unfocused meetings
Team members get too much information in meetings and forget it as soon as the meeting is over.

2 Team members with different working styles
There are 'personality clashes' in the team – some members just don't get on.

3 Lack of communication outside team meetings
Team members do not say what they think directly, and think that hints are enough.

File 41 | Unit 9

Case study, Task, Exercise 5, page 77

Dear Steering Committee

There has been a press leak concerning our plans for our Nigerian plant – see below. We're not sure who the source can be as the facts are wrong. However, in the light of this, we need to consider carefully what our next move should be regarding the project.

'QP Plastics is to close its main factory in Nigeria, putting 1,300 staff out of work. The site at Port Harcourt, in the south of the country, is to close while it looks for a buyer. QP Plastics said the move was not linked to the increasing wave of violence in the oil-rich Niger Delta where kidnappings of western workers has become increasingly common.'

Obviously, our main concern is the social unrest in the area and the safety of our staff. We should also consider our shareholders and reputation. Please discuss this asap and let me know how we should proceed.

Many thanks

Jason Fletcher

File 42 | Unit 10

Working with words, Exercise 4, page 79

Team leader A

Please evaluate the following:

(1 = excellent, 5 = poor)

	1	2	3	4	5
Ability to achieve results	✓				
Commitment to the project	✓				
Honesty and openness			✓		
Ability to make decisions	✓				
Willingness to consult team about decisions					✓
Flexibility in dealing with change				✓	
Communication with team				✓	
Understanding of team's needs and concerns					✓
Allowing team to do their work unsupervised			✓		
Self-awareness					✓

Team leader B

Please evaluate the following:

(1 = excellent, 5 = poor)

	1	2	3	4	5
Ability to achieve results	✓				
Commitment to the project	✓				
Honesty and openness	✓				
Ability to make decisions			✓		
Willingness to consult team about decisions	✓				
Flexibility in dealing with change			✓		
Communication with team	✓				
Understanding of team's needs and concerns	✓				
Allowing team to do their work unsupervised			✓		
Self-awareness			✓		

File 43 | Unit 10

Case study, Task, Exercise 2, page 85

Students A and B

Issue 1: The cost of cocoa beans

The company currently uses Criollo cocoa beans because they are known to be the best quality bean. However, they are also the most expensive bean.

The chocolate made by the company always has a high percentage of cocoa solids in it, at least 70%; some items have 85%.

You have to cut costs and you have two options with approximately the same cost-saving benefits. Decide which option to take.

- choose to use a cheaper, lower-quality bean
- reduce the cocoa content in the chocolate

When preparing your briefing, be aware that this decision will not be popular with the product managers and marketing managers because they have invested a lot of hard work in building up the company's brand image based on the quality of the products.

File 44 | Unit 5

Case study, Task, Exercise 2, page 45

Student B

Outlet manager

You've been at the company since it began. You started work as a server and moved up to a management position. You've been chosen to represent all outlet managers at this meeting. The main objective for outlet managers is to improve team spirit and prevent more staff from leaving.

Your suggestions

- Re-establish the 'all-for-one' principle – reduce the amount of paperwork that outlet managers are expected to do so that there is more time to work alongside staff.
- Give servers the opportunity to take part in training courses to improve their skills and allow them to move up in the company.

Ideas that you do not support

- You do not support any change in the company's organizational structure. You see the original structure as one of the company's strengths.
- You do not think that servers should have influence over what sandwiches should be sold. These decisions should be based on customer feedback and sales figures.

File 45 | Unit 11

Working with words, Exercise 2, page 86

Statement 1 = Microsoft

Statement 2 = Tata

File 46 | Unit 11

Working with words, Exercise 9, page 87

Student A

Company X fact file

- produces coffee, chocolate, and related food and drink products
- sources cocoa and coffee beans from a variety of producers in different parts of the world
- has used the Fairtrade label on a small number of its key products, suggesting that it treats its suppliers well and pays a fair price for the goods it buys

Company X in Fairtrade scandal!

Company X has used the Fairtrade labelling in a bid to enhance its reputation, and has seen sales and profits on many of its non-Fairtrade products soar as a result. But is this about to change? An independent report has revealed that Company X does not abide by the terms of the Fairtrade agreement for most of its products, and actually puts pressure on producers to accept lower prices, driving many growers into poverty.

Company X's situation following the news article
- Company directors moved quickly to limit the damage – they issued a press statement playing down the situation.
- Despite the press statement, the share price has fallen very quickly, and sales figures for most key products are much lower than expected.
- Customer surveys suggest the company is no longer trusted.

File 47 | Unit 7

Language at work, Exercise 6, page 58

Discuss what the speaker could say in situations 1–5.

Example: I was going to bring a sample of our new product, but unfortunately I haven't brought it with me today.

Past	Present
1 I intend to take a sample of the new product to the meeting.	I'm at the meeting. I have forgotten the sample of the new product.
2 I have to give a presentation at the conference in Moscow next week.	My boss has asked me to cancel all other arrangements and go to New York for a meeting next week.
3 We think we will make a profit this year.	Our products haven't sold as well as expected.
4 We're aiming to get a 10% discount on all orders over €20,000 during the negotiation.	They are telling us that they can't offer more than an 8% discount on any order.
5 I'm having lunch with Maria tomorrow.	Maria has cancelled our lunch appointment because she's too busy.

File 48 | Unit 12

Case study, Task, Exercise 1, page 101

Student C

Doing business in Brazil

- Remember that relationships are one of the most important elements in Brazilian business culture.
- Cultivate close personal relationships and build trust – you will then have a greater chance of successfully doing business in Brazil.
- Be aware that great importance is placed on the family in Brazil. This means that you will often find a number of family members working for the same company.
- It is common practice in Brazil to hire a *despechante*, or middleman, to help you in your business dealings. A *despechante* will help you navigate Brazilian bureaucracy for a nominal fee.
- DON'T rush business dealings with your Brazilian colleagues and avoid pressing for final decisions.
- Allow time for socializing before and during meetings – this is an important part of the relationship-building process.
- DON'T publicly criticize your Brazilian counterparts. If you need to tell them something negative, do so in private so they do not lose face in front of others.

File 49 | Unit 5

Business communication skills, Exercise 10, page 41

Student C

Situation 1
You are working on a project with very tight deadlines. Student A is expecting a piece of work from Student B tomorrow. Student B is unable to meet the deadline. Help them to discuss the issue, and to reach the best solution for all concerned.

Situation 2
You share an office with Student A and Student B. The office has to be manned constantly so you can't go out at the same time, even for a few minutes. Think of a very important reason which means you have to be somewhere else at 3.00 p.m. tomorrow. Student B will be on annual leave. Talk to Student A and see if she / he can look after the office for you while you are away from your desk.

Situation 3
You work in a team with Student A and Student B. You are very dissatisfied with some work that Student B has just carried out. It's true, she / he followed your instructions, but the quality is very poor and the work seems rushed. You don't want to accept the work, and you would like her / him to do it again.

File 50 | Unit 11

Business communication skills, Exercise 9, page 89

Student A

Employee

You are extremely busy at work and you have an hour's commute every day. You want to start working from home in order to save commuting time and avoid unnecessary interruptions at work. You have an office space at home and an Internet connection, so you feel that your work would not suffer at all from this change and you might even become more productive.

Student B is your line manager. Explain what you want and discuss the possibilities of this arrangement. State your position, try to negotiate some terms with B, and come to an agreement.

File 51 | Unit 5

Case study, Task, Exercise 2, page 45

Student D

Head Office representative

You have been asked to chair the negotiation. You should do the following during the meeting.
- Invite each person to make their suggestions.
- Check that you have understood each suggestion.
- Ask the other participants for their opinions.
- Keep the discussion on track.
- Ask the participants to compromise and agree on at least two suggestions that you can take to Head Office.

File 52 | Unit 11

Case study, Task, Exercise 2, page 93

Students C and D

What we would recommend
- Carbon emission reduction, rather than offsetting. It tends to be more popular with investors and customers.
- For a reduction programme suggest: paper-free bills, conference calls to replace some international travel, hybrid company cars to replace standard cars.
- A policy to educate customers as part of the reduction programme is recommended. Previous clients asked customers to charge phones only when the battery has run down and to unplug the charger once it has charged.

What we wouldn't recommend
- If the company insists on offsetting, investing in forests is not recommended. Studies show that forestry projects are less reliable in offsetting carbon emissions than first thought. This is because trees are vulnerable to a number of problems, e.g. fires. It would be better to invest in renewable energy.

File 53 | Unit 12

Working with words, Exercise 4, page 95

1

2

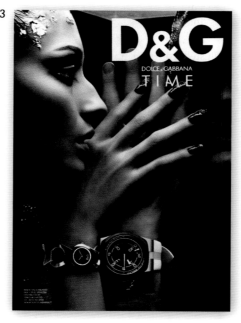

3

File 54 | Unit 6

Business communication skills, Exercise 5, page 49

Students C and D

Choose two of these ideas to discuss in the meeting.
- Provide free coffee and biscuits for staff every day.
- Introduce a yearly paid bonus for all staff.
- Offer all staff three extra holiday days.
- Offer staff the option to work their hours in three or four days, rather than five.

Discuss the advantages of the ideas and how they would work. Think of possible disadvantages and prepare a counter-argument.

File 55 | Unit 12

Case study, Task, Exercise 1, page 101

Student A

Key performance indicators

FJR Immo's Key Performance Indicators (KPIs)

KPI = ensuring customer satisfaction – monitored in the form of a survey

KPI = focusing on investors – returns are judged on measures of profitability and efficiency

KPI = focusing on employees – measuring productivity and employee satisfaction whilst rewarding good work and offering opportunities for education

KPI = measuring standards of the suppliers (i.e. local agents) and ensuring our high standards are met, e.g. customer care, documentation, communication, etc.

These benchmarks give a quantitative indication of how the company is performing and if it is achieving the targets it has set itself.

Objectives can be readjusted from time to time depending on progress.

File 56 | Unit 4

Case study, Task, Exercise 3, page 37

Pair B

Possible strategies

Information and education
- Take steps to inform the public about the quality of AST's products.
- Emphasize the cleanliness of preparation factories.
- Educate the nation about curry and its benefits.
- Make spokespeople available for talk shows.
- Get articles into magazines.
- Use advertisements for information-giving.
- Offer supermarket taste tests.
- Position ourselves at the front of the healthy-eating movement.
- Other options?

Product development
- Introduce new US-only lines.
- Improve product ingredients to allay fears.
- Remove all artificial additives.
- Reduce fat levels.
- Make sure all fats in products are 'good' ones.
- Consider specializing in a purely vegetarian range.
- Source more local, natural, or even organic ingredients.
- Other options?

Sell differently
- Find a US partner – i.e. work with a local food producer and combine our expertise in Asian food with their trading name and reputation.
- Focus sales drive on regions or cities with large minority populations who are most likely to buy products.
- Other options?

Start up production in the US
- Buy or rent production capacity and have US-sourced products.

Exit the US market
- Focus on the markets we know best and stop the haemorrhage of money before it becomes too serious.
- Find ways to expand in Europe instead.

CD 1

Unit 1

01

1

Kimberley So, on my first day here, it was at the afternoon meeting, and I was introduced to my colleagues. They were pleasant enough, but it was kind of annoying at the beginning, because to be honest, I found them a little dull and … well, pompous. I guess I could have been more open-minded. I was too quick to judge – it was just different to what I was used to, but with time I think my impression probably changed …

… Er, the building itself is in this out-of-the-way, purpose-built, industrial zone, as they call it here. In fact it's pretty upmarket and I think it has pretty much everything you could ask for …

… One thing I found very time-consuming was the constant greeting and wishing people farewell. I can appreciate the need for formality, but it got kind of tedious, all that kissing and shaking hands every day …

2

Igor When you're working here, you have to take into account the wide variety of cultural influences. It's quite amazing to me, really. I mean, it's so up-and-coming, investment is pouring in from everywhere. And it really is a melting-pot culture, so business tends to be more formal, which, personally, I think is not a bad thing. People dress smartly, and they are confident, you know, self-assured and outspoken …

… Where I come from many things are out-dated and in some cases quite run-down, but over here it's the opposite. Everything is new and state-of-the-art …

… I suppose a predictable outcome of this difference in cultures is that communication can sometimes break down, you know, in negotiations and business deals. So what happens is that language and concepts get simplified, which can lead to meetings that are, you know, run-of-the-mill – quite dull, really.

3

Ho Lee Park When you arrive in New Zealand, there are so many new things to take on board. A lot of new information to process. But New Zealanders are very down to earth people, and very easy-going … I was surprised at first, but I like it …

… Coming from a big city, I guess it's not surprising that New Zealand lifestyle is more low-key … Yes, this helps to make it relaxing, but there are times when it can feel quite a lonely place.

… One of the most unexpected things for me was how entertaining the people can be. Laughter and joking are very much part of the culture, and it's nice at work sometimes, when people are not so serious. It helps to cheer me up.

02

Extract 1

Johanna Hi, Peter, how was your trip? I've skimmed through your initial findings and I'm very impressed.

Peter Oh, well, I wondered what your reaction would be. I have to say, I had lots of help, and I'm actually quite excited about what I saw …

Johanna OK, well, er, just before you start, can I just fill you in on what the client has said while you were away?

Peter Yeah, of course.

Johanna Well, basically, the client has told us that the site is likely to be around the Krakow area, so can we go over your thoughts on those sites first? Apparently, it seems that Krakow is quite an up-and-coming place.

Peter Yes, it is. I started off in the city centre, which I have to say is really beautiful and very lively. I get the impression that there's a lot going on there. According to the local tourist office, they're really pushing the area for development; however, from what I could see, there are already a number of hotels catering for the business market and I gathered from the locals that there were several interesting sites worth considering nearby. I had been looking around Krakow for a couple of days by that point. I had planned to spend an extra day in Krakow itself, but as it was made clear that I should go exploring, I cut this short so that I could visit other sites.

Johanna Sounds intriguing …

03

Extract 2

Johanna How did you feel about the mountain site? What was it called again? Zakopane?

Peter Zakopane, yes.

Johanna Apparently, you weren't that keen?

Peter No – to be fair, it could have been worse. It does have absolutely breathtaking scenery, but then that's not everything. And I've got to say that I have my doubts. I'm just not 100% convinced. I would say it's more of a ski resort than a business centre. Plenty of sport – guests can really do whatever they want in their free time – skiing, walking, saunas, plenty of that kind of thing. I'm not saying that's a bad thing, it's just that it's not really an ideal location for this type of hotel – and it's not even especially close to the airport – at least a couple of hours' drive. All in all, it's going to be a bit more complicated than we anticipated.

Johanna Yeah, I take your point. So are we saying this is still a serious contender, or not?

Peter I wouldn't like to say, really. Basically, I'm happy to do a bit more research if you're still interested, but I can't promise anything.

Johanna I see, OK, er … Well, any other potential pitfalls? What's your impression of the local workforce, for instance?

Peter Well, I wouldn't go so far as to say that they don't speak English at all, but I did run into a couple of problems. I know English might not be their *first* second language – it's not that it's a bad thing that their German and Russian are pretty good, it's just that English will be a major factor as well, so I'm a bit wary of that. I'm a bit reluctant to recommend the site at this stage. But, look, why don't you come out and see for yourself?

04

Extract 3

Johanna What about the third site? I understand you went back to Krakow at the end of your trip to visit a potential location on the edge of the city?

Peter I've never seen anywhere quite like it. I've got to say that I'm totally convinced by its potential – it has just about everything you could ask for. The major advantage is that the infrastructure is already all in place. I'm sure you'll agree that the local facilities are first class – I've brought some pictures and schematics to show you …

Johanna … Erm, you mentioned an abandoned factory?

Peter Yes. It's this old brewery which I'm fully confident our client can acquire and refit. Basically, the pros definitely outweigh the cons.

Johanna I'm not sure whether the budget will stretch that far …

Peter No, OK, but surely that's not a reason to delay. As you'll see from my projected figures, the purchase value of the disused factory definitely makes it worth considering! We can't go wrong, really, not with the way property values are increasing. Anyway, I thought you'd be impressed, so I'd like to set up a meeting with the owner.

Johanna But we haven't talked the figures through in detail yet.

Peter Yes, but that needn't stop us at least making some further enquiries about the building. It's only a preliminary meeting.

Johanna Well, OK, but by then we need to have pinned down any other potential difficulties, don't we?

Peter I'm pretty sure I've covered everything in my analysis. I'll be writing everything up later this week.

Johanna Then … it shouldn't be a problem.

05

a The major advantage is that the infrastructure is already all in place.
It has just about everything you could ask for.

b As you'll see from my projected figures, the purchase value of the disused factory definitely makes it worth considering.
I'm sure you'll agree that the local facilities are first class.

c Basically, I'm happy to do a bit more research if you're still interested, but I can't promise anything.
I'm a bit reluctant to recommend the site at this stage. But, look, why don't you come out and see for yourself?

d That's not a reason to delay.
That needn't stop us at least making some further enquiries about the building.

e I'm just not 100% convinced.
It does have absolutely breathtaking scenery, but then that's not everything.

f It's not that it's a bad thing that their German and Russian are pretty good – it's just that English will be a major factor as well.
I would say it's more of a ski resort than a business centre.

06

1

Hi, my name's Holly Cheng. I'm from the Singapore office, and, well, I'm accountable for everything that goes on in Production Planning. I'm pleased to say that after two years in the job I've now managed to get on top of things and can see ways of further improving our ability to deliver on time. Lately, I've been concentrating on local production, but with the worldwide strategy gathering speed, it's becoming more and more important to look at the global picture. What's the point of me being here today? I guess I'm ready to take on board anything I can about how to improve communication between my team and our counterparts around the world. I do have a tendency to talk too fast so, please slow me down! Or stop me if you can't understand what I'm saying!

2

Hello. For those of you who don't know me already, I am Elke Seifried from Graz in Austria. My responsibilities include optimizing the quality assurance procedures at our plant there to ensure that we only produce parts of the highest standard. I'm empowered to jettison any sub-standard products and have the task of working out what went wrong. I'd like to point out that over the years, I have been continually improving procedures, and I hope to share some of my ideas with you here.

3

Hi, there. As most of you will know, I'm Harvey Benson from Atlanta. What can I say? Well, it might surprise you to know that we've had a few great years and we're just rolling the stuff out. The point is, we're finding it really tough to keep on top of demand, but, well, you gotta give the customer what they want. Basically, my role is to coordinate what happens between departments, making sure that communication is optimal – this entails a lot of talking, mailing, getting on people's cases, and so on – so I might not be everyone's favourite person! You'll be happy to know that we've been selected as a benchmark for best practice, due to the process that I developed. To get to the point, we want to help out all the sites around the world in optimizing their communication processes – I can't wait to share our expertise with you and to help you embrace the changes you'll be facing over the next few months.

07

Hi, it's James here … Thank you very much again for agreeing to do this for me. Basically, I just want to get an overall impression of the place from an outsider's perspective, and obviously, the restaurants and the local delicacies will be of particular interest to us. Er, let's think, what else …? Er, well, any info about tourist numbers and origins would also be very useful. But probably more importantly for us, specific information on what type of business visitor the city gets. And, erm, what are these visitors doing there? You know the type of thing – what kind of trip is it? Are they coming alone, or with colleagues? Obviously, this means it would also be useful to gather more first-hand knowledge about the local economy – type of business or industry, international connections, etc. … Erm, we really need to establish early on who our target market would be, as this will affect our pricing and marketing strategy. And, erm, I guess the obvious question – is there any competition? And then are there any language or cultural issues which I need to bear in mind? Erm, OK, I think that's everything. Thanks.

Unit 2

08

Interviewer … and today I'm joined by Susan Whittaker, who's a career coach … Susan, more and more people seem to be exploring less traditional career options. Realistically, what are the alternatives to a traditional career?

Susan Well, yes, people are beginning to realize that if you want to move forward you need to take responsibility for your own career development. And if you want to make a real change, you have to be prepared to take some risks. Talking yourself into that promotion, and climbing another rung on the vertical career ladder may not necessarily be right for you. If that's the case, then you have to take a serious look at your options, ask around for advice and see what you can do about following less conventional paths.

Interviewer So what kind of options are people looking for when they're contemplating a change?

Susan Well, there are several ways of approaching the issue. For example, you may want to stay in your current field, but with a change of role. Some people opt for a lateral move, I mean moving across or horizontally into a new role at the same level you're currently at – so that you can gain more experience in a similar position. Moving back or down is also possible – to explore a new direction, open up new opportunities or, increasingly often, to reduce stress. Or you might like to consider an exploratory, often temporary move to another location or department, just to give yourself a taste of what else is out there. But of course, something else to remember is that, over time, you will grow into your role. And then you can develop it on your own terms.

Interviewer Does this really work for everyone? I mean, essentially, aren't most people looking for a change – any change – because they're just a bit bored?

Susan Yes, that's right, there are times when we reach a stage in our careers when we feel stuck – we aren't sure which direction we should be moving in. Within a conventional organization, it's really up to managers to look out for the warning signs that people are looking to move on, and to discuss the options with them. They need to focus on the positives of being assigned to other departments or project teams. It needn't mean you're being sidelined – your horizons are simply being broadened. That sort of approach.

Interviewer And what if the changes suggested by your manager don't match your expectations?

Susan Well, then there's the ultimate step of moving on completely. You want to go beyond the scope of your current job, there's nothing suitable where you are, so you start looking around for an interesting position in another organization.

Interviewer And is a manager ever likely to encourage this?

Susan Well, you and your manager can see when you've looked at all the options and the fit just isn't there. Maybe your skills don't match those required for the job, perhaps your career goals are unrealistic within the organization. In such cases, the manager may just have to let you go, and if the move is done well, you can end up being the best ambassador for that organization after you leave.

Interviewer OK, can we just go back to your point about the move downwards or backwards? How is that supposed to be a progressive step? Surely most of us would find that demotivating?

Susan Good question. I know this can seem like some kind of voluntary demotion, but that's not necessarily the case. It's difficult to explain exactly, but sometimes, in order to move forward you need to take a step backwards to put yourself in a better position for the next move.

Interviewer OK, well, I may have to take your word on that.

09

Extract 1

Heidi … Right, everyone's here now, so let's get started, shall we? I'm afraid we don't have that much time. Now, as you know, the purpose of today's meeting is to look at our current recruitment problems. I've asked Arun to analyse the underlying causes of the difficulties we're currently experiencing in recruiting the right people. So, er, perhaps Arun, you'd like to talk us through some of your findings.

Arun Certainly. Well, this is an issue that has been affecting Coben Walsh for some time now. I've been following up on why so many candidates have rejected job offers. And basically, there's no getting away from it – we face serious competition from the larger, better-known accountancy firms. Top graduates know how much they're worth and they're attracted to the most prestigious, higher-paying firms.

Rachel Could I just say something here, Heidi?

Heidi Yes, go ahead.

Rachel You probably won't like this idea, Andy, but I think that the obvious solution to this problem must be to increase the initial salary package we're offering. I really think we should consider doing so.

Andy I'm sorry, but I don't think we're in a position to do that, Rachel. Apart from anything else, it would mean we'd have to increase all salaries by the same amount to retain motivation in our current staff.

Heidi Can I suggest we come back to this point about salaries a bit later on, Rachel? Andy?

Rachel Yeah, OK.

Andy Agreed. Anyway, I'd rather investigate other options before we go down that route. I'd be interested to hear about your suggestion, Heidi, before we make any decisions.

Heidi Yes, of course. I'll get on to that in a moment. Arun, did you want to talk about staff retention issues as well?

Arun Yes, well, as you know, we're also experiencing a high turnover of staff, again, primarily among our younger employees. Based on what they say in their exit interviews, there seems to be a general feeling that we're a bit specialist, and they'll progress faster in their careers by moving companies. They don't seem to feel any particular loyalty to us. And …

Rachel If I could just come in here for a moment, Arun? What makes you so sure it's an issue that only affects our company? I'd say it's the attitude in all industries these days – people simply don't stay with one company for that long any more.

Andy Of course, you're absolutely right, but we can't just ignore this problem. I know you're not keen on it, Rachel, but I really think we should hear about Heidi's school-leavers plan.

10

Extract 2

Heidi OK, given the current situation, I'm sure you'll understand the need to improve our choice of candidates.

Andy Absolutely, yes.

Heidi Now, I'm not sure what your feelings are about this, but we think we need to move our focus away from university graduates. We were wondering if we could consider targeting school-leavers instead – offering them an apprenticeship with Coben Walsh and paying for them to study for their professional qualifications whilst gaining on-the-job experience.

Arun Er, Heidi, would this be the right moment to mention the conditions of employment?

Heidi Oh, yes, thanks, Arun. Well, basically, the new recruits could combine work and study for five years, during which they would receive a moderate salary. After five years they should then get their full professional qualification.

Rachel But surely the best students will want to go on to university? And won't there be bad feeling if we then recruit a graduate at a higher position with a higher salary?

Heidi Now, it's interesting you should say that, because actually I think the trend is changing. A lot of good students are really worried about the cost of going to university, and the prospect of being in debt. It could be that they would be really happy to take a secure employment opportunity instead.

Andy We'd have to demand very high grades from the school-leavers, you know, to make sure we get the best candidates.

Heidi Yes, quite. Now, coming back to the issue of graduates – they have to complete three years of training once they join us in any case. That means that effectively they'll only be two years ahead of the school-leavers, and since we're paying for five years of education I don't think the school-leavers will complain about their comparatively low salary.

Rachel Mm, I suppose so. But do you really think school-leavers will be able to make such big decisions about their career at the age of eighteen? Given that we need employees who are committed to the profession, wouldn't it be better to focus on ways of improving our graduate intake?

Arun Well, I think a lot of eighteen-year-olds do already have a clear idea of what they want to do. Er … something else we've been thinking about is the introduction of an entry exam …

11

Conversation 1

Arun I'm so glad I finally had a face-to-face meeting with the partners – I haven't had much contact with them so far, and at least now they know who I am.

Heidi Yes, it's just as well I brought you along, Arun – as you're the one who's really going to have to deal with Andy and Rachel if we do go ahead with the changes. If I'd thought about it, I could have brought one of the recruitment consultants we use as well, but there's always next time. It would have been good if we'd made a bit more progress today.

Arun Yes, if only I'd known how Rachel would react to the school-leavers proposal.

Heidi Well, we should have anticipated it, really – we already knew she was quite resistant to the idea.

Conversation 2

Rachel All I can say is, I'm still not convinced this is the right move, Andy. I might have been a bit too forthright, but I need to be sure any change is right for the company. We are partners here, after all!

Andy Well, it could have been awful if we'd just gone round in circles. At least we managed to have some kind of discussion.

Rachel True. But suppose I hadn't been there to present the other side of the argument? What would have happened if I hadn't suggested improving our graduate intake? And I still don't think Arun brought much to the discussion – basically, he relied on Heidi.

Andy Yes, but it's a good thing he came to the meeting, though. It sounds like we're going to be working quite closely with him from now on.

12

Conversation 1

A So, what would you do if one of your key members of staff was off sick on the day of an important presentation?

B Um, well … would it help if I gave you an example?

A Mm. Go on.

B I mean, something like this happened to me in my previous job …

Conversation 2

A Ela, is it OK if we make some changes to those plans you sent through?

B The ones attached with the proposal? I thought they'd all been approved.

A No, I was actually referring to the ones drawn up for internal purposes. Especially the one on page four – it looks a bit odd to me.

B Does it?

A Well, if you look at the scale at the bottom of the page, you'll see what I mean. Surely that can't be right?

Conversation 3

A Sorry, I'm not really sure I've understood. Does everybody need to be informed?

B Sorry?

A Yes, sorry, let me rephrase that. Am I supposed to notify everybody in the department each time I receive one of these proposals?

B No, of course not, you won't have time to do that. What I'm saying is that it's worth sending it to the people responsible for that particular region. I know Alex is looking for new contacts, and so is Thierry. In other words, there's no point in it sitting in your in-tray for the next few weeks.

Conversation 4

A Well, the last year has obviously had its ups and downs for you, but look, the fact of the matter is that I need to see a dramatic improvement in your performance over the next six months.

B But it's been so difficult with all the changes. I'm sure you can appreciate, these are factors which are out of my control.

A Yes, I understand that. It's been difficult for everybody in the group. But the point I'm trying to make is I'd like to see more evidence of how you deal with these challenges.

Conversation 5

A I got some useful feedback from the morning session. Overall it seems they don't feel well informed about the product.

B Really? But don't we keep them informed with our newsletter?

A Yes, but what I mean by 'well informed' is, they'd have liked to be more involved with the product before it came to market. Look … to put it another way, couldn't we consider letting them trial the products in their own markets first, so that they feel their views count?

13

Well, I guess the main reason for working with tpmg is that we needed their help with the design and implementation of the process, but also the necessary IT tools. The software we've worked on with tpmg provided all the information employees and managers needed for the career review interviews, and for the design of career development plans. And perhaps here I should just say, the career development plan is something which the individual employees manage themselves – they can use it to help them plan their progression from their existing role to their preferred new role.

Obviously, our managers needed to get up to speed with the new process, and so the first thing we did was to run a series of briefings. Once the managers were trained, they could begin the interviews with their staff. After all the initial interviews were over, tpmg ran 20 functional meetings, where each functional management team was able to take an overview of their expected requirements and the talent already identified.

And that's where I think this process has been really useful – managers and HR have been better equipped to make fair assessments of who should be offered places on key development programmes, or ultimately offered more senior or key positions. And at board level, this has meant they've been able to talk about high-potential people, using the software to project all the information they needed.

Unit 3

14

Interviewer OK. Can you tell me a little bit about the company?

Iñaki Yes, well, our consultancy, BICG, was set up in 1999. Principally, we do research in the field of new ways of working, which is a fusion of several different disciplines related to the organizational aspects of a company. So we focus on the infrastructure – the information and communication technologies applied to the workplace. We look at the physical environment, architecture and the use of space, the way an office should be built and laid out. And more generally, we deal with the cultural aspects of a company, like working practices.

Interviewer Why does the professional world need new office and workplace concepts?

Iñaki Well, I think it's more like the end of a process, you know. Basically, we help companies to move with the times. I mean, the business world has been evolving rapidly over the last few decades, due to new technologies. Things have changed and it's time for physical spaces to accommodate the new needs and requirements of the world of work.

Interviewer OK. What kind of advantages are there from a management point of view? Is this purely a money-saving exercise?

Iñaki No, not exclusively. I mean, cost-saving is certainly one of the results you can achieve, but it's not the most important. What is essential is being more productive and having more efficient and effective processes, and teams and working practices. Then, also, having more motivated people.

Interviewer Mm. So, I imagine you make quite a few changes to the working environment. How do the people who are actually working there react to that? What problems do you have to anticipate?

Iñaki Well, actually one of the core focuses of our work is to facilitate cultural change within companies. People react differently. Normally the people at the bottom are quite happy to get something new; a more open and creative environment. Those at the top of companies, senior management, they are the champions or sponsors of these new concepts. But middle management tends to be very resistant to this kind of change, so we have to explain the benefits for them as well – it's important to generate enthusiasm for these changes.

Interviewer Yeah. How do you see this situation developing in the future? Are there going to be any more major changes? Or is it more of an ongoing process?

Iñaki I think it's been more or less an ongoing process for a couple of decades. We're getting more mobile and technology is getting smaller and smarter, and this is a trend that is making us more flexible, more and more independent of space. So the office won't be the place where you have to go every day and work eight hours. Work will be something that you can do wherever you are and, really, you'll come to the office to meet people and exchange information and knowledge. So that will probably be the trend in the near future.

Interviewer But if people aren't coming into the office, won't there be a problem with communication?

Iñaki Mm! Definitely, definitely! I mean, this is something you have to take account of, to ensure that people will communicate in the right way and will still have this 'we' feeling – being part of a team. You have to distinguish between the work you can do individually wherever you are, and the kind of work where you need to exchange information, ideas with your colleagues, and therefore you go to the office.

Interviewer Mm. And how do you assess your progress? How do you know whether or not the work you've done has been successful?

Iñaki Since we deal very often with so-called 'soft' factors, it's not that easy to measure the success of these kinds of projects. Nevertheless, there are other ways to measure success. Obviously, you can check the motivation of the people in a company. You can also check measurable aspects, like, for example, the time needed to solve a problem. If you reduce the normal time needed for solving a problem, then you are more productive.

15

Extract 1

… All right, just to fill you in on some of the background, research from Henley Management College in the UK has shown that middle managers are under increasing pressure and it's going to get tougher. Why? Because the flexible working revolution means that management will become more about resourcing and measuring results than about following day-to-day procedures. People are expected to be working more flexibly in the future. In fact, it's estimated that by 2050 most people will have been working flexibly for more than a decade. That's something to think about, and I'll return to this point later …

… So, I´ve divided my talk up into three sections. First of all, I'll consider the current research. After that, I´ll go on to talk about the impact on the workforce as a whole, and I´ll conclude with some comments about how this will affect employers.

16

Extract 2

I'd like to start by saying a few words about some of the changes predicted in a recent report. One significant change will be the rise in 'demuting'. By 'demuting' I mean working remotely from wherever you are, and not needing to travel to an office. So, the opposite of commuting really. It's anticipated that as many as twelve million people in the UK will be working from home by 2020. If the 20th century was about the 47.6-hour week for British workers, the 21st century is going to be about a new generation of 'career nomads'. Now, I don't know if you're familiar with this term? Well, 'career nomads' refers to employees who are changing the rules of time management in ways that suit their new approaches to work and leisure time. … To put it another way, employees who no longer think in terms of a job for life, but move around, changing jobs, and even careers. We need to ask ourselves – is this a good thing, and for whom?

17

Extract 3

… OK, moving on now to look at how this all affects the workforce. One possible consequence of the home becoming the focus of most people's working lives will be a rise in 'binge-time careerism' – this is where employees work non-stop for an agreed period and then take the equivalent amount of time off. Personal development could also benefit as new ways of working give rise to 'shadow careers' – and perhaps here I should just explain what I mean by 'shadow careers' – that's when amateur activities are pursued to professional standards. So for example, …

… Turning to the next point, research commissioned by British Telecom points out that 24-7 access to company emails and information via phones and BlackBerries could simply translate into staff working harder and longer, unless organizations devise formal policies to deal with their new working practices. And as I said earlier, it's predicted that there will be tension between employers and employees over some new ways of working. I'll say more about the effects on employers in a moment.

Just to digress for a second … The report suggests that the trend towards home working could have other positive social side-effects. It points to the fact that three-quarters of people questioned believe that flexible work patterns and the rise of home-based businesses are likely to revive local communities. And six out of ten people believe the shift will make larger communities and cities more personal and people-friendly.

18

Extract 4

For employers, however, the flip-side to all this will be the sheer number of alternatives available to individuals. And this brings me to the last point. Whenever I hear employers discussing how they are going to compete for talent, the focus always seems to be on competition with other employers …

… But today's technology-aware workers already have more opportunities than ever before to make a distinct choice between corporate life and working, in whatever capacity, for themselves – and we anticipate that this trend will only increase. And this is my key point – by the mid-21st century a major cultural change will have taken place. The workforce will have acquired the power to make choices, and employers need to recognize this and start planning for it now. To sum up, forward-thinking employers would be wise to view this element of choice as just as serious a competitor as other employers are considered to be. And solving this dilemma must surely become a key priority.

So, that brings me to the end of my talk. Thank you very much for listening. And I'll be happy to take any questions now.

19

1 Yes, I can't see any alternative. I think it's bound to happen sooner or later.
2 It may happen, but it's not very likely.
3 I think it's possible that we'll see new innovations in this area, yes.
4 It may well be that things change in the next few years. We'll have to wait and see.
5 Definitely, yes – there's certain to be a major change at some point in the future.
6 I think it's very unlikely that will happen, to be honest.
7 Oh, most certainly, yes. And it's highly likely to impact on all our lives.
8 It's quite probable that we'll see some big changes in the near future.
9 It's certain that there will be significant changes, yes.
10 Oh, definitely, and there's a good chance most of us will benefit from these changes.

20

1

A Hello?
B Hi, Sophia. It's Manjit. Have you got a few minutes?
A Er, actually I'm quite snowed under at the moment, with the exhibition only two days away!
B I know what you mean. It's quite hectic over here too. I'll only be a few minutes, though.
A OK. What can I do for you?

2

A How was the presentation? Did it go according to plan?
B No, not quite. It wasn't so great, actually.
A Oh?
B Well, there just wasn't enough time to cover everything. And there were quite a few technical problems along the way. I don't think the organization here has been particularly good, actually.
A No, it hasn't, has it?
B I mean, they should have stuck with the original 45 minutes per presentation.
A Yeah. It might be worth sending an email to everyone who came, to cover the parts you missed out.

3

A … It's just that I'm finding it's quite a task to manage my work now that the team has been split up. I spend way too much time passing messages on and not nearly enough time doing my actual job.
B I hear what you're saying. I mean, I know this is a tricky time for a lot of you, but I really think that in the long run, it'll work better as a system.
A I don't know. I feel like I'm just treading water.
B Believe me, I can see where you're coming from. I had a similar problem at my last company, but it did work out in the end.

4

A This is so annoying. Why won't people reply when I ask them to? It's been three days now.
B I know. I still think you should send the request again, though.
A But I don't want it to look like I'm badgering them.
B Quite. Well, you might want to word it so it's not too aggressive, in that case.

Unit 4

21

1

Nowadays, of course, there's a lot more consultation and discussion, but in the end someone has to take the final decision – and that's me. Sometimes you feel nervous putting your signature to a multi-million dollar agreement. If I've got it wrong – well, I prefer not to think about that.

But, of course, I've only reached the position I'm in because I'm not over-cautious by nature. I have been accused of being reckless – for example, when I took the bold step of cutting all our top-of-the-range prices by 30% last November. I was proved right on that one. To an outsider, my decisions may sometimes look rash, but you can be sure I've only reached them after carefully weighing up all the pros and cons. I have a duty to the shareholders not to behave in an imprudent way with their investment. You have to ask yourself again and again: am I being prudent? Or is this course of action basically foolhardy? And, of course, the other side of the coin is that I wouldn't be doing anyone any favours by completely avoiding justifiable risks that carry the possibility of sizeable returns.

2

I think it's what comes with responsibility. Sometimes it feels like the whole of my daily working life is filled with risk – but that's because I have quite a lot of freedom to make decisions. For example, I can decide exactly what deal I offer potential clients on price or discounts. That means I don't always know for sure that I've got it right. Sometimes I put the phone down and immediately I'm wondering how sensible that was.

In many ways, the biggest risk I face in my work is the risk of wasting time. As they say, time is money – it's actually my income. If you think you've got a good potential lead, you can spend days following up, and then the whole thing can just collapse and you end up with nothing. So to some degree you have to be cautious about deciding which leads to follow up.

3

I think most people think mainly of health and safety issues, but it's not only that. My responsibility covers all areas of risk within an organization – financial, legal, environmental, technological …

When I discover a potential problem, my job is to assess the severity of the loss that could result from it – maybe in equipment or time or knowledge, or even human life – and put a financial value on that. I also calculate the probability of that risk actually happening. I can then decide which risks need immediate attention, and which ones are manageable. In many cases you can find ways to completely avoid the risk. For example, if you determine that a staircase is potentially dangerous – you close it down and repair it. But, outside of safety issues, avoidance isn't always the most prudent course of action. If you went to the CEO and advised him to avoid every risk, you're probably gonna get a deeply sceptical response. A totally risk-averse company is never going to make much progress.

22

Extract 1

Jean-Luc … How about now, Greta? Is that any better? Good. Any more technical hitches? No? OK. So, if the document-share programme is now working, you should all be able to see page seven of the proposal on screen … Joanna, could you talk us through this?
Joanna Yes, sure. Well, if you could look at the bottom of page seven, where it says 'Risk summary', you'll see that I've summarized some of the risks involved in this proposal.

Extract 2

Thomas … OK, so that's one problem. And as a result, the price of minibus hire in the locality has increased dramatically over the last year.
Jean-Luc That's interesting, Thomas, thank you, but I think it's probably best left for another meeting. Maybe we're digressing a little. If I could just bring the conversation back to the agenda …
Joanna Am I right in saying that the general opinion is we can go ahead on this?
Khalid Khalid here. Er, I still have serious reservations. Are we really prepared to lose three of our best-selling products, including the Nile Cruise, just to chase this pipe-dream of green tourism? I suggest that we keep all the current tours, but include the opportunity for clients to pay a voluntary charge for carbon offsetting. Now, by doing this …
Jean-Luc OK, thanks, Khalid, maybe we can let Joana answer that.
Joanna Well, if you remember, we did explore this last year – that was just before you joined us, Khalid – and we decided at the time that it wasn't the route to go down.
Jean-Luc You're saying that it's not worth reconsidering?
Joanna I really don't think so.
Khalid With respect Joanna, do luxury travel and green tourism really go together? And do we really believe that our customers will pay thousands of dollars to stay in a mud hut without running water, next to a termite mound? That's what I'm asking.
Jean-Luc OK, Khalid, you've made your point. Greta – I'd be interested in hearing what you think about this.
Greta Well, at first I was very much in favour of Joanna's proposal, but I admit that I'm having some second thoughts about it. Which is why I put forward an alternative proposal that we're going to discuss later on. I think we have to take the long view. There is huge growth in this sector and we …

Khalid What do you think of this? We offer customers the option of paying the carbon offsetting as an extra …

Jean-Luc Sorry, Khalid. Could you let Greta finish, please?

Khalid OK, sorry.

Greta I was just saying that I think if we're going to stay competitive in this market …

Extract 3

Jean-Luc … so that all seems OK. Thomas – I have a question for you here. How likely is it that our current partners along the Mombasa coast would buy into this proposal?

Thomas Can I just check – we are now talking about the alternative smaller-scale proposal suggested by Greta, rather than Joanna's full-scale original idea?

Jean-Luc Yes. I think that's where we've got to. Is that right? Joanna?

Joanna Reluctantly, yes. I'm not fully convinced as yet.

Thomas To me, it sounds a lot more manageable. Our partners can make a transition over a period of years rather than overnight – and depending on customer uptake, we can go faster or slower as appropriate. I think that makes more sense than trying to do everything at once, and possibly falling flat on our faces.

Jean-Luc OK, well, we seem to have some sort of consensus – although we still have to convince Joanna that this is the right course of action …

Extract 4

Jean-Luc OK … I'm not sure this is getting us anywhere! … Well … I'd like to draw things to a close, so can I just ask everyone to sum up their views in two or three sentences? I'll mention any of your remaining doubts or questions to the board when I report our discussion. Greta, can you start, please?

Greta It's been quite hard, but I think we've made the right decision. It would have been too risky to commit ourselves to …

23

1

Thomas … and as a result, the price of minibus hire in the locality has increased dramatically over the last year.

Jean-Luc That's interesting, Thomas, thank you, but I think it's probably best left for another meeting.

2

Khalid I suggest that we keep all the current tours, but include the opportunity for clients to pay a voluntary charge for carbon offsetting. Now, by doing this …

Jean-Luc OK, thanks, Khalid, maybe we can let Joana answer that.

Joanna Well, if you remember, we did explore this last year – that was just before you joined us, Khalid – and we decided at the time that it wasn't the route to go down.

3

Khalid With respect Joanna, do luxury travel and green tourism really go together? And do we really believe that our customers will pay thousands of dollars to stay in a mud

hut without running water, next to a termite mound? That's what I'm asking.

Jean-Luc OK, Khalid, you've made your point. Greta – I'd be interested in hearing what you think about this.

4

Greta … I think we have to take the long view. There is huge growth in this sector and we …

Khalid What do you think of this? We offer customers the option of paying the carbon offsetting as an extra …

Jean-Luc Sorry, Khalid. Could you let Greta finish, please?

5

Jean-Luc OK … I'm not sure this is getting us anywhere! … well … I'd like to draw things to a close, so can I just ask everyone to sum up their views in two or three sentences?

24

1

Steve Hi. You must be Reza.

Ali Reza Yes. *Ali* Reza, actually.

Steve Sorry. Ali Reza. It's Steve, isn't it? I've seen your picture on the website.

Steve Right. So, you've come over for this meeting?

Ali Reza Yes. I just arrived this morning.

Steve How was the journey?

Ali Reza Not too bad. I managed to sleep a little on the plane.

2

Sophia I thought I recognized that voice. Hello, Harry. How are you?

Harry Sophia. Nice to see you. You're looking well.

Sophia Thank you. It's really nice to see you. I wondered if you'd be coming.

Harry Yeah, well, I may be old, but you can't get rid of me that easily.

Sophia So, they're keeping you busy then?

Harry Absolutely.

Sophia And are you still enjoying it? Really?

Harry Ah. Well …

3

David Kornelia! I had no idea you were coming over for this event.

Kornelia David – hello! Good to see you. It must be two years or more since we last met.

David Wasn't it at that conference in Egypt?

Kornelia Oh yes, on the Red Sea – it was really beautiful.

David Yeah, but do you remember that taxi ride back to the airport?

Kornelia Yeah – I thought we weren't going to make it.

David And then to make matters worse, the airline lost all our bags!

Kornelia Yes – that was no laughing matter!

David So anyway, how are you doing?

Kornelia Fine, thanks.

David Someone said you'd had a difficult year.

Kornelia Well. Yes. I have had a few ups and downs.

David Ups and downs?

4

Pietro Hello. May I join you?

Janos Yes, of course. Have a seat.

Pietro I'm Pietro Agnelli from the Turin office.

Janos Janos Rezmuves. From Szeged in Hungary.

Pietro Good to meet you. Wait a minute … You're not the Janos who pulled off that big Integra deal, are you?

Janos Well, it wasn't just me. There was a whole team involved. And anyway, Pietro, I've heard quite a lot about you, too. You got the gold award last month, didn't you?

5

Marc Well, I'd been working in the Paris office for five years when senior management decided I needed to see more of the world. So I've been in Manhattan for the last … oh, six or seven months, I guess. In a luxury apartment overlooking Central Park.

Maria Lucky you!

Marc Yeah … it sounds good, I know, but the job's pretty challenging. But I'm enjoying it.

Maria Challenging in what way?

Marc Well, it's a well-established team and they had their own way of doing things, so as far as they're concerned I'm still the new guy …

25

Well, yes, McCain is an interesting example of a company that's been able to respond well to some significant changes in the world around it. I think you could categorize their actions under the two main headings of Product Development and Information.

In terms of their actual product, McCain have always been innovators – think of oven chips, chips cooked in the oven instead of a pan full of oil. They've now switched all production from using vegetable oil to sunflower oil, which has much lower levels of saturated fat. They've also invested in finding ways to dramatically reduce salt whilst retaining taste.

The other part of their action plan has been to make sure that the public is better informed about their products. Er, McCain have embarked on an education campaign to explain why chips … sorry, French fries … are a healthy and important food. They've even sponsored some in-school promotions and initiatives to encourage product awareness and more informed attitudes to a balanced diet. This is all designed to provide a scientifically-backed and persuasive counter-argument to the 'chips are unhealthy' lobby.

Of course, there is quite a lot of opposition to this approach. But McCain have made a point of stressing in their marketing that they only use simple, natural ingredients: potatoes and oil. They've now labelled all UK products with a traffic light symbol – red, yellow, and green – to show fat, sugar, and salt levels. In fact, all McCain chips are able to show a green light that indicates low saturated fat. There isn't a single product which carries a red light. More unusually, they've even worked alongside the fire service on campaigns to 'ban the pan' – aiming to reduce the number of kitchen fires caused by the oil in the pan catching fire. It's surprisingly common.

So, all in all, I think McCain have tackled what could have been a very risky period for their products quite boldly, taking on their detractors with innovation and positive arguments. Market research shows that people still want exciting and tasty foods – but, increasingly now, they also want healthy products. McCain are an example of one company that is constantly adapting to satisfy this demand.

Unit 5

26

1

I'd say I'm very sales-focused, very much so. As I've already outlined, I sell more than anyone else in my current job. I just love the challenge of the sale. Of course, I need to drive the other members of my team as well – yes, they might find me a bit demanding at times, but I think it's important to work together as a team to get results. Otherwise we just wouldn't achieve our sales targets, would we?

2

What do I bring to the team? Let's see … Well, given my current position, I obviously know the products inside-out. I think I'm also quite good on detail – I'm generally able to pinpoint the cause of a problem as soon as it arises, and deal with it, of course. I think I'm capable of handling most complications by myself. That's why I prefer not to delegate. I mean, I certainly wouldn't want to neglect my responsibilities.

3

It doesn't matter what project I'm working on, my priorities are always to deliver what's been asked of me, and on time. That's why I prefer to avoid any last-minute changes, although obviously I need to discuss these suggestions with the other team members before deciding how to proceed. Generally though, I'd say it's best to stick to the initial brief, especially where there are particularly tight deadlines to meet.

27

Extract 1

Jenny Right, guys, can I just make sure I've understood this correctly? Paul. Would I be right in thinking we agreed not to use the logo with the knife?

Paul Yes, precisely! Which is why this whole thing is just so frustrating. What really concerns me is the way this has been handled so badly by the printers. I said from the very beginning that I had my doubts about using this contact instead of our usual printer. But Riccardo must have had his reasons.

Jenny OK, OK. Let's try not to get personal here. We've got a problem to sort out. Can we try and stay focused on the facts?

Riccardo And it's worth bearing in mind, the error isn't necessarily on the printer's side. To be honest, I'm a bit worried about some of the other artwork as well. The quality isn't as good as it could be. I mean, the printer may not have received all the latest versions of the files – do you understand what I'm trying to say?

Paul Look, Riccardo, not only do we have a major error on our hands, but we're also not sure how this happened. As I said earlier, I'm really not happy with the way this has been

handled, and it's the Vienna convention which really worries me. I'd just like to point out that we are flying out to Vienna in less than a week, and we don't even have a decent set of brochures to hand out. The real issue here is that we're just not prepared. The printing should have been done months ago!

Riccardo You're quite right, Paul. I don't know if you are aware, but the reason the printing didn't go ahead earlier was that we were waiting for your department's approval on the prices.

28

Extract 2

Jenny Well, Riccardo, how do you propose we deal with this issue?

Riccardo OK – firstly, before going back to the printer, I really just wanted to try and establish how the errors happened. Did somebody on our side hand over the wrong files? I mean, it's a possibility.

Paul Look, Riccardo, the thing that bothers me is that we just don't have time. To be frank, I'm sorry, but I can't just sit around and wait for you to sort this out. And I just don't understand how you could even be contemplating a reprint with only a few days to go, not to mention the extra cost. I say, send the brochures out to Vienna as they are – we can get the errors corrected in the next batch. For now, we'll just have to tolerate them as they are.

Riccardo OK, Paul, I see what you mean, but surely we need to get this right now? The reason why I say this is because if we get it right this time, any future campaigns should run more smoothly.

Paul Oh, come on, that's just not practical. I just won't be able to go ahead with the launch in Vienna if I don't have the brochures by Wednesday. This is what I've been afraid of from the beginning of this project. Think of the repercussions – our key clients have been waiting for months for this new range.

Jenny Look, Paul, Riccardo, can we try to avoid any serious setbacks here? How we resolve this is the issue now.

Riccardo I agree with Jenny. I was really hoping that we could find a solution that suits all of us here. Thinking about this sensibly, the problems with the artwork I'm prepared to overlook, if we could just sort out the problems with that logo. I mean, look, would it help if I gave the printer another call? See if it could be changed in time and get some costs?

Jenny That sounds sensible. Paul, I need to know we've got your approval on this?

Paul OK, fair enough. I'm prepared to wait and see what you and the printer come up with.

Jenny In which case, Riccardo, can I leave you to liaise with the printer, if we *do* do a reprint?

Riccardo Yes, of course. If you both agree to this solution, I'd be more than happy to oversee everything personally. I promise you, nothing will go wrong this time!

29

1 The reason why I say this is because if we get it right this time, any future campaigns should run more smoothly.

2 Which is why this whole thing is just so frustrating.

3 How we resolve this is the issue now.

4 It's the Vienna convention which really worries me.

5 In which case, Riccardo, can I leave you to liaise with the printer …?

6 What really concerns me is the way this has been handled so badly by the printers.

7 The problems with the artwork I'm prepared to overlook.

8 The thing that bothers me is that we just don't have time.

9 Not only do we have a major error on our hands, but we're also not sure how this happened.

30

Conversation 1

A Tomasz, I'm glad I bumped into you. I've had a chance to run through that document you asked me to look at. So … whenever you want to discuss it …

B Great. Have you got time now?

A Yes, I have a few minutes before my next meeting.

B It shouldn't take too long. And look, I really appreciate this, I know how busy you are. So what were your thoughts?

A Mm, I think my only real doubt is the line you've taken on absenteeism.

B OK …

A I don't think they'll accept this approach.

B Oh, really? Why do you think that?

A Basically, … it … it's not strong enough.

B So how do you think I could improve it?

A I'm not sure about including all those transcripts of interviews with staff. Couldn't you just summarize the key issues that came up?

B Oh, I see. Well, it seems a pity to have to cut them, but maybe you're right. Was there anything else?

A Mm. Yes, a slight problem – I think some of your data is confidential.

B Oh, really? I'm sorry, I didn't realize – thanks for pointing that out.

A Sorry, I hope this doesn't sound too negative.

B No, that's fine. Actually, I'm very happy to have some honest feedback. I'll just keep working on it.

Conversation 2

A David, look, I've been meaning to say something …

B Yes?

A It's just … I'm kind of worried about that proposal you're circulating at the moment.

B OK. What's the problem?

A Well, essentially I like the idea, but you know how controversial it might be, don't you?

B No, I'm sorry, I don't see what you're getting at.

A I feel you could be making life difficult for yourself. You know, this may even go to the workers' council.

B Look, you're entitled to your opinion, but at this stage, you know, it might not be a bad thing if it did. And to be honest, I just don't have time to rework it at the moment.

A Look, David, I'm just trying to help. And I'm not expecting you to start again. I've said there's nothing wrong with the idea – you just need to approach it in a slightly different way.

B I see what you're saying, Roberta, but the reason I'm taking this approach is because I think this plan will work in the long run.

A No one's denying that, but I really think you're going to cause yourself a lot of trouble in the short term.

B Fair enough, but it's a bit late now. Maybe you should have said something earlier.

Conversation 3

A Phew. That was hard work!

B Yes. And it's good thing you brought an extra copy of the proposal.

A Yeah, that was lucky. So, how do you think it went?

B Pretty good, I think – they signed, anyway. And that last question – you handled that really well.

A Thanks. Though I have to admit, I got the idea from Jenna – apparently the same issue came up last week and she got caught out. So what about that new guy?

B The one we hadn't met before? Hassan? Yeah, he was really tough.

A Definitely. By the way, thanks for backing me up with the figures.

B Hey, no problem. I could see you were getting kind of lost.

A I know, I'm afraid that was down to nerves.

B Don't worry, you did well. You just have to build on that experience now.

A Thanks for your support – it's good to know I'm on the right track.

Unit 6

31

Interviewer Today we're continuing our theme of innovation, and I'm joined by our business analyst, Jost Van der Saar, to talk about a dilemma faced by many large companies. How do you run an efficient company, but also create space for those new, innovative ideas, without cutting into the bottom line? Jost, it's not always that easy to get the balance right, is it?

Jost No, that's right. If you take a company like 3M, for example. They tend to be associated with creativity – as you know, they invented the Post-it note among other things. Now, they underwent some significant changes when James McNerney took over as Chief Executive Officer – he was the first outsider to lead the company in its 100-year history. The company certainly needed knocking into shape at that time, and McNerney set out to boost earnings from the start. One of the first things he did was to cut the workforce by 11%.

Interviewer What kind of a reaction did he get to these changes?

Jost Well, he caused quite a stir. McNerney's approach to raising profitability certainly satisfied the shareholders. He was clearly attempting to shift the emphasis from innovation to quality control. And from his days at General Motors, he introduced Six Sigma. Now this is a programme aimed at improving quality, controlling costs, and increasing efficiency and it doesn't tolerate mistakes easily. It demands precision, and the main idea is to eliminate production defects.

Interviewer Well, McNerney left the company some years ago, of course. What's the situation at 3M since then?

Jost Well, people are asking whether McNerney's efficiency drive hasn't in fact stifled creativity. As you can imagine, that's quite a serious concern for a company whose very identity is built on innovation.

Interviewer Is there any hard evidence to support these fears?

Jost Well, it's interesting. In the past, one-third of sales came from products released in the five previous years – today this figure has slipped to one-quarter only. The current CEO, George Buckley, is convinced he can outperform the competition by reigniting top-line growth. He's reeling back on Six Sigma just enough to get the creative juices flowing again …

32

Extract 1

James So, even though it's been a surprisingly difficult year for Skion PCs, hopefully today will help generate some ideas for improving our position in the market. Would anyone like to start?

Sue Well, yes … I mean, couldn't we consider ways to develop our image, to show that we're a genuinely caring business?

James Sorry, I should also say, I don't think we need to do anything that's radically different. Also, it's not clear to me what you mean by 'caring'.

Sue Well, for example, what about moving into the area of recycling? Most people have no idea what to do with old computers and components – they either keep them or end up throwing them out. I would have thought it would be possible to collect a customer's old computer when we sell them a new one and implement a policy of recycling.

Jessica Oh, I see, so you're thinking of something charitable, like maybe, we collect in used parts and send X% off to developing countries, am I right?

Sue Well, not necessarily that … I haven't really had a chance to think it through properly, but that's not such a bad idea. Thinking about it, we could even set up a programme where staff can choose to spend some of their holiday time working on a project in a developing country, but we'd pay to make sure it's well-run and responsible. I've done something similar myself. It was actually one of the most rewarding things I've ever done.

James Gareth, what do you think?

Gareth To tell you the truth, I'm not totally convinced. I'm concerned about how that would work in practice, and I can't help wondering whether it would really be cost-effective.

James So is that a definite 'no'?

Gareth Well, no, but I would certainly need to know that it's profitable, before taking it any further.

Sue It's not about cost-effectiveness, it's about acting responsibly …

Jessica Well, can we try and take this just a little bit further after this meeting? I mean, obviously we'd need to do a lot more research before reaching any final decisions.

33

Extract 2

Jessica It's an interesting idea. In terms of marketing I think it has potential. It's certainly worth thinking about. In fact … well, I'm not sure how this would work in practice, but how about a wider policy on environmental issues, you know, similar to the idea about being 'the company that cares', but more focused on energy-saving as well as recycling?

James OK, would you like to expand on that?

Jessica Well, I was thinking along the lines of solar-powered laptops, for instance.

Sue Solar-powered?

Jessica Look, I only say that because there's big money in energy-saving and if we became well known as specialists in this area we wouldn't just sell to domestic customers.

Sue Sorry, are you saying that we could open up market share with this idea?

Jessica Er … well, yes … look, could I just explain in a bit more detail? I think this is where our website could play a major role, I mean, we could target small businesses, educational institutions, and public sector organizations around the world. Places where electricity supplies are sporadic. Does that make sense?

James Well, yes, but I don't really think we could get away with that – do you? It's such a departure from what we're doing at the moment. I mean, it's potentially quite high-risk. If I've understood correctly, you're saying that we should become energy-saving specialists.

Jessica Well, I just thought that in a way maybe we'd gain competitive advantage, you know, something innovative … after all, the technology's there. People are already doing it. Why not us?

Gareth I'm sorry, I'm just not convinced. Look, shouldn't we be thinking more about straightforward, commercial developments? I think we should get back to discussing what we can do realistically, now, with the capacity that we have at the moment, and focusing on the bottom line.

34

Extract 3

James Maybe you're right. What did you have in mind?

Gareth Well, something similar to Sue and Jessica's ideas earlier, about recycling. Supposing we were to sell recovered parts through brokers back to the manufacturers or clients who needed 'obsolete' parts?

Sue Obsolete parts? Right, erm … What makes you think that would work?

Gareth Actually, it's not nearly as complicated as it seems; we might even be able to set up links on our own website …

James Mm, you've obviously given this some thought …

Gareth And there's nothing stopping us from setting up as brokers ourselves, is there? We could buy up unwanted parts and sell them on ourselves, to our regular customers.

James Yes, that's true. You may have something there. Well, it's easily the best idea I've heard so far. And we could probably be more competitive on service than some of those larger brokers.

Jessica Mmm, I don't know, I'm not so keen on the idea.

James We should at least consider it, though.

Jessica Yes, OK. But wouldn't we be doing exactly the same as Green PCs? I've been looking at their website and it's pretty much the same idea …

35

1 Could I just explain in a bit more detail?
2 You've obviously given this some thought.
3 I'm not totally convinced.
4 It's been a surprisingly difficult year.
5 It's easily the best idea I've heard so far.
6 I'm just not convinced.
7 It was actually one of the most rewarding things I've ever done.
8 Look, I only say that because there's big money in energy-saving.
9 I'm not so keen on the idea.
10 I don't really think we could get away with that – do you?

36

1 a Could I explain in just a bit more detail?
  b Could I just explain in a bit more detail?
2 a Surprisingly, it's been a difficult year.
  b It's been a surprisingly difficult year.
3 a It was actually one of the most rewarding things I've ever done.
  b Actually, it was one of the most rewarding things I've ever done.
4 a I really don't think we could get away with that – do you?
  b I don't really think we could get away with that – do you?

37

Conversation 1

Anna Tom, I'm in the middle of preparing for the sales conference.

Tom Oh, yes?

Anna Yes … and I have to do a short presentation.

Tom Ah. Lucky you!

Anna I know! More worrying still is that it's only a month away!

Tom Yeah, it does seem to come round pretty quickly …

Anna Yes. Anyway, I've got a few ideas, but I still need to bring it all together. I was wondering if you remember what you said last year?

Tom Oh, erm, let's see … Something about how well we were doing, I think! Er, hmm … you've put me on the spot here. I'm not quite sure now, it seems like a long time ago. I seem to remember talking about defending our strategic position – something like that, in any case.

Anna OK. And did you talk about the local markets? Erm. Any kind of analysis?

Tom Yes, I'm sure I would have done. Erm. And I remember starting off with a short quiz to break the ice … I'm trying to think what I would have done with that. I could certainly find it, though, and email it to you if that's any help?

Conversation 2

Eva So what do you think of my draft proposal? I'd be grateful for your feedback.

Dan Yes, it's not bad. I'd say you're on the right track. In any case, it's the kind of thing we're looking for. It just needs a bit more development.

Eva More development …?

Dan You know, explaining the rationale behind the proposal, why now, and so on.

Eva OK … what about the opening paragraph? Is it strong enough?

Dan Something along those lines … Yeah, you certainly need something like that, to help set the right tone, don't you? Again, I'd say it just needs a bit more work, really.

Eva More work? Could you be more specific?

Dan Well, I could give you a few general pointers, but I'm afraid I haven't really got time to get involved in the detail. Anyway, I thought Rob was supposed to be helping you with this?

Eva Well, yes, I did email him last week, but he still hasn't got back to me.

Dan Well, he'll probably get back to you before the end of this week – that should still give you time to revise your draft.

Conversation 3

Federico Dominique! I thought you were in Germany?

Dominique No, I got back last night.

Federico How did the research go? Did you see any interesting interiors?

Dominique Actually, overall it was quite disappointing.

Federico Oh, really?

Dominique Yes. Still, there was one place that was quite interesting … I haven't got my laptop with me now, otherwise I could show you some photos.

Federico Was it typically German? The style, I mean.

Dominique No, not really. It's difficult to explain, really. It almost had a hint of something oriental – oh, and lots of black and white … it was kind of minimalist.

Federico A lot of lacquer?

Dominique Yes, panelling, partitions, you know, that sort of thing … In fact, you remember that Japanese restaurant we went to in London?

Federico Yes, of course.

Dominique Well the partitions were a bit like that, but not quite as decorative.

Unit 7

38

Interviewer Would you say that staff in your organization are encouraged to take a 'systems thinking' approach?

Jane Well, we don't explicitly encourage staff to take a systems thinking approach. But if you look at the content of some of the training programmes, a lot of it is geared towards them thinking about the implications of what they do outside their immediate area of responsibility. So, for example, our finance training is very much about getting people to think about how their decisions impact on the bottom line, the profit and loss account, and the implications for other departments. We also have one particular course that all staff in one of our divisions are expected to attend, and it's designed to put people's jobs into the wider business context, so that they can see the bigger picture. So, from that point of view, yes, to some extent we do try to get people thinking more broadly than their immediate remit, but it's not a specific or an explicit aim.

Interviewer So, how would you describe the approach to learning and training across your organization?

Jane The approach that we take is that we divide training into job-specific training, and then more generic training, and we approach the two areas in slightly different ways. The majority of our training is job-specific and we get information on what this should be from what we call a bottom-up approach, where we look at individual training needs. This is normally triggered by the appraisal process, and the delivery of the training then tends to be driven by line managers. They'll often provide that training on the job. So if people need to learn specific skills like design or marketing, that happens locally. Departments often find their own training providers and they have their own budgets to do that, so we take quite a decentralized approach in that way. The generic training would be related to skills that are relevant right across the business, like management skills, communication skills, or IT training. It's also training in response to any current themes that relate to particular business challenges. So, for example, at the moment there's quite a big push on project management training because of the need to manage projects more effectively. This kind of training is often generated by senior management, so it's more of a top-down approach, and the training itself is more centrally-driven.

Interviewer What are the advantages and disadvantages of doing things the way you do them?

Jane Well, I think one of the advantages is that because, primarily, we have a very decentralized approach to training it means that each division gets what it needs from the central training department. So we're quite responsive to their needs and that's a real advantage. Also, we provide a range of learning opportunities, not just courses. We have reading materials, DVDs, books, and also online links that people can use. We're trying to make training more self-directed. Line managers don't always have time to spend with staff, talking in detail and planning their training, so the more we can encourage people to take responsibility for their own development, the better. It's also an advantage because it means staff take ownership of their own learning and, therefore, they're much more likely to put more effort into what they're learning – and that learning is more likely to stick and be transferred into their jobs. Disadvantages? Well, from our central point of view, one drawback is that we get stretched very thinly, because rather than being able to take a one-size-fits-all approach right across the organization, we end up customizing a lot of what we do for each division, which is great for the divisions, but it's not always an effective use of central resources.

CD 2

39

Conversation 1

Tamara Hello, Kirsten. Er, we didn't finish our discussion about next year's training programme.

Kirsten No, you're right. We didn't. Do you want to carry on now?

Tamara Well, we need to have a concrete proposal for the meeting on Friday.

Kirsten Did you say *Friday*? I thought it had been brought forward to Thursday afternoon?

Tamara Well, er, that makes it even more urgent, then. Anyway, I'm not quite clear about your last suggestion. Could you run it by me again?

Kirsten Yes … OK, well, faced with the need to be fully compliant with the new legislation by early next year, I think we have at least 70 staff who need to be up to speed by the end of this year.

Tamara How many did you say?

Kirsten Seventy … seven-oh. But instead of training them all, I suggest we buy in training sessions and offer these to a few key managers. Working on the principle that they can all pass the content on to their own staff, we should have everyone trained up by January.

Tamara How many were you planning to offer it to?

Kirsten Just the eight heads of department. Make a single group.

Tamara And, er, what you're saying is, you don't think we have enough of our own trainers to provide this internally?

Kirsten No, it's not that we don't have the trainers. We don't have the expertise.

Tamara OK, well, on that point, it may not be entirely relevant, but I've heard some negative feedback recently on other internal training sessions.

Kirsten That's interesting. Could you clarify exactly what the problems were? Oh … Actually, no, it doesn't matter – I guess it's a bit off-topic right now.

Tamara OK. I think you suggested a provider. What was their name again? Consuelo, did you say?

Kirsten That's right. Given the limited number of companies offering this training, we don't actually have much choice.

Tamara No, that's right. Oh, that reminds me. Have you heard that Leon's leaving to go and work for another training provider?

Kirsten Yes, I heard. Knowing how demotivated he's been about his job recently, I'm not too surprised!

Tamara Yes. Anyway … sorry. That's a bit of a digression. Let's get back to the main issue. Are there any other loose ends? Er, what haven't we dealt with yet? Shall we talk about the proposal for distance learning?

Kirsten Yes. We need to do that. And we haven't looked at the question of timing yet. Or dealt with the cost!

Tamara I know. By the way, talking about costs, I haven't seen that report on the e-learning project yet.

Kirsten Ah, yes, I remembered that yesterday. I was going to write it this morning, but …

Tamara OK, OK, I know you're busy …

40

Conversation 2

Kirsten Hello, Kirsten Marr.

John Hello, this is John Powell from Consuelo. You left a message for me?

Kirsten Ah, yes, hello. Thanks for getting back to me so quickly.

John No problem. So, I was wondering, could you clarify exactly what sort of training programme you were hoping to run?

Kirsten Yes, of course. We need to ensure that our company is fully compliant with the new legislation and procedures regarding the transport and handling of hazardous biological materials. We had intended to do this ourselves, but having discussed it with the relevant people we now think we need to ask an external training provider to do this.

John Could I ask you to spell out some details – how many participants, when you wanted this to happen, and so on?

Kirsten We were thinking of having eight managers for a one-day workshop, ideally some time around the middle of next month.

John OK, a day should be OK. But, look, I'm very sorry, but you do know that we only run tailor-made workshops for a minimum of twenty participants?

Kirsten Oh, really? No, I didn't know. That's a bit annoying.

John Well, it's to do with cost, I'm afraid. Inevitably.

Kirsten No, I understand that. What I'm saying is, it's annoying for us because we just don't have that many people. So, do you mean that you can't do this training for us?

John Well, we could do it, but we'd have to charge for twenty people, even if only eight came.

Kirsten Mmm. I see. OK, well, maybe we have no choice.

John Sorry, I'm not quite sure I understand. Are you saying that you'd like to proceed with the booking anyway?

Kirsten Er … No. That's not what I mean. What I mean is that we'll have to run this internally after all.

John Look … Just a thought. It may not be entirely relevant, but we do have some spaces available on our open training day on the 3rd. Would you be interested in registering any participants for that?

Kirsten The 3rd, did you say?

John Yes.

Kirsten I think we'd probably be interested in that. But I need to confer with my line manager. Can I get back to you on that?

John Yes, of course.

41

1 Just a thought. It may not be entirely relevant, but …
2 Actually, no, it doesn't matter – I guess it's a bit off-topic right now.
3 Oh, that reminds me. Have you heard that Leon's leaving to go and work for another training provider?
4 Anyway … sorry. That's a bit of a digression.
5 Let's get back to the main issue.
6 By the way, talking about costs …

42

1 Faced with the need to be fully compliant with the new legislation by early next year, I think we have at least 70 staff who need to be up to speed by the end of this year.
2 Working on the principle that they can all pass the content on to their own staff, we should have everyone trained up by January.
3 Given the limited number of companies offering this training, we don't actually have much choice.
4 Knowing how demotivated he's been about his job recently, I'm not too surprised!
5 Having discussed it with the relevant people, we now think we need to ask an external training provider to do this.

43

Conversation 1

A So, what do you think of it so far?
B It's not very interesting, is it?
A That's the understatement of the year. I haven't learned anything I didn't know before.
B It's not *that* bad. Though I have to admit, I'm not getting much out of it.
A And the pace is so slow! It's doing my head in!
B I know what you mean. It's really testing my patience, too.
A In fact, I think I've reached my limit. I'm going to slip out after this coffee break.
B Won't you need to show you've attended?
A No problem. They've taken our names already! Are you staying?
B Well, I agree it hasn't lived up to expectations so far – but I need to learn something about the topic. Maybe it'll get better.
A OK. I'll see you later.

Conversation 2

A Was there something, Sue?
B Well, yes. I've been looking at Lou's new brochure design. I have to say that I was expecting something a bit more professional.
A What do you mean exactly?
B Well, the cover, for example – it's just not up to scratch. I don't find the choice of image appealing. And to be frank, I'm not very happy with the wording, either.
A I see what you mean, but it was a rush job. Maybe we should get Lou in and talk over some of the alternative design ideas.

Conversation 3

A Right. It's four o'clock. Let's move on to the next item.
B I'm sorry. I'm going to have to leave at this point.
A Oh. Is there a problem, Jacques?
B Well, if you're moving on to health and safety issues, I'm not sure how much I can contribute. I can't really see the point of staying.
A Well, I'm sorry you feel that way. It's a very important issue and I think it would be useful to have your views.
B To be honest, I'm finding it a bit frustrating that I have to be here at all. I've got a lot on at the moment and I just don't think this is the best use of my time.

44

I think it's true to say that Leyland Trucks have put developing their employees at the heart of their strategy – they've shown a real commitment to the people who work for them. We can see this quite clearly in how they've responded to the current and potentially very serious skills shortage.

The starting point was the realization that seeking to employ qualified staff from outside the company was not the only possible solution to the problem. Those people already working for the company, although unqualified, had the relevant experience, interest, and potential to make up for the shortage of trained professionals. If they could be helped to take training courses in the relevant areas, and achieve recognized qualifications, it would benefit both the company and the employees themselves. Crucially, Leyland recognized that just because these employees had joined the company straight from school, it didn't mean that they weren't capable of higher levels of study. Now, in fact, their experience of working for the company gave them an excellent basis from which to embark on a course of study to become a professional engineer.

Anyway, Leyland entered into a partnership with two colleges who designed tailor-made courses for their staff. Thirty employees from a wide range of areas of the business were encouraged to apply for a two-year Trainee Design Engineer programme. Seven were accepted, and when they've finished the programme they'll have a qualification that they can use towards completing a full engineering degree. And another thirteen employees are taking a foundation degree in automotive manufacturing equal to the first two years of an engineering degree.

Now, much of the success of these programmes lies in the fact that the participating colleges have created courses that precisely fit the needs of the company, and at the same time they also satisfy the employees' personal aspirations. I think this kind of partnership between industry and academia is excellent, and it shows the potential for similar training schemes in different industries.

Unit 8

45

1

Interviewer What is it that you look for in prospective employees?

Interviewee Well, basically, a strong candidate for us would be … would demonstrate qualities of enterprise. And I should say somebody who can really apply themselves … But equally importantly, they need to demonstrate the ability to take the initiative. I have to say, we do value people who can think for themselves and who are able to seek out opportunities, the *right* opportunities … to make the most of their career with us.

Interviewer And once you've found the right people, how do you help them develop?

Interviewee Well, organizational learning is very important, of course. De Beers believes in the need for continued investment in its people, and I have to say, they generally show a willingness to make the most of any training opportunities. Then, also, at De Beers we encourage not only cross-divisional, but also cross-functional lateral moves – as you can imagine, it's a great way of really developing your career and it's good to see our people showing a desire to benefit from this kind of diversity.

46

2

Interviewer So, what does Credit Suisse expect from future employees?

Interviewee Well, we like people who can offer a combination of specialist know-how and personality. They need to be committed to individual achievement, and to the success of the team. We expect all our employees to support the bank's strategic goals … Erm, basically, you've got to be able to build up rapport and personal credibility with the client as well as your colleagues.

Interviewer And can you sum up, what's in it for the employee?

Interviewee Well, briefly … erm, provided that you live up to our expectations, you get to share in the success of a powerful company, a company that holds a leading position in the market, and I should say, a future-oriented company.

Interviewer And what's life like for employees at Credit Suisse?

Interviewee Our employees are encouraged to strive for a healthy work-life balance. That doesn't mean you'll never be under pressure, so obviously you've got to be able to cope with stress! But, of course, we'll provide training and on-the-job support to help you do this.

47

3

Interviewer What is Orange looking for in an employee?

Interviewee I should say the ability to think on your feet is really essential. The working environment at Orange certainly puts people to the test – by that I mean, you need to learn fast and adapt easily to new ideas and technological concepts. And then, as you'd expect, our employees have a real understanding of the importance of great customer service – of how to go beyond customer expectations, in fact. And I should add, also important – a good sense of humour.

Interviewer A sense of humour? Not something often associated with a multinational company, perhaps?

Interviewee No, that's right, but what we've created is a place where people can be themselves … where they can be professional and informal at the same time. Of course, they are motivated, and committed. But also, quite simply, they actually enjoy coming to work. You know, we like it here!

48

Extract 1

Ian … And that brings us to training. Since Anya's here, perhaps we can look at the new training initiative requested by the various team leaders? Anya, can you give us an overview of where we are with this?

Anya OK, yes. Well, to be honest, we haven't got as far as I'd hoped. Erm, where we are at the moment is … er, we've just completed the initial consultation stage. However, what I can tell you is that the initiative will be complete and in place before the annual review. I'd like to be able to give you a more precise date, but unfortunately I can't do that at the moment. You'll appreciate that I still need to run the details by Jean-Paul and the team leaders first …

So, now, perhaps it would be a good idea if I just went through some of the other training programmes we are running.

Ian Yes, OK.

Anya Good. Now, how can I put this? We have a quite 'flexible' approach to our training programme this year – we're trying to tailor it more to individual and team needs. So if it's OK, I'd just like to sketch out the core elements of the plans … Just feel free to interrupt me with any questions. Now … I don't know if you've heard of a 'balanced scorecard'? Let me just touch on this approach and how it works in practice …

… and that's more or less it … I think that's covered everything. Er, and it's just occurred to me that …

Ian Anya, you haven't said anything about management training?

Anya I was coming to that. Erm, it's obviously a key area, and I have to admit that we haven't got as far as planning the specifics yet – we just haven't had the time. But yeah, you're quite right, we need to address this … it might not be a bad idea to send out a questionnaire to the senior staff for their recommendations.

Ian And you've still got time to do that, have you?

Anya That's a good point. I think so. Let me check, and I'll get back to you. And how about if I send you a draft, too? I'm pretty sure that I could do that before the end of the week.

49

Extract 2

Ian … Pavla, I'm sorry to put you on the spot, but would you like to run through the union complaints briefly? We've really got to do something about job descriptions and pay scales. What ideas has your team come up with so far?

Pavla OK. How long do I have?

Ian As long as you need.

Pavla Right. Well, it's probably best if I just highlight some of the ideas we came up with, don't you think? Erm, it was basically a brainstorming session. So, the first thing is, we feel that people are simply time-serving and spending too long here. I don't know if you agree, but I'm pretty sure that this isn't great for productivity in the long run. And I think you should be aware that it's not limited to one department …

… it's crucial in the current climate. So that's one key point right there – we need to look at attitudes across the organization. Er, OK, next point, and I think this is a really important point: we need to start looking carefully at the current pay-scales …

… and, er, I don't think there's anything I've forgotten, erm … so, the main thing to remember is to listen. OK, I think that's about it.

Ian Good, thank you for that. I assume everyone participated in the brainstorming, did they? If it was just one or two individuals, then just how useful are the results?

Pavla I can't remember exactly, but … off the top of my head, I think everyone had something to say. That's quite a significant factor, though … I can double check if you like?

Ian Yes, email me later.

Pavla I was wondering if there was anything else you'd like to know about the origins of the ideas?

Ian No, that's fine, but it might also be worth touching on the numbers of complaints per business unit.

Pavla Well, I don't have the exact figures, but what if I run through the rough numbers we've come up with so far?

50

1

A Ah! Thierry! Just the person I was looking for! Is it true you're considering reducing the amount of staff car-parking?

B Ah … Look, Rachel, I'm afraid I'm really not in a position to talk about that.

A So it is true, then?

B No, I'm sorry, but I can't answer that.

2

A These demonstrations are quite serious, aren't they? You must be worried about the political situation at home?

B I'm sorry, I don't know what you mean.

A Oh, come on. It's all over the news. Your government is taking a very hard line – I just want to know what you think.

B I'm sorry, Karl. I would prefer not to talk about it.

3

A Can you tell us a little more about the proposed office move?

B I'm afraid I'm not up to speed on the most recent developments.

A Oh, I can't believe that. Someone with your connections?

B It's not for me to say. Sorry. This is HR's responsibility.

4

A Look, I just need to know. Have they agreed to work with us or not?

B Well, it's not that straightforward. There are still things to consider.

A Oh, come on. It's a simple question. Yes or no?

B Honestly, Kris. I'm afraid I don't know any more than you do.

5

A So, is our budget likely to increase in the next financial year?

B It's hard to say at the moment.

A But the decision must have been made, surely? If I find out that you knew …

B Look, it's nothing to do with me, OK?

6

A That was a surprise, wasn't it, Enzo leaving so suddenly?

B Mm … I can't really comment.

A I heard that he didn't resign – he was fired.

B I'm afraid I can't disclose that information – it's confidential.

51

Felipe … so what I want to do is bring the Katisha in line with the other hotels in the group as soon as possible. And obviously, that's with the help of GS International.

Oscar Of course, that was part of the agreement.

Felipe Yes, but I think there's actually a greater sense of urgency than during our initial debriefing.

Oscar In what sense, exactly?

Felipe Well, since the initial burst of optimism following news of the takeover, staff motivation seems to have fallen again. Basically, there's quite a lot of scepticism among the staff over whether they'll fit in with the new regime. This is especially true of the middle managers – and I'm afraid their doubts are resonating with the frontline staff.

Oscar I see. What effect is this having on staff retention?

Felipe Well, it's still early days … But obviously, the most significant thing is the potential loss of the middle management layer. Not only are we having to fill the gaps with untrained people, but we're also losing our skilled managers to other hotels. Naturally, they're only too happy to take advantage of the training we've given them. Inevitably, this has had a knock-on effect on our staff training – those who are left are either not experienced enough or too busy to maintain the level of service that we strive to provide.

Oscar Yes, yes, I can see that's an immediate problem, and obviously we don't want it affecting the GS International brand. How's the financial situation looking?

Felipe Well, bookings are holding up, thanks to the group's centralized reservation service and the goodwill attached to the GS brand. But we're still only just above break-even occupancy and our growth is only about 1%. But even this figure is a misrepresentation.

Oscar What do you mean?

Felipe Well, the 10% increase in occupancy, which we can directly attribute to joining the GS group, is offsetting the organic decrease we're experiencing. So in reality, it's a 9% decrease.

Oscar Right. Any other factors contributing to the decrease?

Felipe Competition's tough at the moment. The global brands have taken significant market share from us through corporate loyalty programmes. But I think the most significant thing is the falling rate of repeat bookings. People just don't seem to be coming back. Actually, guest satisfaction levels are at an all-time low.

Oscar I see. It's not looking good, is it?

Unit 9

52

1

Personally, I'm actually against this trend for CSR policies. I mean, why should I – a shareholder – allow the equity that I've built up to be spent on so-called social responsibility? I feel a lot of these projects are set up purely for short-term gain, and in the long run they can become a huge drain on resources. I mean, how do we know if the money to be invested in, say, a school project in a developing country, is actually going to the right people? We don't. If I want to donate my money to something like this, then that's my business. What I want is a good return on investment – for me it's all about the bottom line.

2

In my experience, having a sound CSR policy actually increases the market value of a company. By that, I mean a company's reputation is one of its key assets – it can have a significant impact on the success of the brand. Take Coca-Cola, for example: 96% of their value is made up of intangibles – the brand itself is worth a fortune, obviously. But if they made a major error, socially or environmentally, the reputation of the company would suffer and it could take a very long time to recover. To dismiss CSR policies on the basis of short-term profit doesn't make much business sense to me.

3

We're in the textile industry and we run a number of CSR projects with our suppliers, who are mostly from Asia. These range from helping to improve the working conditions in factories to helping the local community to look after native species. Before our suppliers become CSR partners we require a cost-benefit analysis from them to make sure that the costs can be covered or offset, and to ensure the long-term viability of the project. Once we've checked the project's feasibility, we draw up guidelines outlining the scope of work for the partners, and we agree goals and objectives. We then require regular access to the site, er, plus monthly reports and reviews with quantifiable data.

53

Extract 1

Margit So, looking at the situation from a long-term perspective, if the IT system is updated, you'll be more efficient in terms of your customer admin, and you'll be able to continue your expansion plan. Is that right?

Judit Exactly. We need to develop a clear strategy to move the business forward. At the moment our systems are old, they're outdated, and we don't have a clear overview of our customers' transactions.

Margit Zoltan …

Zoltan Well, we have a number of options. We've already commissioned three proposals from reputable IT companies. Provided we check out the feasibility of these options thoroughly, I'm convinced we can find a system upgrade that will work for us.

Margit OK, that's all very positive, but I think we need to look at the bigger picture. Do we actually have the resources for this? I mean, there's no point in investing in a system upgrade if we don't have the space, the personnel, or the finances to carry it through.

Zoltan Yes, but …

Margit Let's take a look at our physical resources. Will the new system be linked to production? I mean, you have a lot of real estate here, but the facilities are pretty run-down. Is it practical to set up a hi-tech system in such an old place?

Judit Well, if we'd invested in our production facilities five years ago, like we wanted to, we would have knocked down the old building and had one purpose-built. It's useless to speculate about that now, of course …

54

Extract 2

Margit … OK, so you already have the infrastructure you need to support the new system, even if it's not directly connected to the production facility.

Zoltan, Judit Yes, sure.

Margit Now, what's the situation regarding personnel?

Judit Well, they'd need training. I think our options are quite clear here. It doesn't really matter which system we choose – if training isn't on the agenda, we should forget the whole idea. I mean, you can't expect us to …

Zoltan Yes, but we do have some employees who've worked on SAP-type systems in previous jobs. If we made them our key users, we could gradually train up the rest.

Margit I'm not sure that would work. Do you really have a sufficient skills base to meet the needs of this strategy? You can't just rely on one or two people and you can't run two systems in parallel. How would it work if you took on some younger people? I mean, if you'd recruited more young employees at the start, they would have had some IT knowledge from school.

Zoltan Well, but we do have some well-qualified workers. And we're in a great location, so I think we're in a really strong position to find new staff. I don't have any worries about the human resources aspect.

Judit No, Margit's right. If we only had a couple of people initially who could use the system, how could they cope with the extra work? It would be terrible! Basically we don't have much choice for a long-term plan like this – we can either provide training for everyone, which will be a substantial investment, or we accept that it's totally unfeasible.

Margit OK, I accept that point. What about if we just look at a basic programme of …?

55

Extract 3

Margit … OK, so the HR options are looking quite positive. Now, what about financial resources? We have to bear in mind the long-term viability of a commitment like this. I can see that you have the capital to purchase the system, but how does the return on investment look? Realistically, would we be able to finance this strategy? Obviously, I'm not just talking about the initial outlay and set-up costs.

Zoltan OK, well, let me show you a couple of projections we've made. Look at this, this is a graph showing us in five years' time. This is a worst-case scenario – it shows that if we *hadn't* invested in the system, we'd be way behind the competition. We just couldn't compete with them using the system we have at the moment.

Judit Zoltan's right. We can't afford not to invest. Assuming we decided to commit to the full amount, we could also look at ways to save money in other areas.

Margit Such as?

Judit Well, for example, we could think about reducing expenditure on …

56

Extract 4

Margit OK. So the general consensus is that long-term we have the human resources for the strategy. The question that needs addressing is how to implement the system in the short term. Is everyone OK with that?

Zoltan, Judit Yeah, fine.

Margit OK. And finances are in place for the immediate purchase. The long-term strategy is that with the system in place you can cope with more customers and in turn increase your turnover, and hopefully your profit. Are there any other points to consider?

Zoltan Well, only that I think we should also look at this investment in terms of our intangibles. If we work more efficiently with our customers, our reputation can only improve too.

Judit Yes, I agree.

Margit Right, so we're decided. There are still some issues to be resolved and a more detailed cost-benefit analysis will need to be done, but basically we can go ahead.

57

1

A So you want Mr Khan to be picked up from the airport?

B Well, I thought it would be nice for someone to meet him.

A But he arrives in the middle of the night! I've got to work the next day.

B Oh, I was thinking more along the lines of sending Sami, and then giving him the following morning off.

A Oh, I see. That's a good idea.

2

A According to those figures you gave me, that particular product hasn't done as well as we predicted.

B The amount may seem low, but actually this is the net profit and our earlier calculations were based on gross. Sorry if I didn't make that clear.

A Ah, that explains it.

3

A A team-building day sounds great – canoeing and rock climbing!

B I didn't mean that! It would be indoors, much more businesslike. More of a team meeting.

A But how would that motivate people?

B What do you mean?

A I thought we were doing something related to staff motivation?

B I don't know what you're talking about. We spoke about this two days ago – it's a team meeting in a neutral location. Read your emails!

4

A So we're changing from our normal working day to 24/7?

B That's right. Should be up and running for us by March.

A So *everyone* will be expected to do *all* the shifts in March?

B That's not really what I meant. What I actually wanted to say was, we'll phase it in. First night shift, then weekends too.

A What – one week night shift, then weekend shifts?

B No, what I meant was we'll have a few months of nights, to get people used to it, then move on to …

5

A Hello. I'm calling to chase up an order for a delivery of mineral water. The order number is 811992.

B OK, let me just check for you. Er, right, we received your order for four cases and it's being delivered to your head office in Soho.

A No, that's not right. We wanted *fourteen* cases delivered to our studio in *Chelsea*.

B OK, I'm sorry about that. But it definitely says Soho on our system.

A Yes, that's because … Look, you've got it wrong. We definitely asked for it to be sent to Chelsea. Are you suggesting that this is our fault?

B No, that's not exactly what I'm saying, erm, but … er … I'm afraid the delivery address came through as Dean Street in Soho.

A Look, can I put this straight? We want *fourteen* cases to be delivered to Lots Road in *Chelsea* as soon as possible, otherwise …

58

Interviewer So how have the employees of the cooperative benefited from your input?

Michelin Well, obviously they've benefited from having secure jobs and from learning more about the business. But we've also been able to improve living conditions by being involved with a project to build a housing area, with a school and medical centre for the employees and their families … so a community is developing here.

Interviewer It sounds great. And is the cooperative actually making any money?

Michelin There's no doubt the plantation project is a success – the figures speak for themselves. For example, the turnover hit $3.1m in 2006 – this beat the forecasts by $600,000. We've now forecast that this will rise to $10m in 2023, with 8m of that coming from rubber and the rest from cocoa. Erm, we don't normally like to talk about profits, but projections indicate that our project should bring in some $40,000 a year for a medium-sized landowner.

Interviewer Well, that's pretty impressive! I mean, the cooperative seems to have done well out of this deal, but what's in it for Michelin?

Michelin We know that we have to buy the rubber because we need it for our products. So, although the project doesn't have to sell its output to us – we know for a fact that 40% of it goes to our competitors – we *do* have an exclusivity clause, whereby a percentage of rubber produced has to be sold to us. It's a win-win situation. Look at the facts: current demand for rubber in Brazil is 230,000 tonnes a year, but only 100,000 tonnes is produced and prices are rising. This means rubber producers are profiting because there's a lot more demand than supply, and with this project we as a company have a guaranteed source of raw material.

Interviewer Some people might say you're only interested in this project to help boost your image – to satisfy the green lobby.

Michelin Yes, it's clear some people take that view. We're working in a so-called 'dirty industry' so the green lobby will never be satisfied with our advancements. But at the end of the day, I'm afraid we can't get away from the fact that, yes, it is a business project designed to make a profit. But it's one that both sides are gaining from.

Unit 10

59

Lydia I've been asked to take over a failing team that has been without a leader for several months … They're quite demotivated, and they've got used to operating as a self-managing team. They're a very disparate group of people, very different in their ways of working, although very good at what they do. The problem is, they're currently functioning as individuals, not as a team. I can already see there's massive duplication of effort and they're not being productive Erm … In that sense they're quite dysfunctional … They're used to a very specific leadership style and they're extremely loyal to their previous team leader who was a big personality, hands-on, very charismatic. She was extremely supportive of them, individually, and they were quite dependent on her. She left suddenly and they miss her. So … I'm starting from a pretty challenging position.

So how am I going to approach this? … OK, I know I can't just walk in and take over and expect everything to be fine. There will be issues. It won't be confrontational – that's not my style. But there are two things I need to do, and they're going to take time.

The first is to establish my authority with them as team leader. But I need to get them to accept my authority, not force it on them, so they in a sense give me permission to lead them. I need to get to know them individually, find out what motivates them, and consult them on key decisions. I'll have to be consistent in my expectations and feedback, and just generally make them feel valued. Unless I can instil confidence in them that I'm up to the job, and that I have the interests of the whole team at heart, it won't work.

Secondly, I have to get them to work as a team again. It won't be easy … Essentially, I have to try to build a culture of trust between the individual team members. I sense that at the moment they don't have this, that they're all competing with each other. I need to find a

way to get them to work together. I don't know exactly how this will happen, not yet, but it's essential for me to develop a sense of cohesion within the team. Otherwise nothing will change and the team will continue to fail.

60

Bruce I'd spent fifteen years as a manufacturing engineer, eight of them as a manager. And suddenly here I was, co-leading the team that would design a new fuselage for our latest passenger plane. The technical demands were awesome: stretch the plane by eight metres, add lots of functionality, do it in less than two years. The human demands were just as challenging – my job was to coordinate the work of 300 team members. Most of them didn't report directly to me, almost none of them knew me very well – and vice versa. It's a kind of daunting prospect!

The first thing was, I had to establish my credibility. I had lots of credibility as an engineer, but now I was responsible for all kinds of areas that weren't in my background. 95% of my people get their paychecks from other departments, so all I can do is influence them. I realized pretty quickly that what the experts say is true. Team leaders don't lead teams: they lead a collection of individuals with different strengths and weaknesses, different workstyle preferences … There's no way you can get a team to work together unless you learn how to work with each person on a one-on-one basis. You have to deal with people based on how they want you to deal with them – that's how you get them to follow you. It's about generating mutual respect.

Look, if you want to exert influence over hundreds of different people, few of whom work for you directly, the only way is to work with them on an informal basis – walk around, ask how it's going. But do it subtly, in a non-interventionist kind of way.

Avoid the temptation to micromanage. It's easy to criticize people if you don't understand their roles and their constraints. Take a step back. Most people want to do a good job. You have to let them know that you're there to help, not just to tell them what to do.

I basically have one message to everyone on the team – it's designed to reinforce a sense of team spirit and collaboration: 'We're all here to build airplanes. If the plane could talk, what would it tell us to do? And what can we do to make that happen?'

But I also make sure that I recognize individual achievement within the group. Let me give you an example. Recently, one of my engineers was taking his time authorizing a decision. I said I'd get him a dozen doughnuts if he'd deliver the signed form that day. At 4.00 p.m. it was on my desk. He got his doughnuts the next morning. It was neat to see the look in his eyes, like, 'You really did that?'.

61

Part 1

Jim … OK, you're all aware that a decision was taken at last week's strategy meeting that affects all of us. I hope you've read the briefing document … Yes? Good, so you know what's involved. I understand you may feel it doesn't

address your particular situation, and that's part of the reason I'm here. I'm sure you have quite a few questions and concerns, and I'll do my best to answer them. But first off, let me bring you up to speed on some of the key points …

… As you know, it has been agreed that we are going to combine our e-banking systems into a single integrated network – this involves the creation of what is called a 'middle layer' to the network, enabling us to bring all our applications together. What this will allow us to do is offer our clients a more personalized and customized service – something we couldn't do before.

Another great thing about this development is that it will allow us to grow our business in our core markets more rapidly. We can get our applications and new products into the market more quickly and more cost-effectively – which is obviously good for the business as a whole. There may be some short-term inconvenience during the implementation and the switchover phase, but it will be well worth the investment.

In the longer term, the benefits are clear. We all know that this is a competitive sector – our customers want a fast, efficient service, and this is going to allow us to provide this and to stay ahead of the competition.

So … you and your teams are crucial to the success of this strategy. That's why I want to involve you now in planning the implementation process at a local level. It is proposed that we hold a series of seminars for team leaders at the regional training centres well in advance, to ensure that everyone is familiar with the system and the procedures. If we're going to succeed, we need to realize that we're all in this together. Each one of you has a key role to play in making the new system work.

What I need you to do, first of all, is to commit to making this project a success. If you are committed, your teams will realize that and they'll get behind it. I'd like to see all of you being proactive and taking a lead in this. Set up regular meetings or teleconferences, to share ideas and coordinate your plans. I'd also like you to work together to develop a schedule for training – familiarizing your teams with the new applications and how they work.

Another way you can help is by keeping your team informed, and asking them for their ideas and opinions. I would encourage all of you to do this. Make them feel involved, make them feel that their views count – which they do.

Well, now, I'm sure you have some concerns, so let's just talk about …

62

Part 2

Jessica Jim, I'd like to raise an issue – I imagine it's something all of us are worried about. I understand the reasons for upgrading the system, that's clear, but I'm slightly concerned about the timing and its effect on my team. Will we have enough time to prepare properly? And will there be an increase in workload? I wonder if you have any information about this?

Jim Well, I understand your concerns, but I think we need to look at the positive side. We've been given a deadline of the 30th of

September, which is still more than three months away. As I understand it, the switch over to the new system will be coordinated centrally and you'll be briefed about it well in advance – so it shouldn't have an impact on the way you work. As long as your team have had the training in time, I don't think you need to worry.

Thomas Well, that's something I wanted to mention. You said you wanted us to work together, and I like the idea of regular meetings and sharing ideas, but I'm not very happy about having to schedule and coordinate the training for my team. I don't really feel I have the expertise to do this. Can you give us an assurance that we'll get the appropriate level of support?

Jim Of course. That's a valid point, but again I really don't see this as a problem. My understanding is that you will receive all the instructions and materials you need to help you implement this.

Thomas Yeah, well … I guess that should be OK. But I also have some concerns about the impact on customers. I mean, how do we ensure that we continue to provide a proper service? What assurances can you give us that it will work?

Anna That's a good point. And can we address the issue of costs and budgeting? I think the basic idea is good, but I have some reservations about the cost implications. I mean, whose money are we talking about here? Are there any guarantees that we won't be asked to contribute to this out of our operational budgets?

Jim Well, I understand where you're coming from, of course. The core investment comes from central funding, obviously. It's been suggested that the regional centres should contribute a certain amount of the training costs, on the basis that this will be recouped in increased business later on …

Anna What?

Jim Yes. I've been told that the costs need to be shared around. Apparently the intention is to make everyone's lives easier and better – including yours. Anyway, the decision has already been made. I know it's not great, but come on, let's give this a chance to work.

63

Conversation 1

A So what did you think of the meeting?

B I thought it was quite productive. But to be honest with you, I think there are still some things to sort out.

A Oh? Such as?

B Well, for example, we still don't really know how the new assessment system will work in practice. And personally speaking, I don't see how we can agree to something that we haven't even been consulted about.

A You're not in favour of the changes then?

B It's not that. I'm actually quite enthusiastic about them. But it's the lack of proper consultation, the lack of any real discussion. I have to say I find that quite difficult to accept.

A Yes, I can understand that …

Conversation 2

A I was interested in what you said earlier about working in Kenya.

B Yes, it was a good experience for me, especially so early in my career. I learned a lot.

A What did you like about it in particular?

B Well, the people were fantastic – positive, friendly, incredibly hard-working. But what I really liked was the independence. It was just me and a team of locals in the field office – I was accountable to Head Office, of course, but I was pretty much free to make my own decisions.

A Even so, it must have been challenging at times?

B It was challenging, yeah. But to tell you the truth, I really enjoyed it. To be perfectly honest, I'm not particularly good at working in a big team. I much prefer to be my own boss.

A I can see that that would have been quite attractive. So … how does it feel to be back at the centre of things?

B Honestly? It's fine, the job's good, but what I'd really like to do is run my own operation, my own projects, with no … well, interference. That would be even better.

A Yes, I know what you mean …

Conversation 3

A You were saying earlier that you'd been on a team-building course.

B Yes, the whole weekend.

A I heard some people thought it was a waste of time.

B Yeah, well … maybe. Personally, I think that's down to their attitude.

A What do you mean?

B Well, I look at it like this: you get out of these things what you put into them.

A You mean, if you approach it positively, you'll get something positive back?

B Exactly. And vice versa. Even if you aren't 100% sure, at least give it a try.

A So …?

B Look, my attitude is, if you expect something to be a bad experience, you go in expecting it to be pointless, chances are it will be – for you. Don't get me wrong, I know when something's not working. But I do think I have the ability to make the most of my opportunities. It's one of my strengths.

A Well, good for you.

B Yeah … look, anyway, how was your weekend?

Unit 11

64

Host … So, Carla, just outline the issue for us, if you would.

Carla OK. A recently-published study of consumer attitudes worldwide clearly shows a marked decline in respect for American values globally. This study was carried out by the market research company NOP World. And the implications for the American economy cannot be ignored – this view of America is having a potentially disastrous effect on the image of major US brands such as McDonald's, Coca-Cola, Nike, and Microsoft.

Host It's really that serious?

Carla It could be. NOP World interviewed 30,000 people in markets around the world. According to their findings, there are a number of factors that have all had a profoundly worrying effect on their perception of American culture and, as a consequence, on many of its major brands. Just for the record, these include recent American foreign policy, which many people see as controversial, corporate financial scandals, and a comparatively poor environmental record. There's a real sense that America has lost its moral authority in recent years.

Host Doug, any thoughts on this?

Doug Well, I just don't buy this direct link that's being made. Yes, it may be true that America's image has suffered, but so have those of many other countries, for all kinds of reasons. I'd like some better evidence, frankly. OK, there may be a downturn in uptake of certain US products – but that could be due to any number of economic factors. It doesn't have to be because people don't like America.

Carla Well, there's evidence that the number of people worldwide who like and use US-branded products has fallen significantly, and at the same time brands perceived to be non-American have remained relatively stable. It's not a disaster – yet – but it is clearly a warning sign. And in the long term, if attitudes to America become appreciably more hostile, they are saying, the effect on American business could be irretrievably damaging.

Doug Yes, but, come on …

Carla OK, right, well, wait, let's look at some figures. Until 2002, NOP found that brands such as McDonald's and Coca-Cola were achieving healthy growth, year on year, in terms of their popularity in international markets. But by the middle of the decade the growth in popularity of *all* major consumer brands – including those from Europe and Asia – had stalled. And recently, this previously positive trend has gone into reverse, with US products the hardest hit.

Doug But you just said yourself it's not only American brands that are taking a hit …

Host …OK, well, let's try and move this on. Carla, you said that the NOP study found that this unexpectedly rapid decline in interest in and respect for American products was reflected in consumers' views of American cultural values. What values are we talking about here?

Carla I'm talking about core values like honesty, freedom of expression, and tolerance. Internationalism, if you will. Increasingly, consumers around the world are questioning whether these values still hold true, and whether they want to be associated with them. And this is reflected in the choices they make about the brands they choose to buy. It's kind of complicated.

Doug I'm not sure it *is* complicated. We're at a time of economic and political change, the balance of economic power in the world is shifting. We already know that there are certain countries in the Middle East and Latin America, for example, where consumers with increasing buying power are – and, incidentally, always have been – unlikely to share American cultural values.

Carla But the study also found that people in a number of major European markets felt that their own values were significantly different to American ones. For example, only 65% of British consumers say that they identify with

American cultural values. In Italy and France it's 63%, and in Germany it's only 55%. This is a downward trend we're looking at.

Host Well, whether or not this image of America is right, it's clearly the way we are being perceived. And presumably it will become increasingly difficult to reverse the trend the longer it goes on. So the question is, what if anything are we able to do about it …?

65

Part 1

Hyun-Ki Hello?

Laura Hello. Is that Hyun-Ki?

Hyun-Ki Yes. Hello, Laura. How are you?

Laura Very well, thanks. Are you both there?

Jin-Ho Yes, I'm here too. Hello, Laura.

Laura Hi, Jin-Ho. Andrew is with me, too.

Andrew Hello.

Hyun-Ki, Jin-Ho Good morning, Andrew. Are you well?

Andrew Pretty good, thanks. And you two?

Hyun-Ki We're well, thank you.

Laura Good. So shall we talk about this email? Can you clarify the situation for us, please Hyun-Ki?

Hyun-Ki Yes, of course. This is very embarrassing for us, but we are having a few problems here – not only has one of our contracts just trebled their order, but another new contract has just come in. We now have a big backlog of work and we are in a very difficult situation. I'm afraid we have reached the point where we have no other option than to ask for an extension on our deadline.

Laura I see. Well, that's not going to be easy for us. We have a fixed date to meet, which I think we made clear at the start.

Hyun-Ki Yes, that's quite true and I can only apologize. But I'm afraid this is beyond our control now. I was hoping we could discuss a new arrangement.

Andrew Hyun-Ki, this is not good news for us. As Laura says, we need stock in Berlin in seven weeks. So I think I have to say no to a new arrangement. If we have no product there'll be no product launch, which means serious problems for the company. Do you understand that?

Hyun-Ki Yes, yes. I understand how important this is for you. But please understand also I could not have foreseen this extra work. I wish I could meet your order, but I'm afraid it is just not possible for us now.

Andrew No, no, look … this is not good enough. At no time have we suggested that we can be flexible on these dates. We have our company reputation at stake and without wishing to sound pushy, you are under contract to …

Laura Yes, yes, OK, Andrew, please. We all know this is not ideal, but we are stuck with this situation, so let's try to find a way round this. OK? So, Hyun-Ki, if I understand you correctly, you can't meet the full order in time for the Berlin exhibition …

66

Part 2

Laura … OK, we really need to sort this out. Tell us what you were hoping to get from this discussion.

Hyun-Ki Well, I think we need an extra three weeks to get the stock to you.

Andrew Three weeks? No, no, that's out of the question. Even two weeks late and we'll miss the exhibition completely.

Hyun-Ki How about publicizing the product at the exhibition and promising to supply customers at a later date?

Andrew No, that just won't work. It'll damage our reputation even more. If this launch is going to be a success, we need our clients to see how good the product is.

Jin-Ho Well, I could probably try to streamline the transport process by a few days. Would you consider accepting delivery by the final day of the exhibition?

Laura Hmm. That's not out of the question. We could even hold a launch party on the last day.

Andrew No, I'm sorry, Laura, but I refuse to budge on this. Not everyone will be there on the last day – we need the product from day one. Can you really not get it to us on time?

Hyun-Ki I'm afraid not. The earliest possible date for us to have all stock ready would be five weeks from now.

Andrew Which doesn't leave enough time for shipping. You see, Laura, this really isn't acceptable. If we can't launch the new range we risk going under. I have to stay firm on this – I think if we can't get the product in time, we'll have to use a different supplier – a local one so the shipping is quicker.

Hyun-Ki No, no, you don't need to do that. I'm sure we can come to a solution between us. Could you make do with some samples of the product?

Laura Er, well, it depends what kind of samples you're talking about.

Hyun-Ki I was thinking of the first samples we produced a few months ago. We still have a few stored away.

Andrew We can't possibly do that. That was a trial run, the packaging wasn't finalized, and on top of that, they're six months old.

Laura OK, look, we're not getting anywhere here. Erm, let's have a rethink …
… No, no, no, I agree. Listen, let's go back to this suggestion of doing some samples. What would you say to doing a smaller run for us to meet the Berlin deadline? Say 500 samples of each cream? That would be a tenth of the original order.

Hyun-Ki Yes, I'd be willing to prioritize that. Jin-Ho – wouldn't you agree that we could do that?

Jin-Ho I think so, yes …

67

Part 3

Jin-Ho OK, but I will need to check the dates and confirm.

Laura Fine – we can follow this up by email. But let's just go over what we agreed. Hyun-Ki, you'll produce 500 samples of each cream on the first run and send them direct to Berlin.

Hyun-Ki Yes, that sounds feasible.

Laura Good. And the rest of the order will follow three weeks later and go to the warehouse. Are we all agreed?

Hyun-Ki, Jin-Ho Yes.

Andrew Yes, I'll go along with that.

Laura Great. Thank you, everyone.

Hyun-Ki And thank you too for making these allowances. Had I been given more notice on these other jobs, this wouldn't have happened. I'll make sure it doesn't happen again.

68

Extract 1

A Tania, can I have a word with you?

B Sure, of course. What's up?

A Look, I don't mean to sound rude, but could you try to be a bit quieter when you're on the phone?

B Oh … yes, sorry. I didn't realize there was a problem. I'm really sorry.

Extract 2

A Carlos? About this presentation you're giving …

B Yes?

A Er … What are you planning to wear?

B What I usually wear, of course. Why?

A OK, well … Look, this is a bit delicate. Please don't take offence, but … do you think it would be possible for you to wear something a bit more appropriate? I mean, … it's just that it's quite a formal situation and I think a suit, or at least a jacket and tie, would be, well, smarter than what you normally …

B You mean I'm not smart enough? Are you telling me I look scruffy?

A Er, well, yes, I'm afraid so. A bit. Most of the time it's fine, but on this occasion …

Extract 3

A Ah, Fiametta, I'm glad I've caught you.

B I was just going. So, what did you think of the report I sent you?

A Ah, yes, the report … Look, please don't take this the wrong way … I know you spent a lot of time on it.

B Yes, I did. All weekend, in fact.

A Did you? Right … You see, the thing is, it really needs a bit more work.

B Does it? I see. How much more?

Extract 4

A Maria, come in.

B Thanks. Have you got a minute?

A Yes, of course. Is something wrong?

B Well, sort of. I'm not quite sure how to put this, but, well, I'm really delighted about my promotion, but I wanted to mention the overall package. It just seems a bit mean considering the increased responsibility I'll have. Could we talk about it, do you think?

Extract 5

A … and that's the reason why this is such a great opportunity for us.

B With respect, Thomas, I have to say that I don't think it's quite as simple as that.

A What? What do you mean? I just explained to you exactly why we should invest in this project.

B Well, actually, I don't think you've explained very much at all. You haven't told us what these figures actually mean, or what the long-term implications are. The fact is, there is still an enormous number of unanswered questions.

Unit 12

69

Jacob It's possible to identify differences in approach with regard to advertising around the world, simply because of the diverse consumer profiles. Erm, if you take the United States as an example … erm, life is generally pretty competitive in the US, and so you tend to find that a larger percentage of consumers are quite aspirational. There's a strong imperative to get on and improve yourself in material terms, and that's the message advertisers are feeding the public on a daily basis. This in turn encourages people to consume more, obviously. As there's very little to distinguish between most competing products … cars, washing machines, whatever … advertisers have to find ways of persuading the public to buy them. This is increasingly done by focusing on what we might call the consumer's status-anxiety. It's not enough to put forward the facts about the product, they have to use motivational language in order to persuade the consumer how much they'll benefit from having it. This could be in terms of social status, health, youthfulness, and so on. Erm, for many people, it's become really important to be able to keep up with their neighbours in terms of what they have, what they own and are *seen* to own – whether it's a car, the latest kitchen gadget, whatever. It's all about relative social status. Now, in contrast, if you take a country like Denmark, there are clear differences. Denmark … and, OK, I'm generalizing here, but still … overall, Denmark is a much less competitive society than, say, the US or Britain. There's more emphasis on cooperation, on social relationships, and the gap between rich and poor is far smaller. This comparative economic equality and lack of competitiveness is reflected in the low level of conspicuous consumption. Market penetration of luxury items is relatively slow, because most Danes aren't showy people, they're just not so materialistic. Consumption is based more on need than on want, so there's no imperative to own a particular product until it's reached an affordable price.

And then at the other end of the spectrum are the relatively new consumer economies like Russia and China. And here the whole concept of advertising and persuasion is completely different because most high-end consumer products are relatively new to them. This means advertisers don't need to use those more, shall we say, exploitative strategies to hook consumers, nor do they need to focus too much on the product's USP. The majority of new consumers won't already own the particular product being sold, so advertisers tend to focus on facts about the product and its usefulness, rather than drawing comparisons with another similar product on the market. Now, being aware of these differences between more and less mature markets is essential for advertisers. Getting the approach right – or not – can make or break a product entering a new market …

70

Extract 1

Ranjit Hi, everyone. Thank you for finding the time to join me today. I know it's a busy period for us at the moment.

We're here today to seriously consider our future. I know that, like me, you're concerned about where we're going. I've been doing some research into our position in the market and what opportunities are available to us, and to tell you the truth, I'm excited. Why? I'm excited because what comes across from talking to you is your collective enthusiasm in what we do and your genuine wish for us to succeed. After all, without your support, my plans won't be possible.

So what are my plans? Well, it's become apparent that without moving on from the successful field we're in, work is going to dry up. Admittedly, things are going well now, but I'm thinking five years down the line. We could be missing out on a great opportunity if we don't diversify – mind you, this won't be cheap and it won't be easy. I'm talking about multimedia advertising. Let me explain …

71

Extract 2

Ranjit So that's my idea. Of course, I can't expect you to buy into this plan without some facts. Why should we go into multimedia? Basically, studies show that most companies only invest a small percentage of their advertising budget in print media. As a matter of fact, most of our customers want agencies that offer a variety of advertising media – they want options. Obviously, this information should ring alarm bells for us. If we move into multimedia advertising we not only benefit from keeping our existing customers happy, we also gain from potentially attracting new customers.

OK, that's the first benefit. Now, the second point is where we stand in the market. At the moment, we're third in our region for print media. Quite honestly, I'm not happy with that. Compare us to numbers one and two in the market and, to put it brutally, our service falls short. We must offer something more or different to ensure our survival. Not only that. It's also essential that we increase our customer base. We can't rely solely on the cash cows. I think multimedia advertising is the answer. In addition to that, I'm convinced our team will enjoy the challenge. So, here are some facts and some projected figures …

72

Extract 3

Ranjit Right, OK. That's a lot to take in, but having said that, it's important to remember we won't be doing it single-handedly. Ravi, our key account manager, actually comes from the field of online advertising so he's going to be our guru, so to speak. This means we have an in-house specialist. You could argue that we'll be short-staffed if he's moved off the key accounts, but on balance this won't be the case if we appoint Sumitra – his assistant – to take on his clients.

Now, as I was saying before, we've secured external investment for our diversification plan and we've employed a consultant. I accept that you may not like an outsider telling you what is the right thing to do, but we have to recognize that this person is an expert, and they may well see things, opportunities, that we might not. Anyway, he's on our side. OK, any other points you want to raise?

Audience Yes, I was just wondering about …

73

Extract 4

Ranjit So, I think we're in an extremely strong position. Why? Because we're reacting now, rather than waiting until it's too late. Diversifying into multimedia advertising *is* achievable. No question. Our team will make it work! We're committed, we're motivated, and we believe in what we do. You can't get better than that!

So, as I said before, investment is in place and I'm very clear that this is the right thing for us to be doing, so I very much hope that you'll support these changes. Please give serious consideration to how we move forward together. We can't afford to miss this opportunity, which is why I'm calling on you to work with me to draw up the schedule and …

74

1 I've been doing some research into our position in the market and what opportunities are available to us, and to tell you the truth, I'm excited.

2 I'm excited because what comes across from talking to you is your collective enthusiasm in what we do and your genuine wish for us to succeed. After all, without your support my plans won't be possible.

3 Admittedly, things are going well now, but I'm thinking five years down the line.

4 We could be missing out on a great opportunity if we don't diversify – mind you, this won't be cheap and it won't be easy.

5 Of course, I can't expect you to buy into this plan without some facts.

6 Basically, studies show that most companies only invest a small percentage of their advertising budget in print media.

7 As a matter of fact, most of our customers want agencies that offer a variety of advertising media – they want options.

8 Obviously, this information should ring alarm bells for us.

9 At the moment, we're third in our region for print media. Quite honestly, I'm not happy with that.

10 Ravi, our key account manager, actually comes from the field of online advertising so he's going to be our guru, so to speak.

11 Now, as I was saying before, we've secured external investment for our diversification plan and we've employed a consultant.

12 I accept that you may not like an outsider telling you what is the right thing to do, but we have to recognize that this person is an expert, and they may well see things, opportunities, that we might not. Anyway, he's on our side.

75

1

A Thanks for chairing the discussion. That was great. A very worthwhile meeting.

B Thank you. I felt it went well. We were actually able to make some progress today.

A Yes, it makes a real difference when an outsider …

2

A Good morning, Paola. You're back again?

B Hi. Yes, we've got another regional meeting.

A You're looking well.

B Thanks. I was on a skiing holiday last week.

3

A Are you ready for the meeting?

B Yes, I've got the handouts here.

A Oh, I like your shoes! I've been looking for some like that.

B Thanks – they're Jimmy Choos. They cost me a fortune!

A Ah … So, anyway, let me show you the handouts …

4

A I was hoping I'd have the honour of meeting you. I thoroughly enjoyed your talk – it was very interesting. In fact, it was the best talk of the conference!

B Oh, well, considering it's only day one, I don't know how you can say that, but erm, thanks anyway. I'm glad you enjoyed it.

5

A Gina, I've been looking for you everywhere. I just wanted to tell you how much I like that new logo. Great design. I love the colours.

B Oh, thanks, I was hoping it would be well received. It took my team ages!

A I can imagine! Well done, you all did a great job.

6

A That was a long meeting last night, wasn't it, Magnus? Where's the coffee?

B Oh, hi, Marcie, yeah – coffee's over there … I didn't know you wore glasses.

A I don't, normally. I have contact lenses, but my eyes are killing me today – late nights, you know.

B Mm. But you have very nice eyes, you know.

A Oh, thanks … Right, OK, has anyone seen the sugar?

76

Michelle Hello?

Yves Hello, Michelle?

Michelle Yes. Oh. Hi, Yves. You're phoning about the Brazil project, right?

Yves Exactly. We really need that financial backing so we're going to have to prepare our arguments carefully. I've been thinking about it a lot and I've drafted some ideas.

Michelle Yeah, yeah, me too. Erm, you go first.

Yves Right, well … I thought we could play on our KPIs – you know Key Performance Indicators. Use the ones they're familiar with and highlight how these can tie into our doing business in Brazil.

Michelle OK, OK … I'm not sure I know enough about them, actually – we have KPIs in so many areas.

Yves That's OK. I'm putting together a summary of the ones we might want to mention. I mean, being able to measure the success of major areas across a business is a really useful tool, not only for PR. It must be recognized that our control mechanisms will be in place regardless of which country we expand into.

Michelle Yeah, right, I think you've got a point there. Can you send them to me in an attachment?

Yves Sure.

Michelle Great. Now, I've been trying to anticipate what questions or concerns our stakeholders may have. I've spoken to one of them already in an off-the-record meeting to establish what we might be up against. Now, one area is whether we're ready for this. Apparently, we're still considered a very new and young company – 'young' meaning our employees are pretty inexperienced. Er, you know we only actually have about five senior managers who hold the majority of the knowledge. They see this as a risk. Another problem is that the market is very competitive. In Brazil we'd be up against larger international property companies, plus all the local ones. The questions they'll be asking are, is there the demand for another one? And do we know enough about doing business there – the business culture, the local economy, all of that?

Yves OK, where do we start?

Michelle Well, I've done some research into the Brazilian property market, so we have some up to date figures. I've also spoken to a few of our local agents over there, including the law firm who've done some work for us before. They all seem extremely keen to work with us again. So that's all very positive. I'll send you the Brazil info, and I suggest we read it through and meet next week. I think it might help if we do a kind of SWOT analysis. Er, you know, to see exactly where we stand internally and externally before we decide how to tackle the presentation.

Yves OK, I'll call you on Monday, once I've had time to read everything …

OXFORD
UNIVERSITY PRESS

Great Clarendon Street, Oxford OX2 6DP

Oxford University Press is a department of the University of Oxford.
It furthers the University's objective of excellence in research, scholarship,
and education by publishing worldwide in

Oxford New York

Auckland Cape Town Dar es Salaam Hong Kong Karachi
Kuala Lumpur Madrid Melbourne Mexico City Nairobi
New Delhi Shanghai Taipei Toronto

With offices in

Argentina Austria Brazil Chile Czech Republic France Greece
Guatemala Hungary Italy Japan Poland Portugal Singapore
South Korea Switzerland Thailand Turkey Ukraine Vietnam

OXFORD and OXFORD ENGLISH are registered trade marks of
Oxford University Press in the UK and in certain other countries

© Oxford University Press 2009

The moral rights of the author have been asserted

Database right Oxford University Press (maker)

First published 2009
2013 2012 2011 2010 2009
10 9 8 7 6 5 4 3 2 1

ISBN: 978 0 19 476819 1

Printed in China

ACKNOWLEDGEMENTS

*The authors and publisher are grateful to those who have given permission to reproduce
the following extracts and adaptations of copyright material:* p06 extract from www.
culturosity.com. Reproduced by kind permission of Kate Berardo, Founder,
Culturosity.com. p12 information on company Adventurous Appetites
Ltd. Reproduced by kind permission of James Fraser, Company Director,
Adventurous Appetites Ltd. p14 extract from 'How to Climb the Corporate
Ladder' by Prof. Ben (C) Fletcher, and photograph of Prof. Ben (C) Fletcher.
© Professor Ben (C) Fletcher, 2002. Reproduced by kind permission of the
author. p20 company information from www.tpmg.com. Reproduced by
kind permission of The Performance Management Group. p22 based on
www.flexigrid.net © HOP Associates. Reproduced by kind permission. p23
interview with Iñaki Lozano from BICG – The Business Innovation Consulting
Group. Reproduced by kind permission of the interviewee. p28–29 from
Dieter Spath, Peter Kern: Office 21: Push for the Future, better Performance
in Office Environments. First published by © Egmont vgs Verlagesellschaft
2004, Köln. p36–37, 155–156 extract from www.thetimes100.co.uk © MBA
Publishing Ltd. Reproduced by permission. p38 Team-Role Descriptions
from www.belbin.com © e-interplace, Belbin Associates, UK. 2001.
Reproduced by kind permission of Belbin Associates. Photograph of Dr
Meredith Belbin © Rupert Jefferson. Reproduced by permission. p46 extract
from 'Creativity Lab helps businesses accent thinking outside the box'
by Graham Norris, 13 January 2006, from Taiwan Journal. Reproduced by
permission. p55, p158–159 Interview reproduced by kind permission of the
original interviewee, Lorna Bevan. p160 fictitious interview. Reproduced by
permission of Orange. p160 fictitious interview. Reproduced by permission
of Credit Suisse. p160 fictitious interview. Reproduced by permission of De
Beers Group. p68 Company Profile The Ritz-Carlton. Reproduced by kind
permission of The Ritz-Carlton Hotel Company, L.L.C. p70 information
and logo reproduced by permission of Marks and Spencer plc. p75 from
'Michelin searches for 'green gold' in Brazil' by James Gard, 20 June 2007,
from www.guardian.co.uk. Copyright Guardian News and Media Ltd 2007.
p78 from 'Asian and American Leadership Styles: How Are They Unique?',
27 June 2005, by D. Quinn Mills. Reproduced by permission of Professor
D. Quinn Mills. p84 from www.ryor.cz. Reproduced by permission. p86
'Our Values', source: www.microsoft.com. Reproduced by permission. p86
'Five Core Values', source: http://www.tata.com/aboutus/articles/inside.
aspx?artid=CKdRrD5ZDV4, August 28, 2008 © Tata Sons Ltd. Reprinted with
permission from Tata Sons Limited. p92 Case Study on The CarbonNeutral
Company. Reproduced by permission of The CarbonNeutral Company
(TCNC). p166 adapted from Affluenza by Oliver James, Vermillion 2007 ©
Oliver James. Reproduced by permission of Aitken Alexander Associates.
p141 'Investment Property in Brazil – Economic Factors' from www.
propertyshowrooms.com. Reproduced by permission.

*Although every effort has been made to trace and contact copyright holders before
publication, this has not been possible in some cases. We apologize for any apparent
infringement of copyright and if notified, the publisher will be pleased to rectify any
errors or omissions at the earliest opportunity.*

Sources: www.usatoday.com; www.blogsouthwest.com; www.southwest.com;
www.godubai.com; www.businessweek.com; Chiumento's Happiness at
Work Index; www.google.com; www.innocentdrinks.co.uk; www.bbc.co.uk;
www.ngl.com; www.bpsoutdoor.com; Abraham Maslow's Hierarchy of Needs.
www.communicaid.com

Illustrations by: Martin Sanders/Mapart.co.uk pp28, 29

*We would also like to thank the following for permission to reproduce the following
photographs:* The Advertising Archives p148 (© Yeo Valley Organic/Yeo valley
Group), 148 (© United Colors of Benetton), 148 (© Dolce&Gabbana); Alamy
pp7 (meeting/IS479/Image Source Pink), 8 (Walter Bibikow/Jon Arnold Images
Ltd), 14 (kites/Martin Bennett), 16 (ImageState Royalty Free), 40 (Ralf Mohr/
apply pictures), 56 (Terry Vine/Blend Images), 76 (G P Bowater), 85 (Lynx/
Iconotec), 86 (Ikea/WorldFoto), 86 (Shell/imagebroker/Bodo Schieren), 86
(Microsoft/vario images GmbH & Co.KG/Stefan Kiefer), 88 (Tetra Images),
96 (PhotosIndia.com LLC); Arcaid p28 (James Balston); Axiom p54 (The Irish
Image Collection); Corbis pp6 (bridge/Inigo Bujedo Aguirre/Arcaid), 23
(warehouse/Michael Prince), 30 (man with computers/Comstock/Value RF),
36 (R. Hamilton Smith), 70 (M&S/Homer Sykes), 100 (Daniel Lainé); Eyevine
p62 (Xinhua News Agency); Courtesy of Ben Fletcher p14; James Gard/The
Guardian p76 (Michelin 'Green Gold' project); Getty Images pp11 (Jen
Petreshock/Stone), 19 (Andy Ryan/Stone), 20 (Lester Lefkowitz/The Image
Bank), 22 (Michael Orton/Photographer's Choice), 26 (David Lees/Iconica),
30 (hanging from plane/Gordon Wiltsie/National Geographic), 31 (Thomas
Lohnes/AFP), 32 (Tim Graham/The Image Bank), 37 (Kate Mathis/Stone+), 43
(UpperCut Images), 46 (U. Bellhaeuser/ScienceFoto), 47 (Toshifumi Kitamura/
AFP), 48 (Jon Feingersh/Iconica), 52 (Eightfish), 53 (Car Culture), 57 (amana
productions inc.), 58 (Matthew Antrobus/Riser), 63 (Hill Creek Pictures/Riser),
68 (Glowimages), 78 (Art Wolfe/Stone), 79 (man/AAGAMIA/Iconica), 79 (woman/
ColorBlind Images/Iconica), 80 (ColorBlind Images/Iconica), 83 (Reza Estakhrian/
Stone), 86 (Starbucks/Daniel Berehulak), 86 (Nestle/Justin Sullivan), 86 (Skoda/
Andreas Rentz), 91 (Daniel Allan), 99 (AAGAMIA/Stone); iStockphoto p76
(close-up of bark/Patrick Roherty); Courtesy of Iñaki Lozano p23; Nature
Picture Library p70 (Andrew Parkinson); PA Photos p86 (GAP/Paul Sakuma/
AP); Photolibrary.com pp12 (Dennis Gottlieb), 72 (Rosalind Simon/Garden
Picture Library), 84 (Emotive Images), 86 (Philippe Ughetto); Punchstock
pp24 (Thomas Barwick/Digital Vision), 27 (Image Source), 30 (man with
computers/Comstock/Value RF), 35 (Purestock), 41 (A. Chederros/ONOKY),
51 (STOCK4B-RF), 55 (Diamond Sky Images/Digital Vision), 59 (Will Woods/
Digital Vision), 64 (Image Source), 67 (Tetra Images), 68 (Glowimages), 68
(Glowimages), 75 (Blend Images), 94 (Mark Oatney); Reuters p38 (Stringer
Shanghai); Rex Features p86 (Tata/David Pearson); Science Photo Library p92
(John Mead); South West Arlines pp44, 45; Courtesy of Mrs. Eva Stepankova,
Owner and President of Ryor a. s. p84; Still Pictures p60 (Jesco Denzel/VISUM);
TopFoto.co.uk p54 (Peter Senge)

Images sourced by: SuzanneWilliams/Pictureresearch.co.uk

Cover photo by: Chris King

Photos on p5 courtesy of Cranfield School of Management

*The authors and publishers would also like to thank the following individuals for their
advice and assistance in developing the material for this course:* Catherine Gower,
Shaun Wilden, Gordon Doyle, Gillian Paterson, David Rose, Allan Dalcher,
Piotr Swiecicki, Cindy Hauert, Oliver Sandon, Sylvia Renaudon, Francis
McNeice, Rhona MacRitchie, David Livingstone, Gail Pasque.

*The publisher would also like to thank the faculty, course participants, and alumni
of Cranfield School of Management who contributed so much to the development of
the course. Particular thanks are due to David Simmons, Director of International
Development, whose enthusiasm, generosity, and persistence really have made all the
difference.*